THE
HISTORY
OF
JAMAICA
from 1494 to 1838.

Sous l'œil de Dieu.

Special thanks to Tafar-I Williams.

- *The History of Jamaica, from 1494 to 1838*, by Thibault Ehrengardt.
ISBN 979-10-94341-01-8 / *Dread editions - Jamaica Insula 07.*
Text & translation copyright © 2009-2015 Thibault Ehrengardt /Artwork & illustrations © Dread editions
Contact : dreadzine@free.fr

The

History

of

Jamaica,

from 1494 to 1838.

By Thibault Ehrengardt.

ISLAND of

JAMAICA,

Translated from the French by the author.

The Jamaica Insula series
www.jamaica-insula.com

Also available in the
Jamaica Insula series

- GANGS OF JAMAICA,
by Thibault Ehrengardt
The author was granted the exceptional authorization to follow some police patrols to the most volatile areas of Jamaica. An in-depth inquiry into the underworld of crime.

"Insightful, investigative and written with sheer brilliance - Essential."
The Gleaner (Ja.)

- JAMAICA INSULA: An Atlas,
by T. Ehrengardt
A gorgeous collection of some of the first maps of Jamaica from 1528 to the early 19th century. Coloured reproductions.

- JAMAICAN GREATS, *by Thibault Ehrengardt*
10 portraits of artists, criminals or politicians to draw the one of a boiling island!

"It is a hell of a literary ride - Essential."
The Gleaner (Ja.)

www.jamaica-insula.com
dreadzine@free.fr

Introduction

About the author:
Thibault Ehrengardt
has been the Chief
Editor of *Natty Dread*
magazine from 2000 to
2011. Ehrengardt has
been travelling to the
island Jamaica, voyaging
for more than 15 years.
He is currently running
DREAD Editions which
is the only European
publishing company
dedicated to the island.
He has published 5 books
in the **Jamaica Insula**
series (this is the third
to be translated into
English) and 2 in
Le Moine marin
series.

The last consequent *History of Jamaica* published in French dates from 1751. Contrary to what most French bibliographers think, it is not the translation of Hans Sloane's work[1], but of *A New And Exact Account of Jamaica*[2], by Charles Leslie (Edinburgh, 1739). The confusion does not solely result from an ignorance of Sloane's work, but also from the fact that Leslie's translation is a pirate edition that purposefully blurred things. No author is mentioned and the place of printing, *London*, is a forgery. Built on a series of letters sent by a traveller to a friend in England—curiously, the French edition does not reproduce the map of Jamaica but comes with 6 engravings of natural history—, it gives a thorough description of the tribulations of this 11,500 km^2 Caribbean island south of Cuba. At the time, the French were deeply concerned with the affairs of the English in the New World. Just like in Europe, the 2 nations were neighbours, St-Domingue (Haiti) being only 160 km away from Jamaica. And they soon became competitors on the sugar market. They created

1 - *A Voyage to the Islands of Madera, Barbados, Nieves, S. Christophers and JAMAICA...* (London, 1707).
2 - Reprinted in 1740 under the title *A New History of Jamaica...*

commercial links, indeed, but when war broke in Europe, the colonies became fierce and merciless opponents. The juicy trade of the Spanish dominions in the New World was at stake. Spies, furtive raids or organized looting were the order of the day. As a matter of fact, the French of St-Domingue, who could not afford the necessary material to exploit sugar, stole it from Jamaica in 1694.

Nevertheless, one century later, the geopolitical map of the Caribbean was redrawn. First, the rebellious slaves of St-Domingue set the island on fire to bring it back to life under her free name of Haiti. Then, because of the harsh competition of the sugar beet, and the pressure of the abolitionist societies, sugar was not profitable any more. Jamaica then entered a dark period, and disappeared from the French horizon. If it were not for reggae which was made popular by Bob Marley, or Usain Bolt, only a few French people would have heard about this little 'wasted paradise' in the Caribbean, nowadays a mere resort for American tourists.

This *History of Jamaica* thus breaks more than 250 years of silence[3]; and it was born out of music. Indeed, reggae music first brought me to this *far, far away land*, where I eventually fell in love with the people and the culture. Furthermore, I discovered a totally unexpected way to deal with history. Far from the regular European sanctuaries, history in Jamaica is like a neglected *Dame*, who gives herself away to whosoever watches out for her. The island stands among the most dangerous countries in the world, and can't afford to linger too long over the past. She lives at the present time, somewhat neglecting her heritage. There are some active and serious historians in Jamaica, but they lack resources. Thus left by herself in the middle of chaos, history is drifting on a sea of indifference. Children swim at the foot of the 300 years old mill in Nueva Sevilla, and the Iron Bridge of Spanish Town (1801), the last representative of its kind in America, is nothing but a frontier between two rival gangs. Meanwhile, the magnificent tombstone of Lewis Galdy—a French Protestant who sought refuge among the Buccaneers of Port Royal, where he was swallowed and then miraculously thrown back into the bay of Kingston during the earthquake of 1692—restlessly tells the story of its host in a small isolated churchyard; you just have to kneel down to touch it. History in Jamaica usually catches you off-guard, hitting you with full force. But it can be insidious too, as you keep on passing by the same places, over and over, until they become familiar—I remember whistling the few notes of the instrumental *Rock Fort Rock* (Studio One, 1972) any time I passed in front of the Rock Fort on my way to—and from—the Norman Manley National Airport in Kingston; until I decided one day to stop. And I soon discovered that it was built to prevent my French fellow men to invade the capital of Jamaica in 1694! This book tries to

---

3 - In 1818, De Drouin de Bercy, a Creole from St-Domingue (Haïti), published his *Histoire civile et commerciale de la Jamaïque* (Paris). But it contains 144 pages only, the vast majority being dedicated to the state of the trade in the island.

transcribe this frontal impact. Thus, I focused on ancient testimonies such as those of the 'holy trinity' of the history of the island—Charles Leslie, Edward Long and Bryan Edwards. I have not ignored the crucial works of modern historians such as Vivian E. Black, Franck Cundall, Rex Nettleford or those who regularly publish in the *Jamaica Journal* (The Institute of Jamaica); but priority has been given to ancient writers. Deeply committed Christians, patriots to the excess, and eyewitnesses of some of the stories related in their books, they must be cautiously read. Nonetheless, far from the *rigor mortis* of many modern writings, their books turn the statues into flesh and blood, and the ruins into magnificent cities. In this regard, their works are irreplaceable. Of course, I have kept their sometimes offensive words or expressions since they are the reflections of their state of mind, and of their time. Most of the quotations are directly taken from books that were published in English; nonetheless, some I had to translate from the French publications. They are followed by (F) when listed.

To get as close as possible to my subject, I have also added reproductions of contemporary engravings that must be regarded as witnesses of their era.

The first French edition of this *History* dates from 2009. It aimed at *pleasing* the readers. May we consider with the French second edition of 2015 and this English translation, that it has reached its goal? Let's hope it will meet an ever-increasing readership, willing to share my passion for the remote and mysterious island of Jamaica.

Thibault Ehrengardt

Contents

1

Conquering A New World

On October 12, 1492, the silhouettes of 3 Spanish vessels appeared on the horizon of the Lucayes islands, north-east of the Gulf of Mexico. The *Pinta*, the *Nina* and the *Santa Maria* came from the blue like mythological creatures, with their lungs swelled with the Trade Winds. A hundred men were on board, who had left the old Europe for over a month, sailing a dreadful sea which was said by the Ancients to be populated by monsters. It was also supposed to brutally plunge into a world of darkness at the ends of the world. Their senseless enterprise challenged more than 4 centuries of scholastic and prejudice; and they did it under the leadership of one man, Christopher Columbus. Their bodies were slimmed, their faces drawn by hardships and fears. None before them had ever been so far to the West. This very day, joy filled their hearts while the prospect of gold stirred their imagination. Those who were sceptical, and who almost threw Columbus overboard at one point, fell on their knees, tormented by remorse, and carried away by admiration. They prepared a row-boat, and Columbus, his drawn sword in hand, dressed in his nicest clothes, and flying the flag of his Spanish masters, set a foot in the New World. Dozens of Natives had gathered on the beach. They went naked and knew nothing about iron. They seemed to be abased at the apparition of these incredible beings with their chins full of hairs, and who rode fantastic aquatic creatures—they looked as if they had fallen from the sky.

Columbus kissed the ground and then took possession of this pagan land in the names of His Catholic Majesties, Queen Isabella of Castile and King Ferdinand of Aragon. In the background, his men erected a cross on the beach. Columbus had just changed the course of history, and he knew it—it had taken him 8 years, travelling from Court to Court all over Europe, mocked and betrayed; but he had finally made it! He had not found a New World—he did not know about that yet—, but a new sea route to the Indies of Marco Polo, the breadbasket of spices and precious metals! None but Isabella had had faith in him. In return, Columbus made her kingdom the most powerful in both the old, and the new Worlds—and he took Europe out of the Middle Age.

The Portuguese, or the end of obscurantism

On the engraving of the 18th century (see illustration), the Infant Don Henri, Prince of Portugal, has a severe and straight look that illustrates his motto, *talent de bien faire*. All, in this flattering representation, tends to depict a learned and pious Prince, who was *born*, writes Joseph-François Lafitau[*], *close enough to the throne to be worthy to occupy it, but far enough from it by birth to live all his life as a subject*. At the dawn of the 15th century, this man hurled Portugal and the entire Europe in its wake into the lights of naval discoveries. Staying far from society, Don Henri devoted himself to sciences and voyages. Being a coastal nation, Portugal had developed a consequent fleet, but navigation remained a stagnant art that had hardly improved since the Antiquity. Without a compass and a sextant, which were, at the time, yet to be discovered in Europe, it was impossible to pull away from the coasts, where navigation was still made perilous by the reefs and ill winds that blew around the capes. Not to mention the psychological barriers erected by the Ancients. They had divided the world into 5 zones. The first 2 ones were the poles which were deemed too icy, thus uninhabitable. On the contrary, the middle zone which was also referred to as the Torrid Zone, was burnt by the sun's fire—the water itself turned to flames. This insurmountable barrier separated the last 2 zones, said to be temperate, and upon which 2 sets of men lived forever separate. In the early 18th century, Father Labat underlines[†]: "*Some famous schools still seriously affirm that the Torrid Zone is uninhabitable (...). We could forgive it before (...) but to say it nowadays is a little bit ridiculous and stubborn.*" Ill equipped and filled with terrors, the navigators of the 15th century were bound to a restraint circle of action—they had never passed the aptly named Cape No.

The fads of Don Henri spread around the Mediterranean Sea. All the sailors, whether Muslims or Christians, came to him to relate their

---

[*] *Histoire des découvertes et conquestes des Portugais...* (Paris, 1734). (F)
[†] *Nouveau Voyage aux isles de l'Amérique* (La Haye, 1724). (F)

daring journeys, asking him to finance their bold expeditions. Any brave heart found a keen ear in this Prince, who was mocked at Court for his fanciful passion. But as soon as 1412, his *discoverers* passed the Cape No. Six years later, they discovered the Madeira Islands. Sailing the unknown oceans as the ambassadors of his visions, *Henri's discoverers* repelled the frontiers of the world. They discovered the Senegal River, and then safely crossed the Torrid Zone! Though revolutionary, the progress remained slow; when Henri died in 1463, the Portuguese had not yet sailed the full West coast of Africa. But the Prince had passed the torch to the young Juan II, who carried on his legacy.

The world owes a lot to the Portuguese navigators, who first passed the Cape of Good Hope in 1497 with Vasco de Gama; they were the first to circumnavigate the globe too, in the person of Magellan—though flying the Spanish flag at the time, he was Portuguese, and had first sailed in the East Indies; they picked up the compass and the sextant during their numerous journeys, thus enabling the navigators to sail off the coasts, and to save precious time. Nonetheless, posterity passed them by as a result of one man, whom they refused to help and then tried to betray; a man who, within a single journey, forever cast their efforts into the shadow. This man was responsible for the misfortune of Portugal as well as the fortune of the rival kingdom of Spain. His name was Christopher Columbus.

Columbus and the Portuguese

The story of Columbus, a Genoa born in 1450 or 1451, is closely linked to the people of the Infant Henri. Raised in a family of sailors, he soon went to sea, while learning geography, cosmography or mathematics—though many have doubted his erudition, reducing him to an opportunist, who had simply exploited others' ideas. In 1467, the ship he was sailing sank off the coast of Portugal, and he reached the shore in extremis. He settled in the country, probably the most exciting one for a young and ambitious sailor of the 15th century. He married the daughter of one of *Henri's discoverers*, Bartholomew de Pestrello, whose archives fascinated him. Thanks to them, he came up with a theory that would change the world. Columbus believed the Earth was round, as many Ancients did—though some believed it was flat and bounded—, and he wondered whether he could reach the Indies before the Portuguese (who took so long to explore the West coast of Africa) by sailing due West. Circumnavigating the globe, he was bound to reach the Indies. He talked about his project to a Florentine friend as soon as

1474—it took him more than 20 years to turn it into a reality. He first went to the Genoa Senators but they were ill informed about the latest discoveries. Furthermore, they did not know Columbus who had been living for so long in foreign. Thus, they turned him down.

Columbus then contacted the King of Portugal, Juan II, who listened to him. The notoriety of Columbus was nationwide at the time, as well as his brother's, a renowned cartographer. The councillors of the King, on hearing Columbus and studying his project, decided to give it a try—behind his back. But the caravel they surreptitiously sent to the sea sailed for several weeks, meeting nothing but hardships and despair. Betrayed, threatened by a failure that the Court unjustly reproached him, Columbus slipped out of Portugal to reach Spain in 1484. The King of France was too absorbed in war to pay attention to Columbus; and the King of England could not be reached. Indeed, Christopher's brother, Bartholomew, was captured by pirates on his way to England, where he intended to expose his brother's project to the King—he remained prisoner for several months, eventually reaching the Court of England to hear about his brother's successful journey.

In Spain, the negotiations with Isabella and the inconstant Ferdinand happened to be long and complicated. Columbus had no personal fortune to invest, and he had no title. On the contrary, he had many claims. After several unsuccessful interviews with the monarchs, he was about to leave Spain when Grenada, the last Moorish bastion in Spain, was eventually taken. This was 1492, the *crucial year*.‡ In the middle of general euphoria that ensued, Columbus' friends convinced Isabella. Before leaving, the navigator obtained the title of Great Admiral of the

---

‡ The Jews and the Moors were chased from Spain, and Columbus discovered America.

Opposite: Christopher Columbus at the top; Prince Henri; a world map from the Middle Age, showing the various Zones.

Septĕtr. frigida.

Temperata noſtra.

Torrida.

erata antipodũ.

ĩoĩda.

Ocean Sea—hence his nickname of *Admiral*—, as well as 10 per cents of all the profits his future discoveries might generate, for life and to be continued with his heirs. The preparations for departure were quick and not costly—no more than £400, according to Robertson[§]. They had 3 vessels. Columbus was sailing upon the *Santa Maria*, whereas three other sailors, the Pinson brothers, were dispatched on board of the *Pinta* and the *Maria*. These vessels were ill adapted to sail the open sea. Yet, carrying 1 month of provisions, Columbus and his 90 men headed due west, soon leaving all known sea routes behind them. The Admiral had to lie to his crew, switching from kindness to severity, back and forth, in order to keep them together—until the night of October 11, when he caught a glimpse at a light. Columbus had just discovered a new world.

Meet A New World

Columbus reached the island of San Salvador, and it was fascinating. His men knew nothing about the vegetation, or about the bronzed bodies the half naked Natives around them. The Castilians focused on the thin golden plates they wore around their necks. They asked them about their provenance, and the Natives pointed their fingers southwards. Columbus was not motivated by greed, but he knew nothing would plead his cause with the King like the precious metal. The 3 vessels sailed to Cuba, where a few false observations achieved to convince them they had reached the land of the Great Khan described by Marco Polo. It was then logical for them to call the Natives *Indians*, since they genuinely thought they had reached

§ *The History of America* (1777).

India. They found no gold in Cuba, so they sailed towards a new island, Hispaniola—today's Haiti/Dominican Republic. But one of the Pinsons suddenly sailed away despite Columbus' warnings. The Admiral feared he would go back to Spain to claim his discovery. Nonetheless, he resumed his journey, making friends with the chief of the Natives of Hispaniola, Cacique⁹ Guacanahari. But Columbus grew suspicious of his being isolated, and of Pinson, who had sailed away; so he decided to go back home. First, he erected a fort in Hispaniola, and called it *La Navidad* (nativity). He left Diego d'Arada and 38 volunteers inside, and departed the Caribbean islands on January 4, 1493. He joined Pinson 2 days later, pretending to accept his evasive explanations not to ruin his glorious trip.

Columbus was first thrown into the port of Lisbon, where people celebrated his success while the nobles were planning his death—fortunately, the king opposed their plot. Then he sailed to the Spanish port of Palos, Spain, where he entered 7 months and 11 days after his departure. The march to Barcelona was magnificent. A handful of Natives from Hispaniola led the way, observed by dozens of thousands of curious. The historian De Paw quotes** Dapper to underline that these Natives had tried to commit suicide during their journey to Europe: "*As they had been tied down so they would not hurt themselves, they entered a sort of rage that did not cease until they died. When they were taken to Barcelona, they scared all the curious with their yells, and their contortions; their movements were so violent, people thought they were frenetic.*" The Monarchs welcomed Columbus as a king—they refused to let him bow before them. The gold and the fantastic tales of his companions excited and charmed the Court. Everyone thought the Admiral had discovered King Solomon's mines! The whole country grew fascinated, and the second expedition was organised in a few weeks' time. This time, 17 vessels set sail, carrying 1,500 people to the New World, including many nobles.

The Pope's Bull

The good fortune of Spain aroused the envy of all other nations in Europe. Fearing for the riches she intended to keep for herself, Spain called upon Rome. The decisions of the Pope, published through bulls, were highly respected at the time. The Supreme Pontiffs, says[††]

---

⁹ "Cacique, in their language, meant 'prince' or 'lord', and the Spaniards turned it into a generic term to refer not only to all the sovereigns in America (...) but also to the chiefs of the smallest villages." Charlevoix, *Histoire de S. Domingue*. (F)

** *Recherches Philosophiques sur les Américains* (Berlin, 1774). (F)

†† *The History of the Reign of the Emperor Charles V* (Complete works, London, 1817).

Robertson, *disposed of crowns; absolved subjects from the obedience due to their sovereigns; and laid kingdoms under interdicts. There was not a state in Europe which had not been disquieted by their ambition. There was not a throne which they had not shaken; nor a Prince, who did not tremble at their power.* And the throne was then occupied by one of the worst Popes ever, the infamous Alexander VI. An offspring of the Borgia's linage—that had already given a Pope to the world, Calixte III—, Alexander VI was elected Supreme Pontiff in July 1492. His pontificate was riddled with crimes and infamies. He aimed at nothing but securing the fortune of his relatives, including his notorious son, Cesare Borgia. *"He had the bizarre idea of having one of his bastards* (Cesare, who inspired several chapters of Machiavelli's *The Prince—* editor's note) *crowned Emperor of Germany* (...) *He imagined that with the support of the King of Spain, he would succeed. Thus he spared no occasion and no flattery, to express his sympathy towards Isabella and Ferdinand. When the West Indies* (the New World—editor's note) *were discovered, he granted America to them, though he did not even know where it was."* Such was the greedy and rogue Pope[‡‡] who issued the Inter Caetera bull that divided the unknown world in two. He drew a line from pole to pole, a hundred leagues to the westward of the Azores, and bestowed all the land east to this line upon the Portuguese, and all those to the west upon the Spaniards. The bull reads: *"Of our own sole largess and certain knowledge and out of the fullness of our apostolic power, by the authority of Almighty God conferred upon us in blessed Peter and of the vicarship of Jesus Christ, which we hold on earth, do by tenor of these presents, should any of said islands have been found by your envoys and captains, give, grant, and assign to you and your heirs and successors, kings of Castile and Leon, forever, together with all their dominions, cities, camps, places, and villages, and all rights, jurisdictions, and appurtenances, all islands and mainlands* (sic) *found and to be found, discovered and to be discovered towards the west and south, by drawing and establishing a line from the Arctic pole, namely the north, to the Antarctic pole, namely the south, no matter whether the said mainlands and islands are found and to be found in the direction of India or towards any other quarter, the said line to be distant one hundred leagues towards the west and south from any of the islands commonly known as the Azores and Cape Verde."* In spite of the respect they had for the Pope—and the fact that they had called upon his authority to secure their own discoveries

---

[‡‡] He died in 1503 after inadvertently drinking some poisonous wine he intended to serve to some of his hosts.

in Africa—, the Portuguese could not give up a whole world without putting up a fight. Threatening to go to war, they forced the Pope to move back the demarcation line, which later enabled them to settle in Brazil.

Left out of the sharing, the other European nations soon defied the Papal authority. As soon as 1497, the Venetian Sebastian Cabot sailed along the West coast of the American continent on orders of the King of England; from the 56°, he went downward to Florida, before heading back to Europe—in 1526, he ran up the Plata River, where stands today's Buenos Aires. William Hawkins, for his part, reached Brazil in 1530. Jealous over their prerogatives, the Spaniards captured every foreign ship they came across in this region. That was what happened to Francis Drake during his first journey to the West Indies. Determined to recoup his loss, he went back to the New World in 1572 to plunder the Spanish colony of Nombre de Dios, and to intercept the *mule train* that carried the gold of Peru to Panama.

In 1580, during another voyage, Drake was forced to enter the South Sea with the Spaniards coming after him; he had no choice but to come back through Asia, thus becoming the first English to circumnavigate the globe. He was made a knight, but was seen as a vulgar pirate by most of the nobility. The Spaniards enraged, produced the Papal bull, and complained to Queen Elizabeth. Thomas Lediard[§§] reproduced the answer of the Protestant sovereign to the ambassador of Spain: "*The Spaniards have drawn these inconveniences upon themselves by their severe and unjust dealings in their American commerce (...) If someone can convince Drake of having broken the laws of humanity, let him be judged (...); though all the gold of Drake does not amount the one I had to spend to calm the uprising caused by your Prince in Ireland and England* (in 1579—editor's note)." The French King François I, for his part, giggled and asked to be shown the article in Adam's will that excluded him from the succession of the New World. But the art of rhetoric and the art of politics where two distinct sciences, and as Elizabeth returned *a considerable part* of Drake's booty, the said Drake went back to the West Indies to plunder more Spanish settlements—he eventually died there, in 1596. None had the right to go to the West Indies but those authorized by Isabella—who first granted this privilege to Castilians only. The reunion of the kingdoms of Spain and Portugal soon enabled the heirs of Don Henri to travel to the Americas, but all other nations were kept away from this formidable cookie-jar. For more than one century, they were outraged by the riches discharged by the Spanish

§§ *Histoire navale d'Angleterre* (Lyon, 1751). (F)

galleons into the ports of Spain, looking for the slightest opportunity to harm this selfish nation. The French, the Dutch and the English were the first ones to defy Spain; first capturing the 'lesser' islands in the West Indies, they soon reached the greater ones, and then the continent itself. Little by little, they redrew the geopolitical map of the New World. Furthermore, the Pope's influence grew thinner and the English historian Edward Long underlines[11] that the proud bull of 1493 made people smile in 1774.

1493, the Second Voyage

When he returned to fort *La Navidad*, in Hispaniola, Christopher Columbus found it burnt and demolished. His men had taken liberties with the Natives, looting, robbing and raping, until they were attacked by an angry group of men, who surrounded them into the fort, where they eventually murdered them—or in a nearby sea inlet they had tried to cross to escape. Columbus quickly renewed his friendship with Guacanahari, but only for a while. The Natives knew nothing about agriculture or breeding livestock, and satisfied themselves with what Nature offered them. Since they considered work as an absurdity, they compensated their lack of activity by frugal meals. But these strange men wearing beards ate 3 times a day! The Natives started to wonder: had these insatiable creatures been driven here by famine? When war broke out again in 1494, the Admiral had just come back from a miserable expedition in the West Indies, during which he discovered nothing of interest but the island of Jamaica—the Spaniards did not care about it until a few years later. The fight was, of course, unfair; the Natives only had wooden spears to oppose the Spanish muskets, and fought disorderly, being soon disbanded by the English and their dreadful dogs and horses—the Natives could not tell the man from the beast, and these 'centaurs' sowed terror among them. Columbus thus easily defeated their army that the historians joyfully estimated to be about 100,000 men; he imposed them a tax in gold. The first plague had just fallen on these lands that the Spaniards subdued with the most extreme brutality, blinded by their thirst for power and glory.

Columbus might not have been a keen politician, but he was a persistent man. Though Ferdinand restlessly tried to spoil him and his heirs, he stuck to his privileges until his death. His discovery was so tremendous, how could Ferdinand invest him with more power than he himself held? Furthermore, the Spanish monarch was rather

---

[11] *History of Jamaica* (London, 1774).

unscrupulous. As soon as the second voyage, Columbus was disgraced. A small bunch of conjurers chased out of Hispaniola complained to the King. These nobles were, to be truthful, terribly disappointed by this New World, where they had expected to grow rich without effort. But they came back with pale faces, weak bodies, and fever. Had this damn Columbus endeavoured to destroy the best of Spain's nobility? The Admiral sensed a change in the wind and hastily headed to Spain to justify himself in front of the Catholic Monarchs, who welcomed him with respect. But the craze of the New World was over; yet, Columbus needed volunteers to populate his colony. He suggested emptying the prisons of Spain to send the convicts to Hispaniola. Villains and murderers then packed his ship, impatient to reach the New World. *"Had this enterprising seaman carried out men of the common stamp, he might, during the voyage, have inspired them with honest principles, if not with high notions of honour,"* guesses*** Guillaume-Thomas Raynal. These new colonists only made things worst in Hispaniola, where the authority of Columbus was contested; when new complaints reached Spain, the King sent the terrible Bovadilla—in 1500. He had Columbus chained, and he sent him back to Europe. Offended in his dignity, the Great Admiral kept his irons until his death, and even demanded to literally take them to his grave. Step by step, he was pushed aside. Other Spaniards went to conquer the New World, including Americo Vespucci, who, following a murky affair of forged dates, was crowned discoverer of the *continent*—or Terra Firma—, named *America* in his honour. Meanwhile in Spain, Columbus was fighting to obtain, and to keep, what Ferdinand had promised him. Everything seemed to be lost when, suddenly, the Portuguese passed the Cape of Good Hope, bringing back astonishing fortunes from India. Ferdinand started to wonder. There might have a shorter way to India beyond the new continent, as suggested by Columbus. Wishing to get ahead of the Portuguese, he granted 4 vessels to Columbus, who, on May 9, 1502, set sail for his 4th and last voyage— during which he wrecked his boats on the coast of Jamaica.

Columbus in Jamaica

Columbus discovered Jamaica[†††] during his second voyage, as related

---

*** *Histoire philosophique et politique de l'établissement et du commerce des Européens dans les deux Indes* (Genève, 1780). (F)

††† The name Jamaica has been the subject of many assumptions. *"The English observe that it is a mistake common to most of our geographers to believe that the name Jamaica derives from the ancient name of the island,"* explains La Harpe in *Histoire Générale des Voyages* (1759). *"Everyone knows, they say, it was named Sant'Iago by Christopher Columbus, which*

by his biography, written by his second son, Ferdinand. The latter, aged 13, was from the 3rd voyage:

> On Saturday the 3rd of May, The Admiral resolved to sail over from Cuba to Jamaica, that he might not leave it behind, without knowing whether the report of such plenty of gold they had there, was in it, proved true, and the wind being fair, (...) he discovered it on Sunday. Upon Monday, he came to an anchor (St Ann's Bay—editor's note) and found it the beautifullest (sic) of any he had yet seen in the Indies, and such multitudes of people in great and small canoes came aboard, that is was astonishing. The next day he ran along the coast to find out harbours, and the boats going to found the mouths of them, there came out so many canoes and armed men, to defend the country, that they were forced to return to the ship, not so much for fear, as to avoid falling to enmity with those people. But afterwards considering that if they showed signs of fear the Indians would go proud upon it, they returned together to the port, which the Admiral called Puerto Bueno, that is, Good Harbour (Discovery Bay—editor's note). And because the Indians came to drive them off, those in boats

means St James; and from this James, or Iago in Spanish, comes the name Jamaica." This explanation was quickly contested by many historians, including Bridges who denounces a gross mistake, reminding that early historians such as Acosta or Benzo already named it *Jamaycque*, more than 100 years before the first English set a foot on it. *"The island (...) had its name at the time of the first discovery by Columbus,"* specifies Sloane. *"The Spaniards write it either Jamaica, Jamayca, or Xamaica."* The Natives called it Xamayca. *"We must (...) suppose that the word* Xaymaca *would probably denote the most obvious qualities of the land to which these Indian savages pointed* (to Columbus—editor's note)," says Bridges. *"On so in fact, it did; for in the speech of Florida,* chabaüan *signified water, and* makia, *wood. The compound sound would approach to* Chab-makia. *This, and, harmonized to the Spanish ear, would be* Chamakia." Bryan Edwards reminds us that some historians such as Oldmixon (author of *The British Empire in America*) had wrongfully supposed that the name derived from Sant'Iago. *"It (...) was called St. Jago* (at one point)," says Sloane, *"but soon obtained again its first name (...). The descendents and prosterity of Columbus were, and are still called* (in 1707) *Dukes of Veragua and Vega, and Marquesses of Jamaica."* Antonio de Herrera tells us that at the time when Sancho de Matienço was abbot of the island after the death of Peter Martyr, he ordered the island to be named *Santiago*—but he dates this change around 1514, while Peter Martyr was the abbot of the island from 1524 to 1526. Hans Sloane writes that Peter Martyr, made abbot, gave back its first name to the island. Then he adds: *"The island of Antego, one of the Antisles or Caribes, had the same name with this island given it by the Indians, but it was soon changed to that of Santa Maria del Antigua from whence the present name is by corruption derived."*

gave them such a flight of arrows from their crossbows, that six or seven of them being wounded, they retired. The fight ending in this manner; there came an abundance of canoes from the neighbouring   places   in   peaceable manner, to see and barter provisions, and several things they brought, and gave for the least trifle that was offered them. In this port, which is like a horseshoe, the Admiral's ship was repaired, it being leaky, and that done, they set sail on Friday the 9th of May, keeping so close along the coast westward, that the Indians followed in their canoes to trade, and get something of ours. The wind being somewhat contrary, the Admiral could not make so much way as he wished, till on Tuesday the 14th of May, he resolved to stand over again for Cuba, to keep along its coast, designing not to return till he had sailed 5 or 600 leagues and were satisfied whether it was an island or a continent. That same day, as he was going off from Jamaica, a very young Indian came aboard, saying, he could come unto Spain, and after him came several of his kindred and other people in their canoes, earnestly entreating him to go back, but they could never alter his resolution; and therefore to avoid seeing his sisters cry and sob, he went where they could not come at him. The Admiral admiring his resolution gave order that he should be used with all civility.

From May till July, the Admiral explored the Cuban coast, and then came back to Jamaica. Sailing along the coast from today's Montego Bay, he found a *pleasant and fruitful* country, with many harbours and villages. The Indians brought some provisions *much better liked by the Christians, than what they found in the other islands.* (Columbus) Every

night, contrary winds forced the Admiral to cast his anchor into welcoming harbours, described as *abounding in provisions, and so populous that he thought none excelled it, especially near a bay he called de las vacas* (Cow Bay—editor's note). There he came in touch with a Cacique, who had come to him half-naked and wearing a head-lace with precious stones artfully put together, and locked on his forehead with a golden badge. The Indian asked Columbus to take him to Spain, but was denied. Eventually, after a full day spent at Portland Bight, Columbus resumed his tour of the island; upon reaching the eastern point, he headed to Hispaniola.

Columbus did not see Jamaica again until 1502, during his terrible 4th voyage. By then, he had been somewhat cast aside of the discoveries of the New World. When he asked Governor Ovando for permission to

Above : Coumbus' ship—detail of his arriving to the New World; the island of Hispaniola by Bordone (1528); the first isolated representation of Jamaica by Bordone (1528); Columbus' coat of arms.

refit his damaged vessel, he was refused. He sailed away, desperately cruising the Caribbean islands. Suffering from the gout—a form of arthritis—, exhausted by all these years of adversity and sickness, he fought against the contrary winds of the region just like he had fought against those of fortune all his life. He describes his state of mind in a letter: "*Hitherto, I have wept for others; but now, have pity upon me, heaven, and weep for me, O earth!*" (Irving[‡‡‡]) Things got from bad to worse. Because of their decayed hulls, the boats were falling apart; they banged into each other during a tempest—the first one lost her bow, the next one her stern and cables. When the Admiral miraculously reached Puerto Bueno in Jamaica, he had no choice: "*The boats being unable to stand the sea any more*," says Herrera, "(the Spaniards) *drew near the shore, within crossbow shot, fastened them, side by side, supporting them with scaffoldings (...). Finally, they were filled with water up to the deck; upon which, as well as at the sterns and bows, they built some apartments to accommodate the men.*" Columbus was first and foremost concerned about providing his men with provisions. Diego Mendez de Segura, *a prudent man of honour* (Herrera), volunteered to walk from village to village in order to enter into arrangements with the Caciques. At the eastern point of the island, he made friends with the powerful Cacique Ameyro, bought a canoe from him, and then sailed back to the Admiral. "*He returned in triumph to the harbor, where he was received with acclamations by his comrades, and with open arms by the admiral*," says Irving. This was yet a temporarily victory. Columbus was aware of it. He took Mendez aside, and told him: "*Mendez my son (...) none of those whom I have here understand the great peril in which we are placed, except you and me (...). In this canoe which you have purchased, some one may pass over to Hispaniola, and procure a ship.*" (Irving) Hispaniola was not that far from Jamaica, but the sea was rough, the currents unfriendly and the Spaniard's crafts derisory. It was a perilous expedition, not to say desperate. Columbus appointed a Genoa named Bartholomew Fiesco to go with Mendez—his orders were to come back to Jamaica upon reaching Hispaniola to keep the Admiral informed as soon as possible. Mendez, for his part, had to jump on the first caravel to Spain to carry letters to the Catholic Monarchs. The Castilians went to the eastern point of the island, and there waited for the best departure conditions with 6 other Castilians and 60 Indians. On July 7, 1503, Mendez and Fiesco embarked with their small provisions and all the water calabashes their frail skiffs could contain. "*The Indians rowed restlessly*, explains Herrera, *and when tired,*

[‡‡‡] *The Life and Voyages of Christopher Columbus* (New York, 1851).

because of the heat or else, they jumped into the sea to refresh themselves, and then they returned inside their canoe."

They lost sight of Jamaica the first evening, finding themselves between the sea and the sky the next day, already short of water and exhausted by their efforts under the boiling sun. Two days and one night later, the islet of Navasa, located on their way to Hispaniola, was not in sight yet. *"They had already thrown an Indian into the sea, who had died out of thirst; others were lying unconscious at the bottom of the canoes, and those who remained, the more resistant, were quite melancholic, and waited for nothing but their time to come,"* goes on Herrera. Having no strength left, they eventually reached Navasa the 4th day, where they recovered their strength before setting off again for Hispaniola. Notwithstanding Columbus' orders, Fiesco followed Mendez to Santo Domingo. Governor Ovando, upon learning about the misfortune of Columbus, did not rush to rescue him—he feared the reaction of the Admiral's many enemies, who lived in the colony. He reassured Mendez and Fiesco, and then sent one of Columbus' enemies to make sure of the latter's situation, forbidding him to rescue him.

Meanwhile in Jamaica, provisions grew few, and everybody wondered about Mendez and Fiesco, reckoning they had perished at sea. The Admiral's troops were restless, and he forbade them to leave the wrecked ships to trade with the Indians. His men were afraid never to leave this place; they were also angry at the Admiral, his brother Bartholomew and his son Fernand, and they expressed resentment more and more openly. One thing led to another and, on January 2, 1504, the dissidents led by 2 brothers, the Porras, came to the Admiral, weapon in hand. Columbus, then lying in his bed after a terrible attack of the gout, allowed them to leave the ships to avoid a blood bath. The Porras then took possession of the canoes bought from the Indians, and headed toward the eastern point of the islands with a majority of the crew. They intended to follow the footsteps of Mendez and Fiesco. But they refused to leave their belongings behind, and took them on board; as a result, the overloaded canoes let water in. The Indians were very good swimmers, and they knew how to make the best use of their canoes; they jumped into the sea when the water started to fill them, reversed them to empty them, and then jumped back into them. But the Castilians could not do the same—because of their belongings, first; and then, because they could not swim. As the water rose, they got scared, and threw away everything they could, including the Indians. The unfortunate were too far from the shore to swim back, so they swam besides the canoes until their forces gave up on them. Ten they asked for the permission to grab the canoes for a while, in order to rest. "*But far from being that charitable,*" relates Herrera, " (the Castilians) *cut their hands off with their swords.*" Eventually forced to turn back, convinced that Fiesco and Mendez coud not have succeeded where they twice failed, the Porras brothers and their men started to roam Jamaica, harassing the Arawak Indians.

Near Puerto Bueno, Columbus and his remaining men were worried, as the visits of the Indians—upon whom they depended for food—grew less frequent. Without them, they would not survive. According to the various historians, the Admiral always behaved correctly with

the Natives—unlike his companions and successors. But the situation was critical. He then had quite a novelistic idea. He summoned all the Caciques to inform them that his powerful God, upset by their behaviour, had decided to darken the moon at night to cast them into everlasting darkness. His scientific knowledge had enabled him to

Above: detail of the battle between Porras and Colombus, as depicted by Theodore de Bry. We notice 2 historical mistakes: Columbus was sick, and did not personally attend the fight. There were 2 boats, and they were wrecked; the fauna of Jamaica; a map of the West Indies (17ᵗʰ century).

foretell an eclipse—when it took place, the Indians threw themselves at the Admiral's feet, begging for mercy. Columbus promised to do his best. The moon reappeared, and he never went short of provisions again.

The ship sent by Ovando appeared at last. Diego de Escobar, one of Columbus' enemies, had a quick talk with the Admiral, and left him a small barrel of food before heading back to Hispaniola to report to Ovando. Columbus offered a portion of the barrel to the conjurers, but the Porras had made up their mind to bring it to a fight. The Admiral could not get up, so his brother took the lead of their small troop. The 2 parties met near Mayma, where the Spaniards later established their first settlement. The fight turned in favour of Columbus' troops. The Porras were taken prisoners, and all their men surrendered. The Admiral granted them his pardon to maintain peace until help arrived. At last rescued from the shore of Jamaica, Columbus reached Hispaniola where the conjurers were treated with a complacent indulgence. But he was too exhausted to take umbrage—he left the Americas on June 18, 1504, never to come back. Upon his arrival, he learnt about the death of his protector Isabella—the end of an era. Columbus died in Valladolid, Spain, on May 20, 1506, without fulfilling his divine mission, which, he believed, consisted in raising an army with the gold of the New World to liberate the Holy Sepulchre. Indeed, Columbus was a mystic man, tormented with visions and furies.

Ferdinand paid homage to the discoverer, appointed his sons to various honourable functions—including Governor of Jamaica for his eldest son Diego—and undertook to slowly rip them off everything their father had earned. The body of Columbus was carried to Hispaniola several years later, then repatriated to Seville. The epitaph of his grave, simple, sums up his life to his most important achievement: *He gave Castile-Leon[§§§] a New World.*

[§§§] A Spanish kingdom united to Castile since 1217.

2

Any Spaniard in Heaven?

Tied to a stake and about to be burnt alive, Cacique Hatuey, who had been captured in Cuba in 1511 after resisting the Spanish invasion, was approached by a Saint Franciscan Father, who urged him to convert to Christianity so he could enter Heaven. The stoic Indian wondered: "Are the Spaniards also admitted into Heaven?" – *The gates of Heaven are open to all who are good and godly*, answered the religious. "I'd rather go to hell than Heaven, for fear I should cohabit in the same mansion with so sanguinary and bloody a nation." He then perished by the flames, pagan but free.

Bartholomew de La Casas

The anecdote of Cacique Hatuey, like hundreds of others, is related in a book entitled *Brevissima Relacion de la Destruycion de las Indias*— or, *Account of the Devastation of the Indies*—, and published in 1522. His author, the Dominican Father Bartholomew de Las Casas, is a key figure of the history of the New World. He grew with an Indian, whom his father had brought back in 1493 from his travel to the West Indies with Christopher Columbus—until Queen Isabella ordered the Spaniards to send back all Indians. A scholar, Las Casas became passionate about the Indians. A feeling that *was excited to tenfold fervor, when, at about the age of twenty-eight years, he accompanied the commander Ovando to Hispaniola in 1502, and was an eye-witness to many of the cruel scenes which took place*, writes Irving. Actually, when he first went there, Las Casas had no other plan but to get rich as quick as possible. In this regard, he had associated with another religious, Pedro de la Renteria.

In his lengthy manuscript*, which remained unpublished for several centuries, Las Casas confesses—talking about himself in the third person: *"He had started to make himself a reputation of being a very interested man, as he was showing (...) readiness to take care of his lands and mines."* To make profits, he shamelessly exploited the Indians appointed to his service—the famous *repartimientos*, bestowed on every Spaniard by the Governor. But all of a sudden, the ordeal of his slaves became unbearable to him; and he became the most zealous defender of the Indians. But he was not the first to care about them. Queen Isabella was their very first rampart against the Castilians. She was so concerned about them, that she dedicated an article of her will to their preservation: *"Ever since the apostolic throne has granted us the islands and the mainland of the Ocean sea, our main intention has always been to bring the benefits of our faith to the peoples of the New World, and to send there some religious to convert them (...). I beg the King Lord and the Princess my daughter to keep on working to make this enterprise a success and to protect the Indians from any harm."* In 1502, she made the exploitation of the Indians illegal, and commanded that they be paid and their works contingent on their decisions. The activity stopped overnight in Hispaniola. But when she died in 1504, the fate of the Natives changed for the worse. The Spaniards reduced them to slavery by any means necessary. The first Dominican Fathers to go to Hispaniola in 1510, including Father Montesino, publicly expressed their indignation in historical preaches. Las Casas described scenes of uncommon brutality, which portrayed his fellow countrymen as bloodthirsty beasts. His testimony was at once translated into several languages all over Europe. The stunning engravings of Theodore de Bry, which usually illustrate his text, reinforced the strength of this incredible piece of work, which put the entire nation of Spain to shame. The 'black legend' was born. Las Casas describes some Spaniards *from the rabble; who call conquests some unjust and cruel wars they fought in the New World where they had entered to exterminate the inhabitants (...). They murder, slaughter, loot, they plunder the countries they cross.* In their voracious hands, the Indians are compared to *ten-year-old infants, naturally simple,* knowing *not malice, trickery or cheating.* Region after region, Las Casas lists the exactions of the Castilians. In Mexico, *they burnt some, had others eaten up by their hungry dogs; they cut off the feet of some, the hands, the arms, the tongues, the heads, just to intimidate them.* In Cuba, a ceremony was given by the Indians in their honour; *but behold on a sudden, some*

---

* *History of the Indies* (Harper & Rowe, 1971).

wicked devil possessing the minds of the Spaniards, agitated them with great fury, that I being present, and without the least pretence or occasion offered, they cut off in cold blood above three thousand men, women and children promiscuously, such inhumanities and barbarisms were committed in my sight, as no age can parallel. The Spaniards were pure rage and fury. They *bred up curst curs (...) they carry these dogs with them as companions where ever they go, and kill the fettered Indians in multitudes like hogs for their food; thus sharing with them in the butchery. Nay they frequently call one to the other, saying, lend me the fourth part of one of your slaves to feed my dogs, and when I kill one, I will repay you, as if they had only borrowed a quarter of a hog or sheep*. Soon, the workers went missing in Hispaniola! Ovando then decided to import Natives from the Lucayos islands—today's Bahamas—, pretending to draw them closer to the Lord. "*By this artifice above,*" says Marcus Rainsford[†], "*forty thousand were decoyed into Hispaniola to share in the sufferings which were the lot of the inhabitants of this island.*" On their journey, the Indians were not fed, and the corpses of those who died were simply thrown overboard. Las Casas affirms that a pilot, sailing the first time from the Lucayos, *without the need of compass or chart*, followed instead the trail of floating dead bodies tossed overboard by the ship before them. The Caribbean Indians were enslaved without any hesitation, as they were convinced of cannibalism—with Queen Isabella's consent, who could not stand such a sin. Yet, the Castilians did not hesitate to encourage their sinful inclination when it advanced their interests. Las Casas reports that, in order to feed an army of Caribbean Indians enrolled by force in Guatemala, the Spaniards *permitted them to feed on the flesh of other Indians taken prisoners in war; and so kept a shambles of man's flesh in his army, suffered children to be kill'd and roasted before his face. They butcher'd the men for their feet and hands only; for these members were accounted by them dainties, most delicious food*. Did Las Casas, a most passionate man, exaggerate? "*I guess* (his) *account is exaggerated in more than one part,*" confesses Voltaire[‡]. "*But even if he reports ten times more than what really happened, there's enough to frighten us.*" Today's historians consider his writings, though of a tremendous emotional strength, to be a partial reflection of reality. Except for one sentence in the introduction of his book, he does not evoke the diseases brought by the Europeans, for instance—and we know today that they decimated a lot of Indians, if not the majority.

---

† *The Black Empyre of Hayti* (Albion Press, 1805).
‡ *De Colombo et de l'Amérique* (Khel, 1784). (F)

Nonetheless, the Spaniards' brutality leaves breathless. Washington Irving depicts them as knights in shining armours, raised on the crusade against the Moors and entering pagan lands like Crusader knights willing to defeat bastions of infidels—some young and fierce dogs, drunk with the power and the glory. Las Casas' work was read all through Europe. Despised and envied, the Spaniards became unanimously decried—no one was more hated, during the 16th century, than a Spaniard.

The Yoke of the New World

The religious instruction of the Natives was the main concern of the Pope and Isabella. But in the West

Indies, the conquistadores had other priorities. They even opposed the conversion *of those they regarded as dogs or beasts* (Las Casas). Indeed, once baptized the Indians were less conveniently put to hard work. Furthermore, the debate was red hot: were these imperfect creatures sons of God? In the Bible, no mention is made of them. How come God remains silent about them? Where were they coming from, anyway—since the entire humanity was descended from Noah and his family,

Above: Las Casas, feather in hand; tortures inflicted on the Indians (engravings by Theodore de Bry).

were they the only survivors of the universal flood? The theologians eventually agreed: the Indians had a soul. Yet, the colonists were looking for any reason to treat them as beasts. Francisco Lopez de Gomara[§], a Spanish historian of the 16th century, does not beat around the bush: "*I think God has sent those poor wretched this servitude of hard work to punish them for their wickedness. Indeed, I think Cham never offended his father as much as these Indians have offended God; thus I think they are his descendants, and that they've inherited the spell God cast on him.*" In the Bible, having seen his father Noah drunk and naked, Cham is cursed by him, and condemned to become *the servant of the servants of his brothers*—the race of slaves, justified by this bizarre anecdote. When it came out, Gomara's book scandalized many people; but it summed up the position of a majority of Spaniards over those pagan and cannibal savages.

The Indians realized that gold attracted their executioners, and threw it into the lakes, hoping to make them leave—or was throwing gold into the lakes a religious ceremony, as recent researches tend to prove? Anyway, the Spaniards found gold mines in Cuba, Hispaniola, and then silver in the dreamlike Potosi, Peru. In order to extract it,

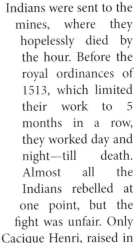

hundreds of thousands of Indians were sent to the mines, where they hopelessly died by the hour. Before the royal ordinances of 1513, which limited their work to 5 months in a row, they worked day and night—till death. Almost all the Indians rebelled at one point, but the fight was unfair. Only Cacique Henri, raised in the prestigious Spanish universities of the New World sustained a long war. He led an upheaval at Diego Columbus's sugar factory in Hispaniola, in 1519. With his men, he then sought refuge in the nearby hills, where he fought against

§ *Histoire Génerralle des Indes Occidentales* (Paris, 1569). (F)

the Spaniards for years, eventually forcing them to negotiate. But this masterpiece of resistance remains an exception. Everywhere else, the Indians were defeated because of their lack of military science, and because of their weak weapons, far less efficient than their foes'. They attacked with courage, but disorderly. Their ranks were quickly broken and their armies dispersed with a disarming ease. It took Fernand Cortes 3 years and 600 men only to conquer the mighty empire of Mexico.

Balboa In Peru

Two men of the famous conquistador Vasco Nunez de Balboa started to fight over a few grams of gold one day, under the despiteful look of a Cacique of the Darian Gulf. Kicking the gold away, the Indian disdainfully affirmed that he knew a place where this metal was used to make the most useful objects. He took them through the jungle across the Isthmus of Panama, to the shore of a previously unknown sea, the South Sea—today's Pacific Ocean. This was 1513, and the New World was yet to fulfil its promises. Which it did, with the discovery of Peru. As a matter of fact, that's where the Cacique intended to take Balboa and his men. But the Castilians were ill equipped and thought the expedition too perilous. Back to his colony of Santa Maria de Antigua, Balboa immediately sent an emissary to Spain to inform the King of his latest discovery—this was probably the worst idea of his life. Far from confirming Balboa's position, as expected by the latter, the King sent him the terrible Pedrarias instead, who soon cut his head off. Described by Charlevoix as *a well born officer of merit, whose gallant reputation took nothing away from his reputation of being a brave man*, Pedrarias was one of the few conquistadores whose names were called in Las Casas' book (at least the French edition). "*When he became Governor of the Indies, he entered these lands like an hungry wolf furiously rushing upon a flock of sheep; he committed so many atrocities, made some many massacres (...); he could have been regarded as a plague sent by God in His wrath to exterminate all Indians.*" Civil war was then devastating the New World. Each emissary from Spain murdered his rivals, wrongly accusing them of treason, corruption or summary executions. Everyday, a new emissary from the New World disembarked in Sevile, carrying the complaints of a conquistador. This inner feud reached their peak in the newly found land of Peru. The mines abounded in precious metals. The Spaniards sent their riches once a year to Panama; then, they transported them by land to Nombre de Dios—and to Puerto Bello from 1584—, and then embarked them again. After a stop in Cuba, the royal fleet crossed the Atlantic Ocean and landed in Cadix, Spain. The hegemony of Spain then extended over the whole Americas, but was it in position to sustain its colonies and, most of all, to defend them?

The Genocide of the Indies

Las Casas, who was appointed Protector of the Indians, restlessly went to and fro the Indies, fighting some powerful clans at Court[¶]. He thus obtained the first set of laws aiming at preserving the Indians. Thanks to his writings and his eloquence, he refuted the thesis contrary to the interests of the Indians—such as Sepulveda's, in 1550. Unfortunately, it was already too late for the Natives of the islands of the West Indies. Las Casas also wrote a *History of the Indies*; but he refused to publish it, fearing it might do more wrong to his nation. He handed his manuscript to the Council of the Indies, which kept it secret until the end of the 19th century; the Spanish writers, including Herrera, inspired so much from it that they established it as a silent reference book. Las Casas was obsessed with the evangelization of the Indians; he built a model society in Chiapa, to prove the world that his creatures, when properly educated, were able to live in a polished and advance society—a failure. He was so passionate, that he even suggested, in 1517, to substitute the Africans to the Indians. *"The clerk Las Casa,"* he says in his *History of the Indies*, *"says in his memoirs that the Spaniards should be granted the right to import (...) a dozen of* (African) *slaves (...) because, with them, they could earn a living in these countries and set their Indians free."* Thus Las Casas, probably the greatest humanist of his time, joined the supporters of the slave trade. Yet, the idea to deport Africans did not please everyone. Cardinal Ximenes, regent of Spain until the majority of Charles V, opposed it—he feared the warlike spirit of the Africans. In his biography of Ximenes, Marsollier[**] writes: *"Chièvres* (one of Charles V's advisors—editor's note) *bought five hundred robust Negroes and* (sent) *them to Saint-Domingue* (Hispaniola). *As soon as he learnt about it, Ximenes opposed the project, and wrote to Chièvres that he knew the spirit of the Negroes; that they were a very robust people indeed, but extremely fertile, that if given time to multiply in America, they would inevitably rebel, and eventually enchain those who had tried to enslave them."* To explain his reluctance, Washington Irving also evokes a desire to tax this new trade.

At the end of the day, Las Casas had the ban lifted and more than 4,000 African slaves were sent to the West Indies. This remedy, yet

---

¶ He was supported by the Flemish, especially Juand de Selviago, personal advisor of the King.
** *Histoire du Ministère du Cardinal Ximenez* (Toulouse, 1694). (F)

another poison, did not stop the genocide in the West Indies. But Irving considers that the decision of both Las Casas and Ximenes—who eventually agreed with him—must be put into historical perspective. At the time, he reminds us, no one contested the idea of slavery itself. Las Casas had yet enough judgement to regret his position: *"The piece of advice to authorize the importation of black slaves in these countries, the clerk Las Casas gave it right away, without thinking about the injustice with which the Portuguese capture and enslave them; had he thought about it, he would have never given it, as he has always considered that these men had unjustly become slaves, since they are entitled to the same rights than the Indians."* The religious took his regrets to his grave, in 1566—he was 92.

Rooted into a dark reality, the 'black legend' was used as a political tool. The Europeans pointed out the savagery of the Spaniards to justify the barbarous way they started to treat them. Indeed, during the era of the Buccaneers, the Spanish settlements in America were plundered, burnt and razed to the ground; and there was no more or less 'noble idea' of conquest then; furthermore, these enormities were perpetrated by Christians upon other Christians. But Europe had been longing for the gold of America for too long. The *cliché* of the bloodthirsty Spaniards had spread out—served them right!

Spanish Jamaica

When Columbus died, a war of succession started between his son Diego and King Juan II, who unjustly spoilt him of his privileges. Supported by his mother, Diego commenced a lawsuit against the Crown before the council of the Indies, which surprisingly ruled in his favour. *"But he King,"* recalls the historian Bryan Edwards[††], *"notwithstanding this distinguished and competent recognition of his rights, confirmed to him only the title and authority of governor and admiral of Hispaniola."* He went to Hispaniola as soon as 1508. But behind his back, the Court gave some lands discovered by his father to 2 other conquistadores, Alonso de Ojeda and Diego de Nicuessa. The former, supported by the worst enemy of the Columbus, the Bishop of Palencia—later of Burgos—, obtained an incredible concession over the continent, where he had already been twice with Amerigo Vespucci. Learning about Ojeda's good fortune, Nicuessa relied on his own connections to get half of the territory granted to him. Nicuessa thus

---

[††] The History, Civil and Commercial, of the British Colonies in the West Indies, (London, 1793).

became the Governor of Castilla del Oro, a territory stretching from the middle of the Gulf of Darien to Cape Gracias a Dios, while Ojeda was appointed Governor of New Andalousia, from the middle of the Gulf of Darien to the Cap de la Vela. Charlevoix underlines: *"Jamaica was granted to both Governors, as a place to furnished* (sic) *themselves with provisions and every necessary thing."* On their way to the continent, the 2 met in Hispaniola, where they had an argument. The boiling Ojeda suggested that they should settle the matter with their swords, but Nicuessa was too cunning, and not good enough a fighter, to comply. *"Jamaica was the bone of contention between the two of them,"* continues Charlevoix. For his part, Diego Columbus took offense to this attack over his sovereignty. He decided to hastily take possession of Jamaica, and sent a former companion of his father, Juan de Esquivel, to the island. Aware of Diego's move, Ojeda swore he would cut Esquivel's throat should he come across him over there.

But when Esquivel reached Jamaica with 70 men in 1509, no one was there to 'welcome' him. Ojeda had headed straight to Cartagena; attacked by some Natives, he was eventually rescued by a Spanish vessel, which found him at the bottom of a mangrove, holding his sword in one hand and his shield pierced with several dozens of arrows in the other. All his men had been killed. During his next attempt, he was injured at the thigh by a poisonous arrow. He forced the doctor to cauterize the wound at both extremities with a red firebrand; he survived after several days of a terrible bout of fever. While down on his knees in the Gulf of Darien, he suddenly saw a ship coming, steered by one Bernardin de Talavera who, *being a fugitive from justice* (...), says Bruzen de la Martinière, *had captured his ship near Tiburon before setting sail without precise destination.* Coming across Ojeda, Talavera was *pleased to find a safe haven, and he engaged with all his men to his service.* Ojeda decided to go back to Hispaniola, but the ship was shipwrecked on the coast of Cuba. He had to walk for 30 days through the swamps, losing half of his men. Finally, almost dying from want, he had no choice but to send someone to the nearby Jamaica. Herrera says:*"Moved by compassion* (...) *and notwithstanding the threats he had received, Esquivel sent for him, received him with kindness, accommodated him in his own house in Jamaica and had him served as himself."* Esquivel even arranged the return of his new friend to Hispaniola, where he arrived exhausted and broke. According to Gomara, he remained several years in Hispaniola, where he died *in such poverty that it was necessary to beg a shroud to bury him.* (Charlevoix) As far as Talavera was concerned, wanted by

justice, he was *too advised to follow* (Ojeda) *to Hispaniola, but not enough
to leave Jamaica quickly enough*. The Admiral—Diego, who also
inherited the title of his father—, *upon learning about his whereabouts,
sent for him, and had him hanged*. (La Martinière)

Nicuessa, for his part, reached Nombre de Dios, where he fought
against famine and warlike Indians; these terrible challenges made him
half-mad. He eventually joined the settlement of Balboa in the Gulf of
Darien. Since it was located in his territory of Castilla del Oro, he
approached with contempt and was chased right away. Forced to run
away in the nearby jungle, he came back after a short while, covered
with shame; then he embarked *in a bad brigantine* (Charlevoix), and set
sail, never to be seen again. "*The fishes ate him up*," says Gomara—thus
perished the 2 first Governors of Jamaica.

Juan de Esquivel

The man responsible for the Spanish conquest of Jamaica was Juan
de Esquivel. Described as a brave officer, this former companion of
Christopher Columbus had made a name for himself by taming the
Indian rebellion in Higuey. "*He was one of the very few Castilians, who,
amidst all the horrors of bloodshed and infectious rapine, were
distinguished for generosity and humanity*," affirms Bryan Edwards.
When he arrived, the island was populated with many Natives, the
Arawaks or Tainos; they were friendly and willing to exchange with the
Spaniards. Scattered in numerous villages, they fed on crabs, parrots,
hen, corn—they even made a liquor of corn—or cassava. Though going
half-naked, they were keen weavers of cotton, and made hammocks that
they traded in the whole Gulf of Mexico. They knew nothing about iron,
could not read or write and had no form of cult whatsoever, though they
were no strangers to spirituality. They had probably come from Guyana.
Columbus himself described them as *a peaceful good natur'd people*.
Even the dreadful Edward Long finds them worthy of praise: "*The
Spaniards looked with astonishment on a race of men, who, in this
sequestered part of the world, by mere dint of natural genius, unaided by
books or information, had attained such lengths towards perfection in
contrivance, delicacy, elegance, and utility, as appeared in their various
fabrics, apparel, and ornaments (...); so apt and lively were their faculties,
that as soon as the Spaniards instructed them in the art of writing, they
immediately wrote they prayers, and traditional odes or songs.*" Juan de
Esquivel first reassured the Arawaks, charming them with presents; but
he had come to conquer. When he set up the *repartimientos*, the Indians

fled to the hills. But the Spaniards and their terrible hound dogs went after them and subjugated them. Las Casas dedicates a short paragraph to Jamaica in his book:

> In the Year 1509, the Spaniards sailed to the Islands of St. John (today's Puerto Rico—editor's note) and Jamaica (...) with the same purpose and design they proposed to themselves in the Isle of Hispaniola, perpetrating innumerable robberies and villanies as before; whereunto they added unheard of cruelties by murdering, burning, roasting, and exposing men to be torn to pieces by dogs; and finally by afflicting and harassing them with un-exampled oppressions and torments in the mines, they spoiled and unpeopled this contrey of these innocents. These two isles containing six hundred thousand at least, though at this day there are scarce two hundred men to be found in either of them, the remainder perishing without the knowledge of Christian faith or sacrament.

Las Casas probably never set a foot in the island; but his associate Pedro de la Renteria did, at the beginning of their association—to find some pigs, corn, and *other things that could not be found in the devastated island of Cuba.*(Las Casas) The figure of 600,000 is not correct, and might come from a misprint or an excess of zeal. Nevertheless, with roughly 60,000 inhabitants, Jamaica was one of the most populous islands of the Caribbean. In 1611, a Spanish report specified that 74 Natives only remained.

Esquivel and his men could not find gold in Jamaica, but they still worked towards the development of the colony that produced cotton. The historian Herrera underlines that the island produced *the best quality of cotton.* They weaved shirts or hammocks, and sold them all over the Caribbean. "*Herds were thriving,*" keeps on Herrera, "*and provisions were abundant. So that people were coming from the other islands.*" The historian Morales Padron draws[‡‡] a positive portray of the envoy of Diego Columbus, reminding that the conquistador did not fail the confidence of the Court until 1512 despite the on-going feud with the Columbus family—he even lightly tells about the way he suppressed the Indian rebellion. Yet, we know Esquivel had used of violence in Hispaniola under similar circumstances. Edwards reminds us of his

---

[‡‡] *Spanish Jamaica* (Ian Randle, Kingston 2007).

magnanimity towards Ojeda, to conclude that *under such a man it is reasonable to suppose that the yoke of subjection sat light and easy on the natives, and that the ravages of conquest were restrained within the limits of humanity.* To be honest, it does not seem less reasonable to doubt it. As a matter in fact, in Jamaica, and like everywhere else, many Natives chose death rather than the yoke, drinking some juice of manioc to commit suicide.

In 1512, the Court reproached Esquivel of his converting the Natives with brutality; but this was just a false pretence, the heart of the matter being the feud with the Columbus. In fact, the King had no reason to complain about the conquistador, who had so efficiently suppressed the Indian rebellion, and put the colony on the path to prosperity. But the laudatory reports of Diego Columbus turned him into a suspicious subject; so the King sent Michel de Passamonte to replace him.

Nueva Sevilla

Jamaica remained a Spanish dominion for 150 years. This period, poorly documented, was not thoroughly studied until the early 19th

Above: a map of 1597, showing Cuba and Jamaica, by Petrus Kaerius. The Jamaican settlements of Oristan and Sevilla are mentioned.

century. There's no doubt that Esquivel came to Jamaica in 1509, but we still do not know about his first settlement. According to W. Bridges[§§], he landed at Santa Gloria, where he established his colony by *the little rivulet there*, just below the Indian village of Mayma, where Columbus had fought against the Porras brothers in 1504 (see chapter 1). "*Diego Columbus had desired him to name the settlement Sevilla Nueva*," resumes the historian, "*to commemorate the successful termination of his suit against the crown, which had been recently decided in the council of the Indies*." According to Cundall and other historians, he first built the colony of Melilla, between Port Maria and Port Antonio, before turning to Sevilla Nueva 1 year later. Charles Leslie also quotes Melilla as the first settlement; but the Spaniards, feeling uncomfortable there, finally left to build Sevilla Nueva and Oristan. Padron thinks that Melilla and Nueva Sevilla were erected at the same time. "*We know nothing of its* (Melilla) *origin, and its actual location is still the subject of conjecture*," he adds. "*According to some commentators, it was situated in Santa Gloria, a view that cannot be supported since it was New Sevilla that was built there. For others (...) Melilla stood on the site of the modern Port Maria. For Francisco de Oviedo[¶¶], Melilla was only an islet that had been taken over by Indian Caciques. We are inclined to opt for Port Santa Maria although the matter is hardly of great importance because the township soon disappeared*." Indeed, the Spaniards moved several times—some blame an Indian rebellion, which fits with Oviedo's testimony; others talk about the terrible bites of red ants, which dwelt under the floors of their houses. "*Ants are said to have killed the Spanish children by eating their eyes when they were left in their cradles in this part of the island*," writes Hans Sloane. "*This is given as one reason why the Spaniards left this part of the country.*" Herrera, for his part, does not even mention this prototype colony; and Clinton V. Black, the Jamaica historian whose book is studied at school, calls Sevilla Nueva *the first Spanish colony in Jamaica*, though it was not built until 1510. Some consider that Esquivel also built Oristan, on the South coast; soon transferred from its original spot—today's Savannah-la-Mar—to the spot of today's Bluefields; unless it was the contrary. At the end of the day, Sevilla Nueva—sometimes referred to as Sevilla del Oro—remains the emblematic colony of the conquest. Its location, near today's St Ann's Bay, is described by Edward Long: "*A place could not have been more happily selected than this by the*

---

§§ *The Annals of Jamaica* (London, 1828).

¶¶ Gonzalo Fernandez de Oviedo (1478-1557), a renowned Spanish historian of the New World, who went there himself, and published *Histori General des Las Indias* in 1535.

Spaniards for building a town. Here was plenty of excellent materials for architecture, abundance of good water, a fertile soil in the neighbourhood, the woods filled with the greatest variety of large and valuable timber-trees, the sea and the rivers stored with innumerable fish, a safe and spacious port, and the distance not remote from their island of Cuba." They built a theatre, a fort, a fortified castle as well as a church, which magnificence was unusual for the West Indies. Its construction was ordered by the famous Peter Martyr of Anghiera (1457-1526), member of the prestigious Council of the Indies, and author of *Decades* on the discovery of the New World. A close relative to Queen Isabella, he was a privileged witness of the discovery, and was engaged in a written correspondence with the Admiral, as well as with the main conquistadores of the time. He sent letters to his many learned friends all over Europe to tell them about the incredible news, being the first one to use the expression 'New World'. Appointed Abbot of Jamaica in 1524, he probably never set foot in the West Indies; yet, jealous of the church erected by another religious in Hispaniola, he wanted his edifice to reflect his own grandeur. The construction started in 1525, thanks to the funds obtained from Charles Quint—they were, at first, supposed to help build a hospital in Nueva Sevilla, but the inhabitants rejected the idea in favour of the church. Unfortunately, it was never achieved. Indeed, in 1534, the Spaniards deserted Nueva Sevilla. Bridges describes their terrible exile as sudden and irreversible. In fact, it was probably progressive, as some French pirates plundered the colony in 1554. In 1688, when Hans Sloane visited the place, the ruins of the church still testified of its ambition. *"The church was not finished, it was twenty paces broad, and thirty paces long; there were two rows of pillars within, overt the place where the altar was to be, were some carvings under the ends of the arches. It was built on a sort of stone, between freestone and marble taken out of a quarry about a mile up in the hills (...). The west gate of the church was very fine work, and stand very entire, it was seven foot wide, and as high as before the arch began. Over the door in the middle was our Saviour's head with a crown of thorns between two angles, on the right side a small round figure of some Saint with a knife stuck into his head, on the left a Virgin Mary or Madonna, her arm tied in three places, Spanish fashion."* The magnificence of this chruch, said to be *exceptional in the West Indies* by Padron, also testified of the prosperity of Nueva Sevilla. Indeed, plenty nobles joined Esquivel in Jamaica, bringing with them *the refinements of taste, and the means of displaying it.* (Bridges) Herrera explains: *"Though the suspicion of the Court against Esquivel was groundless, the mere fact of being a friend of Diego was damaging his reputation; it enabled the Admiral's detractors to discredit him in the eyes of the King— which they gladly did; they said he had not thoroughly searched for gold in Iamayca, and that his reports about what was going on in the island were incomplete (...). Thus the King ordered the Admiral to send someone to remove Esquivel from his duties as soon as possible."* Dismissed on royal orders, Esquivel disappeared from the official papers. He apparently died in Nueva Sevilla in 1513 or 1519.

Diego was aware of the plans of the King, but could not openly fight them. He sent Captain Perea to Jamaica, where he did not stay long, *because of the disorders his arrival created.* (Herrera) His successor, Captain Camargo, did no better as these so-called disorders bordered on rioting. Perea and Camargo were perceived as the creatures of the King, thus hostile to the Columbus. They were chased out of the island. So that the King eventually had to ask Columbus to *kindly accept a Lieutenant, in the person of Francisco de Garay.* Garay, the former Sergeant Major of Hispaniola, was also an enemy of the Columbus, but he was respected. Indeed, *Francisco Garay,* says Las Casas, *was among the first Castilians to come (...) alongside the Admiral Christopher Columbus, who discovered the Indies; he was a man of honour and he possessed many Indians who served him, and thus he earned a lot of riches (...). It is said that five thousand Indians raised his pigs.* Garay was an ambitious man, who first tried to take control of Guadeloupe, where the Natives repelled him. He then insisted to obtain the government of Jamaica. *"He obtained it,"* underlines Herrera, *"providing he gave up half of his herds, profits, provisions (...). Garay worked so hard that he soon increased his heritage; then he found gold, and thus contented the King more than any previous governor of this island."* He reached Nueva Sevilla on May 15, 1515, moved by a tough determination. He did his best to make the settlement prosper, hoping to be rewarded by a prompt authorization to explore the American continent—the *Terra Firma,* the ultimate goal of all conquistadores. But despite its prosperity, Nueva Sevilla was soon abandoned. Some blame the pestilential smells that emanated from the nearby swamps, others an unusually high mortality rate among the infants less than 6 months of age. But if the colony was so unhealthy, why had the inhabitants refused the construction of a hospital in favour of Peter Martyr's church? This exodus puzzled the English. After their capturing the island in 1655, *Governor Lynch sent to the old Spanish inhabitants of it on Cuba, to know what reason they had to leave it, and go to the south side; the answer they made was, that they left it because their children died there, that there were abundance of ants, that there was no good port, and that it was out of the road for the trade of Cartagena, and Santo Domingo.* (Sloane) In fact, this exodus was motivated by 2 things. First were the continuous attacks of pirates— bloody and devastating, they also cut the trading route with Cuba. Secondly, if it was logical to settle as close as possible to Hispaniola and Cuba in the beginning—on the north coast—, the conquest of Mexico, which started in 1519, and then of Peru, remodelled the face of the New World. These new lands overshadowed Hispaniola, and many of its inhabitants migrated to the continent. The colonists of Jamaica naturally adapted to the new trading routes by settling on the south of the island. Nevertheless, the colony was disregarded. There was almost no gold, and the people there were too much dependent on the rare passages of the ships that rallied Cartagena and Hispaniola; it was seen as a mere food provider. Even the fiscal advantages granted by the King seemed unable to wake Jamaica from its slumber.

The Marquisate of la Vega

Garay knew he would not meet his destiny in Jamaica. According to Gomara, he armed 3 vessels in 1518, and sent them to Florida: *"He disembarked his men, who are at once attacked by the Indians, killing or harming many of them,"* says Gomara. *"Thus he did not stop until he reached Panuco, which is more than two thousand miles away from Florida (...). He tried to trade in Panuca* (today's Tampico—editor's note), *but the inhabitants, being great and valiant butchers of men, refused to comply. They were also mistreated at Cila, where the Indians ate several Spaniards they had killed; they skinned some of their victims to decorate their temples with their dried skins, exposed as the trophies of their victory."* The vessels eventually reached Villa Rica, where the rear-guard of Cortes' army was positioned. The encounter was not friendly— conquistadores were wolves to the other conquistadores in this new world. On October 3, 1520, Cortes wrote to the Emperor Charles Quint: *"I received intelligence (...) that four ships had arrived on the coast, and that the captain I had left in command there had gone out to them in a boat, when he was told they belonged to Francisco de Garay, Lieutenant and Governor of the island of Jamaica***."* They were offered to sail to the port of Vera Cruz, placed under the jurisdiction of Cortes; they refused, and started to wander around. Cortes went to meet the 3 envoys of Garay, supposedly to determine the boundaries of their respective

***

*** The presence of Garay himself in these ships is dubious.

territories. *Believing that they must do some wrong in the country,* (Cortes) he took them prisoners, and then forced them to attract the rest of the crew ashore; a short skirmish ensued, which forced the Spaniards from Jamaica to flee. Back to Jamaica, they claimed they had found gold in the Panuco River. Garay then wrote to Spain, and obtained the authorization to leave Jamaica, and to sail for the continent.

In 1523, the wealthy Governor of Jamaica armed 11 vessels with 800 men and 144 horses—as well as many Indians. This was quite an impressive expedition, which tells a lot about the prosperity of the colony at the time. Yet, the dream soon turned into a nightmare. Gomara claims that some warlike Indians killed more than 400 of his men, skinning and eating them up. But his most terrible foe in this expedition was a Christian by the name of Hernando Cortes. The latter wrote to the Emperor: "*Francisco de Garay (...) proclaim(ed) himself, through an interpreter, whom he had brought with him, governor of the country; he told the Indians he would revenge the ills they had suffered at my hands in the recent war, and that they should join with him in driving out those Spaniards whom I had placed here, and that he would help them; besides many other scandalous things which considerably agitated the natives.*" The confrontation was avoided thanks to a decree sent by the King to Garay, which forbade him to enter Cortes' jurisdiction. Had he disobeyed, he would have become a traitor to the King—which meant death. He had no choice but to comply. He asked Cortes to help him in setting an expedition to some remote provinces. But the long awaiting had damaged his ships, and 6 of them could not manage the sea anymore; and his disappointed men rebelled. At the end of the day, Garay forgot all ideas of conquest, and went to join Cortes in Mexico instead, where he was to marry his eldest son to the conquistador's daughter, Catalina[†††]. Padron sums up his situation with no complacency: "*The governor of Jamaica had no choice but to offer unconditionally to Cortes 'his life and his honour'.*" Meanwhile, the revolt that Cortes openly blamed on Garay, spread to the province of Panuco, where the Natives, upset at the intolerable behaviours of the disseminated troops of Garay, and convinced that the Spaniards were divided, slaughtered the Europeans, and marched on Saint-Etienne-du-Port to besiege the place. "(Garay) *was much impressed by this news,*" says Cortes, "*not only because it seemed to him that he was the cause of it, but also because he had left his son in that province with all his possessions; so much so indeed, that his chagrin brought on an illness from which he died within the space and*

---

††† Apparently, they never actually married.

term of three days." In fact, many believe Cortes poisoned Garay. The majority of Garay's men perished during this uprising, which was soon violently suppressed by the formidable Cortes. This was quite an infamous ending for Garay. But Las Casas does not lament over his death: *"As he had to pay, in this world or in the next one, for having destroyed the people of these islands, God permitted that he went to discover other lands (....), where he was to lose all his goods, his wealth, and his life."*

Meanwhile in Jamaica, the former Treasurer Pedro de Mazuelo asked for permission to abandon Nueva Sevilla—and obtained it. Don Diego's men then built several settlements, abandoning them one by one. There was Oristan—today's Bluefields—in the southwest part of the island, Caguya—today's Passage Fort—in the south, Puerto Anton (Port Antonio) in the north west, and, last, Santigo de la Vega (Spanish Town). The legends have it that the latter was built by Diego Columbus himself— he came to Jamaica in 1522, says Oviedo, when Garay left. Standing six miles away from Passage Fort, the settlement was surrounded by fertile plains that produced food in abundance, including indigo and cocoa. The colony soon boasted of 2 churches, 7,000 houses, and several chapels. It went into a decline, though; when the dream of immediate wealth vanished, and when, driven by their thirst for gold, the colonists left for the continent. Fortunately, the island kept its status of pantry. Quickly, some herds of beef and savage cows—first imported to the island—throve in the green plains of the island. In the chapter of his book entitled *Herds of ownerless cattle in the islands of Cuba, Iamaica and others*, the historian Jospeh Acosta writes[‡‡‡]: *"The cattle of Hispaniola and other neighboring islands have multiplied so greatly in this way that thousands of ownerless animals roam the woods and the fields. These cattle are used for their hides; both whites and blacks go out in the country and chase the bulls and cows, and the animal that they hamstring, when it falls, belongs to them."* Once a year, the colonists let their slaves organize an island-wide hunt. They slayed thousands of cows, skinning the dead animals and leaving their carcasses to waste in the sun. *"The hides that are imported into Spain represent one of the chief products of the islands and New Spain,"* concludes Acosta. The first black slaves who got to Jamaica[§§§] made the hunting of these cows their specialty. Left by themselves on an island they explored from top to bottom, they even

---

[‡‡‡] *Natural and Moral History of the Indies* (Edited by Jane E. Mangan, 2002).
[§§§] On August 23, 1513, according to the Jamaican historian Rex Nettleford (*Mirror, Mirror...*, Kingston, 2003),

had some relationship with the last Arawak Indians, from whom they kidnapped women—some think they were no Arawaks, but Indians imported by the Spaniards from the Continent. Living in semi-autonomous camps, they enjoyed a relative freedom—as a counterpart, they provided the colonists with meat and animal skins.

Meanwhile, the legal claims of the Columbus had irritated the King to such an extent that the Admiral's grandson, Don Luis—the son of Diego, who died in 1525 or 1526—, decided to compromise. In 1545, *he agreed to be Duke of Veragua and Marquis of Vega, accepting Jamaica and Veragua, and renouncing all other claims.* (Edwards) Jamaica, now a marquisate, entered a dark period, during which it suffered under the yoke of its new masters. "*It is certainly fact,*" says Charles Leslie, "*the successors of Columbus acted more like sovereign tyrants than any thing else, and used the utmost severity in collecting the stints which they had imposed.*" The successive Governors sent by the Columbus were more inclined to make profits than to develop the colony. In 1582, Francisco Marquez de Villalobos describes the colony, stating: "*They have not made improvement of one inch of this land. On the contrary, the Governors have ne'er made visits, neither have they governed as was their duty. (...) And when after the said Governor(s) becometh rich, the Admiral doth send another servant to be Governor.*" (Padron) The Spanish archives brought

Above: a map of Mexico from the 17th century; details from various Mexican divinities; Hernando Cortes, conqueror of Mexico and Garay's deadly foe.

to light in Jamaica in 1916, confirm the decline of the colony between 1556 and 1597, a time when the island came under attack of French pirates, who plundered Kingston Bay and Salt River in 1555, Port Royal in 1565 and Negril in 1558. The King did his best to help Jamaica; he exonerated certain exported goods, granted some privileges and sent many emissaries. But *the continuous suits* (against the Court of Spain) *in which the heirs of Columbus were to become involved were to obstruct the implementation of any viable policy for the Marquisate (...) and led to the complete neglect of the colony as the years went by.* (Padron) Indeed, the rehabilitation of Don Luis was merely symbolic, as the King kept the final say in political matters. The text underlines that Don Luis received *the isle of Jamaica, named Santiago, and together with all the revenues and duties of whatever kind, while declaring that supreme authority should remain with his Majesty.* (Padron) The heirs of the Admiral were slowly ripped off all their rights. In 1678, their marquisate became an honorific title only. Meanwhile, placed under the authority whether of the King, the marquis de la Vega or the council of Cuba (when there was no governor in the island), Jamaica stagnated. The Spaniards survived thanks to tobacco growing and a few exchanges—of leather, pepper and coconuts—with the rare ships that came by. Burdened with taxes, they did not care working hard to make a cupid and unknown Governor rich. "*Thus these first planters were unworthy of the name of men by their cruelty, and of all society by their indolence,*" states Charles Leslie. The situation apparently affected the colonists, described in a Spanish report from 1650 as *not very intelligent and not very active.* The fiscal yoke of the Columbus, well known in the West Indies, scared the migrants, who carefully avoided to go to Jamaica. Those who already lived there fled to Cuba or Hispaniola despite the governors' strict interdiction. The colonists appealed this decision to the Crown of Spain, but the latter had too many problems to pay attention to this remote colony hardly located on a map. Thus, bitterness and distrust haunted Jamaica, and the colony was reduced to 130 colonists when the English raided it for the first time in 1596.

We must put this chaotic vision into perspective. At the turn of the 17th century, Jamaica enjoyed a regain of prosperity. Its population increased as the new and controverted Governor Caballero established an illegal trade with some neighbouring settlements. Defying the King's ban, he traded with foreign ships, selling back his commodity to Cartagena with great profits. Indeed, Caballero had tight links with the Inquisition headquartered in Cartagena—his wife was also from this city. But *thief do not like to see thief with long bag,* goes the Jamaican saying; and an internal feud arose in

Jamaica when a new Governor arrived in 1649 to replace Caballero. Murders, plots and planned *coups*, Jamaica was bubbling.

The First English Visits

The English got interested in Jamaica long before they captured it in 1655. Captain Anthony Shirley left Plymouth, England, in 1596, with the intention to plunder the island of Saint Thomas. He attacked Santiago and Saint Martha with his numerous men, and then headed to Jamaica, where he landed without any resistance; he plundered and burnt Santiago de la Vega, and even thought, claims Leslie, to capture the place. But he left one month later. In his *History of Navigation*, Thomas Lediard gives a short relation of the expedition: "*When they arrived in the bay of Jamaica on January 29* (the English) *landed and walked six leagues into the country to reach the main city. The inhabitants appeared on horses, as if willing to stop them; but they never engaged our troops. As soon as the English took the place, and the whole island, people submitted, and brought provisions of smoke meat and cassava bread. They were ready to depart when Captain Parker, from Plymouth, arrived in turn on March 2. Captain Anthony Shirley associated with him to sail to the Bay of Honduras.*" In fact, the Spaniards had sought refuge into some nearby caves; they did not come out until the English had sailed away. Their common misery brought them together, says Leslie: "*The Governor relax'd something of his usual severity, and they appeared more easy and content.*" In 1635, Colonel Jackson raided the island in turn, meeting a more consequent resistance at Fort Passage; but the English made their way to Santiago de la Vega where they entered sword in hand. "*And the Spaniards were glad to agree for a certain sum, to save the city from being burnt,*" writes Leslie. Jackson did not lose more than 40 men; yet, a handful of them fell in love with the place, and deserted to start a new life. The resentful English officially demanded that they should be handed to them when they captured the island in 1655.

Not fortified—mainly because of its special status linked to the Marquisate of the Columbus—, the island was an easy prey. What prevented it from more plundering was the fact that, being kept away from the riches of the New World, it was of little interest. As a matter of fact, the English took it in 1655 as a consolation prize. This historical turning point yet launched Jamaica into an era of unprecedented prosperity. Finding a comfortable place on the geopolitical map of the New World, the island became the jewel of Great Britain in the West Indies.

3

Protector and Usurper

O
n May 10, 1655, 2 Spaniards who had gone fishing near Port Morant, Jamaica, witnessed a magnificent but terrible scene as 38 English vessels loaded with 8,000 soldiers entered the Caguaya Bay—today's Kingston Bay! They hurriedly gave the alarm to Santiago de la Vega, but the colonists were then disseminated through the island; some watching their herds, others taking care of their sugar cane plantations. Notwithstanding, the Governor gathered 180 men, and waited for the invaders behind a small breastwork. The weak rampart did not last long and, after a short skirmish, the English landed. The Spaniards ran to Santiago de la Vega—today's Spanish Town—but General Venables did not take advantage of this first success as he decided to camp for the night. This was an ill-advised decision, but this expedition orchestrated by Cromwell was a disgrace from the start.

The Western Design

Oliver Cromwell took the head of England after 7 years of the civil war that had opposed King Charles I and the Parliament. When Cromwell's troops finally overtook, the King was beheaded (1649) and Cromwell became Lord Protector of the Commonwealth of England, Scotland and Ireland. But the war had left deep scars. Charles Leslie, who wrote his *New Account of the Island of Jamaica* after the restoration of Charles II, calls Cromwell a *usurper*—a common designation among historians. A Protestant fiercely opposed to the Papists, and a man of excess, Cromwell tied and untied the Parliament according to his interests, and curbed the Irish revolt with the utmost severity. He was from the gentry, but a zealous believer, and a fierce warrior. Most of all, he happened to be a formidable politician. *"The nations around* (England) *believed her sunk beneath her own ruins, when on a sudden she became more formidable than ever, under the dominion of Cromwell, who enslaved her by carrying the gospel in one hand, and the sword in the other, and the mask of religion on his face, and who in his government concealed the crimes of a usurper, under the talents of an able King,"* claims* Voltaire. Despite the regicide of Charles I that owned him the general disapprobation of Europe, Cromwell launched England on the road to prosperity. He declared war to Spain in 1655, hoping to legitimate his position with war conquests, and to get rid of the Parliament's claims (which had to agree over public expenses) by collecting consequent war booty. France was then too powerful, it was wiser to make friends with her. *"The crafty Mazarin having engaged Cromwell to join with France, and turn his arms against Spain, politickly* (sic) *contrived an expedition to the West Indies,"* says Leslie. The weakness of the Spanish settlements in the Americas was well known, and the powerful English fleet almost unbeatable. But this war was highly criticized. First because a majority of officers reluctantly obeyed Cromwell, whom they saw as a usurper—then, because there was no good reason to break the peace treaty signed with Spain in 1630.

Admiral Blake was in charge of the European front, where he fought bravely before being killed at sea. But Cromwell also fitted out a fleet with the intention to conquer Hispaniola. He jointly intrusted Admiral Penn and General Venables with the command of the fleet and army. This expedition to the West Indies, called *The Western Design*, was deeply inspired by a peculiar man, Thomas Gage. A renegade Dominican, Gage had a lot say about the wealthy and yet poorly defended colonies of the Spaniards in the New World. Cromwell lent him a keen ear since Gage had spent 12 years travelling through the Spanish dominions in America. In fact, as astonishing as it might appear, Gage was the very first non-Spaniard to ever give such a circumstanced relation. Indeed, the Spaniards had so far succeeded in hermetically sealing their kingdom to foreigners!

In 1625, a Dominican missionary named Antoine Melendez convinced Thomas Gage to follow him to the New World. They were to reach the Philippines through Mexico to preach the gospel there. But Gage's true ambition was to escape the wrath of his father, who reproached him his leaving the Jesuits to join the Dominicans; he

---

* *The Age of Lewis XIV* (London, 1779).

considered it as an unforgivable treason—the first of a long series. "*Well considered I the sight of a wrathful father,*" writes Gage[†], "*the power of a furious brother a Colonel who (as now landed in England to search me out, and do me mischief), when Zephyrus with a pleasant gale seconded his Popish zeal, might violently assault me. (...) Wherefore after a whole nights strife and inward debate, as the glorious Planer began to banish nights dismal horror, rising with a bright and cheerful countenance rose in my mind a firm and setled (sic) resolution to visit America, and there to abide till such time as death should surprise my angry father.*" Gage discreetly embarked. "*I was conveyed alone to our ship, and there closely hid into a barrel that was emptied of bisket (sic) to that purpose.*" He had never intended to go to the Philippines, and he parted company with his Dominican friends in Mexico. He then roamed various provinces of the New World for 12 years, coming back to England in 1637. There, he abjured Catholicism and joined the party of the Protector. While getting involved in politics, he met Thomas Chaloner, an influent member of the government, who urged him to publish his memoirs in 1648. "*We owe (Gage) the first description of some vast provinces that the Spaniards alone then explored, jealously defending their access to any other nation.*"[‡] Gage talks about rogue religious living in luxury and lust. Some, he says, had turned their convents into brothels. That led Father Labat, a Dominican himself, and a disgusted reader of his book, to say: "*We can easily make out the character of this author (...): a light spirit, inconstant and double, a lying tongue, a heart filled with ungratefulness, perfidy and greed; in a word, a villain in a religious habit.*" Pragmatic, Father Labat still praises the previously unpublished details given by Gage: "*Those who had written about the continent before, had seen nothing but its shores.*" Gage's book outraged many people in Europe. The famous *Dictionary* of Moréri, for instance, describes it as *riddled with fairy tales about the monks*, and Chaudon & Dandeline consider[§] that *some futilities in style and facts have indisposed people of good taste against the author and his book.* In fact, Gage was hated because, back in England, he started to inform on his former catholic friends. And once unmasked, the Catholic proselytes were not simply arrested, but put to death. In 1642, Gage gave away Thomas Holland, a former friend of his, who was consequently hanged—his body was then cut into pieces, and exposed on London Bridge. Gage's relatives went mad; his brother offered him

---

† *A New Survey of the West-Indies...* (London, 1677).
‡ *Nouvelle Bibliograhie Générale* (Paris, 1815). (F)
§ *Nouveau Dictionnaire Historique* (Lyon, 1804). (F)

money to join him in the Flanders—he refused. Then his brother sent someone for him. *"I was like to be killed in Shoe Lane by a Captain of my brother's regiment who came over from Flanders on purpose to make me away or convey me over,"* confesses⁋ Gage. That is when he met Chaloner—one of the jurors who had voted the execution of Charles I. The publishing of Gage's book was meant to create excitement over the riches of the Spanish Americas. All pretences were good for Cromwell to rally as many people as possible around his warlike project—and covetousness seemed to be a good one.

Gage also wrote a memoir to the Protector to discuss an expedition to the New World. First, he said, the Spaniards had always refused other nations the right to trade in this part of the world, enslaving all British subjects they could get a hold on. Thus, this war would not mean breaking a peace treaty, but fighting back an unjust oppressor. Furthermore, on what grounds did the Spaniards claim exclusivity on the New World? Strength alone had maintained them in their position—why not turn it against them? Should the Natives, the only legitimate owners of these lands, decide to shift masters, would not the new ones become the legal owners of their lands? Tactically, he suggested taking Santo Domingo first—the door to the Caribbean. He assumed that losing their historical colony would be a very bad omen for the Spaniards. Furthermore, since only a small part of the island was populated, it would be easily taken. Cromwell made up his mind. But the powerful *Western Design* suffered from irremediable inner weaknesses from the start.

Cromwell was paranoid. He knew he was surrounded by many people who had secretly remained loyal to the King. He feared they

---

⁋ The RoutledgeCurzon edition of 2005.

Opposite : Oliver Cromwell; the capture of Spanish Town by the English (figurative engraving of 18ᵗʰ century); Jamaica and Hispaniola; detail of the frontispiece of the French edition (1720) of Thomas Gage's voyage.

might plot his death, thus he distrusted everyone. To avoid giving too much power to a sole man, who might then turn against him, he divided the decision-making positions. He appointed an Admiral, William Penn, as well as a General, Robert Venables—to whom he added 3 commissaries devoted to his cause. One of them, Edward Winslow, was a very wise choice. A former passenger of the legendary *May Flower* in 1620, several times elected Governor of New Plymouth, America, and very well aware of the political processes, he knew about establishing a colony. He was Cromwell's right-hand man on board. Unfortunately, he got ill after the disastrous attack on Santo Domingo, and died at sea on May 7, without even laying his eyes on Jamaica. *"No greater loss could have befallen the expedition than the death of the only man among its leaders who knew by practical experience how to lay the foundation of a colony,"* says

C.H Firth**. There were other valuable men in the expedition—but it suffered from ill organization. Venables hardly obtained the agreed equipment, finding only 190 rifles out of the promised 1,500—half of which were not working. A first dispute arose over provisions, which were said to be insufficient; Penn had allegedly sent back a part of it to England, where they were sold for his personal profit.

It took months for the Protector to give the order to embark. Meanwhile, the Ambassador of Spain found out about the project, and warned his compatriots in the West Indies. They accordingly took serious measures that *contributed to the failing of the attack of Santo Domingo.* (Padron) When the order to embark finally arrived, the deadlines were so tight that the ships were hastily loaded in Portsmouth— some unwilling soldiers were even forced aboard by an officer riding his horse! Another officer reports: "*General Disborrow was so strict (not giving us eighteen hours) that many officers and the goods of others were left behind, not seeing servants nor good until we came to the Barbados.*" (Firth) The Colonels were to enrol their troops; but failing to recruit the required 1,000 on due time, they enrolled raw volunteers by beating the drums in the slums of Portsmouth. That is why Venables describes his men as *unruly raw soldiers, the major part ignorant; lazy dull officers that have a large portion of pride, but not of wit, valour or activity.*

The fleet called at Barbados, where it was reinforced with several hundred volunteers. But Venables lamented over their lack of discipline, their cowardice and their dissolute way of life. Reviewing the troops after the failure of Santo Domingo, the officers discovered several women dressed as sailors—*a strict inquiry made after all suspected prostitutes*, writes Long. The fleet captured 18 Dutch vessels anchored at Barbados, and Penn, according to Lediard, decided to take an inventory by himself, refusing Venables' suggestion of a neutral observer. Furthermore, the recommendations of the war council were not respected; the promised provisions were nowhere to be found; the soldiers got upset at the poor quality of food. Last but not least, it was announced that no looting would be tolerated in Santo Domingo. Probably, as guesses Venables, this was because Cromwell did not intend to plunder the West Indies but to conquer them. Thus, the officers and the soldiers would have to satisfy themselves with a raise in their salaries.

Under these bad omens, the fleet left Barbados in March 1655, and reached Hispaniola 13 days later. The island was divided into 2 parts. The French lived in the western part known as St-Domingue, while the

---

** *The Narrative of General Venables* (New York, 1900).

Spaniards lived in the eastern part, Hispaniola. Venables meant to land his men as close as possible to the Spanish capital of Santo Domingo, on the South Coast. But the war council, which comprised Winslow and Penn, opposed his decision. They suggested the mouth of the Hine River, instead; where Francis Drake had disembarked his men some 50 years ago. Yet, once there, Penn refused to sail into a *dangerous and unknown* bay, fearing he might wreck his ships. The army eventually landed at Point Nizao, more than 50 kilometres from Santo Domingo! Lediard goes on: "*The army was exposed to a tedious march (...) without guides, in a country covered with deep woods and quick sands; the horses, as well as the men, fell on the ground, as they could not endure thirst no more (...); they were cruelly tormented by blood flows because they had eaten some oranges and other green fruits for want of wate*r (...). *Thus, many died, and the rest were so exhausted and sick that they were unable to resist, not to mention attacking, their enemies.*" The soldiers, having left without hope of booty and dying from thirst and exhaustiveness, grew unruly. A few hungry ones deserted, and were slaughtered by some ambushed enemies. "*The war council was called,*" resumes Lediard, "*and we realized that many soldiers had eaten nothing but some fruits they had picked up in the woods in four days; and that they had no water as the Spaniards had plugged all their wells.*" While the Admiral's ships remained anchored in the bay, the ground attack was a disaster. It took 4 days for the soldiers to reach Santo Domingo, where the Spaniards were ready and waiting. Sick and feverish, Venables tried his best to motivate his troops—but disgrace was added to defeat, as the forefront suddenly disbanded and ran away. "*The way being narrow,*" explains the General, "*they ran upon my own regiment, who charged their picks at* (them) *to keep them back; but they would not be stayed.*" In the middle of chaos, the Spaniards preyed upon the English, *giving no quarter.* (Venables) The loss was terrible.

Finally, following several unsuccessful attempts and Venables collapsing on the battlefield, the war council declared the take of Santo Domingo impossible. The glorious death of Major General Haynes, underlined by the heroic action of his son, who retrieved his father's body under the fire of the enemy, was the only brave English deed of this sad day. The soldiers crawled back to their ships. "*The injured and the sick were left 48 hours on the deck,*" explains Lediard. "*Their injuries were not bandaged, they were given no food or water, so that their wounds generated worms (...). Venables was told that Penn had ordered (...) to give them no provision; thus the troops were forced to eat the dogs, the asses and the horses left in the camp; some even ate poisonous things, and 40 of them died."* Some disciplinary sanctions were taken in emergency. Adjudant Jackson, who had run away, was heard by a martial court. It was reminded that, when in Barbados, he had already been found drunk among some prostitutes. He was downgraded him and his sword was broken over his head. He was then sent to serve as a ship's boy at the infirmary. *"A sentence too gentle for so notorious an offender,"* concludes Venables.

1655, Captured Land

The instructions of Cromwell deemed the islands of Cuba, Hispaniola or Saint John as prime targets for the Western Design. The name of Jamaica did not appear. In his book, Gage only gives a few lines to the island, where he had obviously never been:

> Jamaica is another island under the power of the Spaniards, which is in length 280 miles, and 70 in breadth, which though it exceed Margarita in sweet and pleasant streams and fountains of water, yet is far inferiour (sic) to it in riches. Some hides, some sugar and some tobacco are the chief commodities from thence. There are only two towns of note in it, Oristana and Sevilla[††]; here are built ships which have proved as well at sea, as those that are made in Spain. The island was once very populous, and now is almost destitute of Indians; for the Spaniards have slain in it more the 60,000; in so much that women as well here as on the continent did kill their children before they had given them life, that the issues of their bodies might not serve so cruel a nation.

This is not a very exciting description, but Venables and Penn knew that the Protector would resent the shameful failure of Santo Domingo. Not to mention that the bad news reached him in two steps. *"Penn had not yet arrived to Hispaniola,"* writes[‡‡] Gregorio Leti, *"that the news spread in Europe that he had taken the island (...) and all the treasures of Peru."* The sycophants came to congratulate him, and the people lit bonfires all over London. Cromwell even proclaimed a day of fasting! Learning about the true fate of the Western Design in the middle of all these celebrations, he hid his disarray behind *an unnatural laugh* (Leti),

---

[††] By the time he wrote these lines, it had been abandoned for almost a century.
[‡‡] *La Vie d'Olivier Cromwell* (Amsterdam, 1706).

but he was mortified. Of course, Penn and Venables were yet unaware of these circumstances, but they knew the Protector would demand some explanations. The aim of the Western Design being to secure a base of operation in the Caribbean, they headed towards the nearby island of Jamaica to capture it as a consolation prize.

Fearing the unruliness of his troops, Venables gave order to shoot deserters at sight, and made it clear that any soldier refusing to comply would be shot. But the Spanish resistance in Jamaica happened to be anecdotal, and the English easily landed. Venables was later harshly criticized for not following the runaway Spaniards to Santiago de la Vega. In his own tale of the events, he invokes the late hour—5 o'clock, but the sun sets at 6 in the West Indies. He also says he wanted to find water for his men first, as well as some guides to avoid ambushes on the way. The next morning, Governor Juan Ramirez de Orellano and a handful of Spanish officials approached the English to capitulate upon terms. But these talks only intended to stop the progress of the invaders, and to give time to the inhabitants of Santiago de la Vega, so they could hide their riches away. "*They amused the English,*" affirms an author quoted by Lediard, "*by providing some fresh provisions to his army and by offering Mrs Venables some of the most beautiful fruits of the island.*" The General had come to the West Indies alongside his wife Elizabeth. Consequently, Lediard describes him as *a man who loved sex*. The just married couple enjoyed spending time together indeed, and Elizabeth sure had influence over her husband. Nonetheless, Venables had always made it clear that he intended to settle permanently in the West Indies, which explains why his wife came along with him. But his detractors spared him nothing, portraying him as a joyful idiot, who rejoiced over a basket of fresh fruits while the enemies where leaving the town with their riches. "*They left a naked town to the English,*" writes Lediard, "*where they found some beautiful houses, but no inhabitant or merchandise. This was grieving for the soldiers, who expected an important booty.*" Outraged, the English razed the city, and melted the churches bells to mould ammunitions. Meanwhile, Governor Orellano discussed the terms of his surrender. Thomas Gage acted as an interpreter. At one point, the Governor who was trying to gain time, suggested postponing the talks until the end of some religious ceremony, but Gage retorted that God, surrounded as He was by angels, could do without them. And when the Spanish governor objected that Jamaica was a legal possession of Spain, Gage answered: *Law does not give possession, only arms.* (Padron) The treaty was finally ratified. According to the terms, the

Spaniards had to embark for the destination of their choice before the 15. But some runaway Spaniards gathered in small groups in the woods around Santiago de la Vega, where they endeavoured to scatter the herds with the intention to starve the English. A Spanish commissioner sent a priest to dissuade them—they hanged him to a tree. Mortified, the commissioner informed the English that, sooner or later, the cows would have to come back to the plains to drink—*which fell out accordingly*, underlines Venables. Thanks to this piece of advice, the situation of the English got a little bit better. Meanwhile, 70 Spaniards embarked to Campeche, including the sick Governor, who died at sea. The others, who considered the treaty to be unacceptable, decided to stay and fight.

The English troops now found themselves on a remote island. What if some Spanish reinforcements should arrive from Cuba? Could they resist, starving as they were? Hunting savage cows happened to be more complex than expected. The soldiers often hit their target, but the injured animals rushed into the thick woods, where they disappeared. To prevent his men from *dying in a cook's shop*, as one of Venables' detractors—who published a libel against the Western Design under the initials I.S— ironically put it, the General forbade them to hunt in small groups, so they would not waste meat. Diseases spread among the troops, and Thomas Gage was among the many victims. There's no official report of his death, that took place early in 1656, *as we know from the fact that in July of that year the Council of State arranged to pay the debts owing to him to his widow Mary Gage and she was granted a pension of 6s 8d. a week*, says Professor A.P. Newton in the preface of the 2005 edition of Gage's work (RoutledgeCurzan). Regarding the 16 months he spent in Jamaica, we do not have much information. Padron says he preached in the church of Santiago de la Vega shortly after it was captured, the day of the Holy Trinity. But nothing remains of his sermon.

Times were so hard in Jamaica that the English even considered leaving the island. But the Spaniards made a mistake of consequence. Thinking the English were about to depart, they sent a troop to reconnoitre—following a short skirmish, the Spaniards were repelled and disbanded. Coming after them, the English found their freshly abandoned camp, several cattle herds and other goods. They also heard of an existing mine of silver, and another one of copper. "*From this intelligence,*" explains Edward Long, "*the army began to be extremely well satisfied with their conquest, hoping, no doubt, that after a little better acquaintance with the country, they might find means to amass a considerable stock of wealth, without much labour.*" While Penn and Venables hurriedly returned to England, the army took possession of the southern and east-southern parts of the island, while the Spaniards occupied the North Coast. Succeeding Governor Proenza—blind, feverish and physically unable to organize the resistance—, the controverted Lieutenant General Don Christobal Arnaldo de Ysassi actively planned the recapture of the island. He needed 500 men, and thus had no choice but to wait for reinforcements. Meanwhile, his men floated around Santiago de la Vega, setting some houses afire, harassing the invaders and slaughtering all isolated English. Their virulent resistance was designed to last—thus, these colonists, described in Europe as *indolent* (Leslie), resisted many years under terrible conditions. Spain had the firm intention to recapture Jamaica. The Captain General of Cartagena was among the first to understand the importance of the island; he sent Ysassi some provisions and materials twice in the course of 1655. He would have sent troops, had the King not forbade, fearing to weaken Cartagena. His zeal came from the tight links he had with Jamaica, being engaged in an interlope trade with the island.

In March 1656, Ysassi ambushed a group of 50 English near Santiago de la Vega, and killed them all. The delighted King of Spain appointed him Governor, and gave instructions to the Governors of Puerto Rico, Havanna, Cuba and Hispaniola, to support him. But a feud arose between Ysassi and Governor Don Bayona Villanueva of Cuba, *an old soldier who had served in Italy*, writes[§§] S.A.G. Taylor, *who had a high opinion of his own ability and qualifications as a military man and he treated with contempt the opinions of those who had become soldiers without graduating from his exclusive school.* Needless to say that he had little respect for the Jamaican resistant, an amateur fighting a guerrilla war. Ysassi was said to be a poor tactician, who could not even properly handle a musket. Yet, he was clear-sighted—he demanded a landing of troops on the *South* Coast, close to Alligator Pond, from the beginning. Thus, the soldiers would walk along the clear shore until they reach Spanish Town; it was shorter and far less exhausting than crossing the Blue Mountains. But Bayona insisted on landing on the North Coast, since rounding the island meant sailing head to wind. Ysassi proved an obstinate and a wise adversary. He understood the crucial importance of the slaves, to start with. When the English captured Jamaica, it was populated by some 1,500 Spaniards and as much slaves. The English thought they would easily turn the latter against their masters by

---

§§ *The Battle of Rio Nuevo* (The Jamaican Historical Review, March 1957).

granting them freedom. But they proved so loyal that the English were not even given the opportunity to talk to them—they systematically hanged those who came too close. And when they seemed willing to discuss, it was to slaughter their enemies more conveniently. They were the ones who provided Ysassi's troops with food while they were hiding in the hills. In return, they were taught the art of war—and they soon made good use of these teachings.

In 1655, Venables was almost 40. A professional soldier, he had fought from 1649 to 1654 in Ireland for Cromwell, before being sent to the West Indies, where he intended to settle. But the failure of the *Western Design* urged him to change his plans. Especially after Penn had left Jamaica—he appointed William Goodson as his successor. No doubt he would put all the blame on him—and this feared Venables. Being sick—he claimed he was almost dying—, he gave his commission to Richard Fortescue, and landed in Portsmouth on September 9, 1655, a few days after Penn. Heard by the King, they were both sent to the Tower of London—officially, for having abandoned their posts and unofficially, for having highly contributed to the failure of the *Western Design* through their misunderstanding. Penn confessed his wrongs, and was soon released; he joined the royalists and contributed to the restoration in 1660. He died in 1670, after a honourable career, only troubled by the political tribulations of his son, William Junior, an herald of the Quakers, who were *sometimes persecuted under Charles II*, writes Voltaire. This was *not because of their religion, but because they refused to pay their due to the clergy, they addressed the magistrate in a casual way, also refusing to swear according to the law.* When his father died, William Jr obtained lands in America from the Crown, as the payment of some debts contracted towards his father. He went there to establish the town of Philadelphia, in the state of *Penn*-sylvania.

As for Venables, freed on October 30, 1655, providing that he abandoned his commission in Ireland—he joined the royalists as well. He was certainly a courageous man; but obviously, as Firth writes, *he was deficient both in strength of character and capacity.* The same author underlines that his commission gave him *sufficient authority if he had known how to use it.* He died in 1687.

Cromwell, who expected to take over the Spanish Americas, was left with an island, a sort of *amends* for the *disgrace of the English*, as stated by Leslie; the same author adds that *chance more than design brought* (it) *into their hands.* Nevertheless, Cromwell understood its potential right away. As war raged with Spain, he forced the Parliament to vote appropriations to sustain the new colony, and published a proclamation that promised lands to the migrants, and guaranteed them the same rights than any English citizen. The Protector describes *a certain island called Jamaica, spacious in its extent, commodious in its harbours and rivers within itself, healthful by its situation, fertile in the nature of the soil,* and affirms that all measures had been taken to insure its security, as well as to grant it a civil government. "*And for the further encouragement to the industry and good affection of* (the colonists)", continues the text, "*we have provided and given orders to the commissioners of our customs, that every planter, or adventurer to that island, shall be exempted and free from paying any excise or custom (...) within the space of seven years to come from Michaelmas⁵⁵ next.*" The Jamaican crops were exempted for 10 years providing that they should be shipped to some nation of the Commonwealth. This proclamation was crucial. In the New World, the real challenge was not to capture places, but to make them thrive. It was very hard to attract colonists. Survival in these regions was uncertain, mostly in the beginnings. Thus Cromwell called upon Robert Sedgwick to bring Jamaica to life. There's no known portrait of Mr Sedgwick; we shall probably never know what this 24 years old man looked like when he left his native land of England for America in 1635. His outgoing personality and his ability to run a young colony made him very popular in Boston, where he first settled and became Major General. Cromwell called upon him a first time to chase the French colonists from Nova Scotia, which he did; then a second time to populate Jamaica. If history crowns Governor D'Oyley *the father of the nation,* it was Sedgwick who took Jamaica out of its deadly slumber. He got there as soon as October 1655, and found a desolate place. He established a triumvirate with Fortescue and Goodson—it did not last long, as Fortescue deceased shortly afterwards—to rule the colony. "*The state of our Army is sad, as God has visited us with a sore hand of sickness, tearing and snatching us away in much displeasure,*" he wrote on November 14, in his personal style full of religious imprecations. "*Major-General Fortescue, Commander-in-Chief, died about 14 days since; believes since he came to this place not less than 700 men are laid in the grave; the greatest part of the Army now sick, and many of our new Regiment that landed in much health, about 50 of them dead. Unless God in mercy stay his hand it will be very sad with us.* » As soon as he set foot at Passage Fort, he realized how desperate the situation was: «*At his first landing found the whole shore covered with butts, barrels, and chests of dry goods, as clothing,*

---

⁵⁵ The beginning of the fiscal year in England.

arms, surgeon's chests, &c., lying exposed, to all the damages imaginable, when a week's time with soldiers or sailors would have built a house to have received them all." The most resistant soldiers walked every day from Spanish Town to get their daily ration—half a biscuit. Furthermore, they drank the water directly from the Rio Cobre, without filtering it. The army of conquest seemed determined to starve to death rather than toiling the soil—especially since they had to do it for the officers' sake.

The soldiers were willing to plunder the nearby Spanish settlements or to go back home. But they refused to turn farmers. "*Many there are who came out with us,*" says Fortescue (Long), "*vaunting as if they would have stormed the Indies; big with expectation of gold and silver ready told up in bags.*» Disappointed and disheartened, the soldiers roamed the island in small hungry groups; some were ambushed and killed by the Spaniards' slaves. Some officers apparently encouraged their suicidal attitude, convinced that on learning about the terrible condition of the army in Jamaica, the Protector would promptly call it back. «*Our soldiers have destroyed all sorts of fruits and provisions and cattle,*" says Sedgwick. (Cundall) "*Nothing but ruins attends them wherever they go.*" Death hit these crazy Europeans, who were not careful enough to bury their dead. Some 140 soldiers were dying every week from fevers, dysentery and various oedemas. Sedgwick even feared an epidemic of plague. It became more and more difficult to find legitimate successors to the officers, who died by the dozen. For decades, Jamaica would be reputed for

Below and opposite: a view of the island in the 18th century; the first coat of arms of Jamaica.

its lethal climate, while the solution was simple. The officers had successfully converted to farming—Colonel Barrington, for instance, had a very prosperous plantation of tobacco and vegetables. But they needed the soldiers to toil the soil. The latter, who had come as conquerors, were now employed as farmers, and resented it. Furthermore, they were treated so bad that the commissioner officially asked Cromwell to send Servants and black slaves to Jamaica, giving as a reason *that their masters, having by this means an interest in their Servants, would be more careful of them, and work them more moderately* (than the soldiers); *by which many lives would be saved.* (Long) To escape the yoke, the soldiers revoked their officers one by one, including Archbould and Barrington, who had opposed a project of granting plots of land to the soldiers. They considered that the soldiers *could and should cultivate as Servants only,* underlines Vice-Admiral D'Oyley in 1656. The said D'Oyley finally sided the soldiers, and granted lands to them. The league of officers, who stood against him on this occasion became so quarrelsome that the colony almost plunged into civil war.

Meanwhile, Sedgwick realized that Jamaica was indeed a fertile island. Since the soldiers refused to work, he called upon his crew to build some shelters at Passage Fort to store the thousand tons of food he had brought from England. But he remained on board of the *Mandruke*, anchored in the bay— the ships were said to be healthier, and he had been feverish for a long while. Sedgwick was an idealist, who had left his wife and 5 children in England to

come to Jamaica. He never saw them again, dying shortly after his arrival, on June 24, 1656. Such was the price paid by these early settlers. Nevertheless, within a few months' time, he had invigorated the colony, saving it from decay. He had a fort built at today's Port Royal, and even convinced some soldiers to plant. However, Jamaica under the English seemed to be doomed. Among the colonists, who had come from the nearby islands, some got sick very quickly, others were horrified at the sight of the country. Many women, who had come to join their husbands, *upon finding them dead, sold themselves into the other islands for Servants, rather than stay with the army.* (Long) Jamaica was said to be an open grave; this bad reputation went as far as Europe, where the Protector was yet doing his best to help the colony. He urged some colonists from New England to move to *a land of plenty, Jamaica.* But the delegation was not convinced. They reported about the profane character of the army, the important death rate, and the unsafe situation of the colonists due to the scattered Negroes and Spaniards. The venture was a failure.

The colonists of other sugar islands such as Barbados, who dreaded a pernicious competition at a more or less short term, also denigrated Jamaica. Cromwell held on tight. He wrote to Luke Strokes, then residing in the island of Nevis. Following the instructions of the Protector, Strokes left with his entire family and more than 1,600 colonists to settle in Port Morant. A heavy rainfall welcomed them, as foretelling the tribulations ahead. Not less than 300 of them perished between December 15, 1656, and January 9 of the following year. A few months later, Stroke died—his wife soon followed him to the grave. Notwithstanding, the survivors throve. They had built 60 settlements by 1671, and one of Strokes' sons became a wealthy planter during the 18th century. Frank Cundall writes: "*Of Luke Strokes, research has failed to reveal any particulars (...). He seems to have been a simple-minded man who did the best he could for the Empire.*"

The Spanish Wars

In the spring of 1657, some Spanish troops gathered in Cuba with the intention to recapture Jamaica. Ysassi knew about the desperate situation of the British army, and urged constant and repeated actions against them. But the Spaniards should have acted quicker; as underlined by the historian Taylor, *by the middle of 1657 it was too late.* On July 5, a first group of Spaniards landed at La Maguana—today's Ocho Rios—, on the North Coast, led by Juan de los Reyes, an experienced officer. But he had an argument with Ysassi, who contested him the title of Sargento

Mayor, already granted to his 18 years old nephew. Notwithstanding this very bad start, they set out for Spanish Town. Five days later, upon reaching Los Vermejales, the men were exhausted, the provisions almost depleted, and the spirits so heated that Juan de los Reyes turned back to build a fort on the North Coast. Ysassi, for his part, went on. But all these misunderstandings gave the English time to prepare.

In Spanish Town, the general situation, though getting a little bit better, remained critical. The soldiers vehemently opposed the officers who had turned planters and oppressors; and the rivalry between the royalists and the faithful supporters of Cromwell threatened to get out of hand. It took D'Oyley all his ability to maintain a precarious balance between the 2 parties. The historian W.J. Gardner stresses the consequences of this political opposition, and accuses D'Oyley of being engaged in a correspondence with the royal family, then exiled in France. But the opinions are otherwise unanimous: "*D'Oyley was one of the greatest and best Governors that ever commanded any province,*" writes Leslie. "*And no colony could possibly be happier than Jamaica was, while ruled by such an able hand.*" Even the fiery Raynal praises him unconditionally, describing him as a *selfless and simple man, friendly in his private life, but in his place an intrepid warrior, a firm and severe commander, and a wise politician.* Though unnoticed during the attack on Santo Domingo and the capture of Jamaica, he revealed to have been an exceptional Govenor. First, he gloriously chased the last Spaniards from Jamaica thereby restoring the honour of the English after the humiliating defeat of Santo Domingo. Then, he remained impartial in the feud between the royalists and the supporters of Cromwell—thus avoiding a civil war. Cromwell yet denied him twice the title of governor; he gave it to Sedgwick first, and then to William Brayne, sent in 1656 with 500 Scottish and 700 Irish. Brayne's governorship did not last, as he died in September 1657. He had time to encourage planting, to start the building of a settlement at the entry of the bay—today's Port Royal—, and he even eased the tension by sending the most turbulent officers back to England.

Grieved at the lack of recognition, D'Oyley asked for his return to England on a wailing tone. Cromwell hesitated to appoint him governor, as he knew he had remained faithful to the King. Yet, D'Oyley apparently did not limit the opinion he had of his nation to the one he had of her masters. Intercepting a missive—Taylor says he got the information from a prisoner from Cuba one day, D'Oyley learnt about the warlike projects of the Spaniards. "*I was resolved,*" he writes, "*to give* (them) *time to fortifie* (sic) *so much, that he might think himself secure enough to stand us (that he might not perpetually be put to the toyl* (sic) *of hunting* (them) *in the woods) and yet so that he might not be able to give us any strong resistance."* (Taylor) Ysassi's troop, while en route to Spanish Town, was located and rapidly disbanded. This was a first victory, but D'Oyley was now resolute to chase the Spaniards once and for all. He sailed to the North Coast, landing his troops a few kilometres from the Spanish fort at Los Chorreras. The English were ambushed shortly afterwards, but later, defeated the Spaniards who ran away to their fort—which was taken in 45 minutes' time. Los Reyes and 200 of his men then fled to the nearby woods, leaving 120 dead on the spot. They remained hidden there for a while, but eventually proceeded to Cuba. Los Reyes, held responsible for the defeat, was sent to Spain where he was prisoned. Yet, the Spaniards had not yet spoken their last word.

A few months later, in May 1658, 1,000 men led by Don Alvaro Raspuru left Mexico to land near Rio Nuevo, in the parish of St Mary. Once more, Governor Bayona had refused to land on the South Coast. He built a new fort on the North Coast instead, where he remained inactive. His attitude is said to be *absurd* by Padron: *"The logical move was a southward advance against the English positions."* In fact, Raspuru was sick, and the heavy rainfalls did not make things easier. Belated by his argument with Bayona, Ysassi joined Raspuru 8 days later; furthermore, an English ship that was sent to reconnoitre, spotted the Spanish vessels. She was fired at, and went back to Cagway to give the alarm. D'Oyley called a war council at once, which decided to send 750 men to the North Coast. *"To advance by land was impossible, for the interior of the island was little known,"* says Gardner, *"(...) and moreover large bodies of troops might easily be cut off by ambuscades which would be easily planned by the fugitive Negroes to whom the mountains were familiar."* On June 11, a fleet left Port Royal. *"As soon as the ships were brought to anchor opposite the Spanish fortifications,"* resumes Gardner, *"the soldiers were landed, and immediately drove in an opposing party, with a loss of four and twenty men. An attempt was then made to bombard the fortress, but it was too high to be reached by the guns of the ships."* At night, the assailants made up some ladders while the prayers of the Spaniards resounded in the air. A dawn, the emissary sent by D'Oyley to the enemies came back with a few presents, and a flat refusal to surrender. Another day passed by, and then 2 ships sailed forward into the bay to fire the fort. Meanwhile, D'Oyley *forded the river at the flank of the battery with most of his soldiers*, explains Gardner, here contradicted by

Taylor, who claims that the English had more likely been through the woods, the river being too raging. Once at the feet of the fortress, they tried to climb the ramparts with their ladders, but were repulsed 5 times in a row. "*The English were becoming desperate; on all sides they attempted to scale the walls.*" says Gardner. "*The Spaniards perplexed by the cross fire to which they were exposed, at length recoiled, and in a moment the English were masters of the position. The carnage was terrible, and as the now conquered Spaniards sought to escape to the hills behind, they were shot down in great numbers.*" The attack left 400 dead—including Ysassi's nephew—, a third of the Spanish troops. "*The loss on the part of the English was inconsiderable,*" confesses Gardner. "*Four officers and twenty three privates were killed. The victory was attended by results that could scarcely be anticipated.*"

The Spaniards called a war council in the woods, and decided to retreat to Cuba. Ysassi disagreed, and decided to stay with a few obstinate. A military advisor came to him from Mexico shortly afterwards, but without the fleet that all strategists were asking for, but which the King could not put together, everything seemed to be lost. At the beginning of the year 1660, *some friendly Negroes* (Long) spotted Ysassi, and reported to the English. In fact, these *friendly Negroes* were the former Spanish slaves, who had suddenly turned their coat. The treason of their leader Juan de Bolas was a turning point in the *Spanish wars in Jamaica.* Not only did they stop providing the Spaniards with food, but they revealed their secret hideouts to their enemies. On February 6, they even ambushed the famous military advisor from Mexico, killing him. D'Oyley rewarded some of them and freed the others after the decisive fight led by the English colonel Tyson. Leslie tells the moving story of one of them:

> It seems this fellow had been slave to one of the most considerable amongst them, and love a young Negroe to distraction. He had several children by her, and lived in an interrupted course of happiness (if the state of slaves can give such) when the old fox his master, with brutal fierceness, tore the fond creature from his arms, and cruelly forced her to comply with his own sordid desires. The husband called on every power to avenge the rape; but his passion was ordered to be allayed by the severities of the whip; he underwent the punishment, but waited revenge; and having found opportunity from the late disturbances, got an

interview with his once adored wife (...); but as their happiness was now forever past, and the former days of love could not return, he would not live to see her another's, when she could not be his; for he could never take an adulteress to his arms; and therefore, closely embracing her, plung'd a poignard to the heart of the unhappy creature; thus, says he, I exert the right of a husband; and after a few caresses, and seeing her breath out her last, fled to the English, and in all their engagements did them eminent service, particularly in this last, where the sight of his former tyrant having inflam'd his desire of revenge, he flew to the place where he fought, and soon laid the haughty Don at his feet.

D'Oyley freed this man, and granted him some lands, *which ever after he lived upon quiet, and rather melancholly* (sic) *than otherwise. He arrived at a vast age, and died only in 1708.* (Leslie)

This last confrontation, concomitant to the one at Point Pedro, spelt the end of the *Spanish wars in Jamaica.* After a few months spent in the hills, the last rebels who were now reduced to only 70, resigned to get to Cuba. On May 9, 1660, they embarked near Robin's Bay, Saint Mary. "(We) *allowed them quietly to embark with their wives, children, and abandon Jamaica forever to the English,*" rejoices Leslie. Sailing some makeshift embarkations, Ysassi and the remains of his army left the shores of Jamaica once and for all. This was a hard blow to Spain, whose hegemony in the New World was shaking. Motivated by several successes of the kind, the European nations took New York, New Jersey and Pennsylvania. Meanwhile, Spain appeared amorphous, as if taking what Padron calls *an historical nap.* Beyond its strategic importance, the victory of Rio Nuevo was first and foremost a glorious one. At last, a virile and straightforward battle justified the presence of the English in Jamaica! D'Oyley offered more than a victory to his nation.

Juan de Bolos, the Spanish slave who had turned to the English, was freed and appointed Colonel of a regiment composed of black soldiers; he started to chase the last groups of indomitable slaves, who were still roaming the hills. Meanwhile in Cuba, Ysassi was making plans to recapture Jamaica; they were never practiced. Yet, Spain was about to get the island back, at one point; by diplomatic means.

1670, The Treaty of Madrid
As England and Spain signed the peace Treaty of Madrid in 1670,

the fate of Jamaica became uncertain. After all, the island had been captured by a *usurper*, who had deliberately broken a valid peace treaty; how could the restored King justify its possession? Thus, Jamaica almost fell back into the hands of its first conquerors. In 1660, 2 years after Cromwell's death, Charles II returned to the throne—after the flash reign of Cromwell's son. As the exhumed and severed head of the *usurper* was impaled in front of the Abbey of Westminster, the fate of Jamaica was at stake. The Spaniards wanted it back, and Charles II was about to comply—the first boats were officially called back from the colony. Yet, he changed his mind. This island seemed promising, after all. Moreover, it was perfectly located on the road from Spain to Honduras, Campeche or Mexico. The Buccaneers—or Freebooters— had already started to take advantage of its location. Upon realizing that Charles II would not return the island, the King of Spain addressed his Council: "(We must) *regard the recovery of Jamaica as a matter of grave importance, since the difficulties* (we are) *experiencing all originate*(d) *from there*." (Padron) In 1660, the Buccaneers sacked and plundered the Spanish kingdom in America. In Europe, Spain held the English crown to account, and demanded the complacent Governor of Jamaica to be dismissed from his post. But Spain was the shadow of herself; crumbling under the weight of her own empire, and corroded by internal feuds, she was unable to impose her will. The English took advantage of the Spaniards' weakness, forcing them to sign the Treaty of Madrid. It was centred around Article 7: "*That all the offences, losses, injuries and harm which the Spanish and English nations have mutually experienced in America, (...) be forgotten, and completely blotted from memory; as if they had never occurred. Apart from this it has been agreed that the most Serene King of Great Britain, his heirs and successors, shall have, hold and enjoy in perpetuity (...) all the lands, regions, islands, colonies and domains situated in the West Indies, (...) which the said King (...) happen to have and hold at the moment.*" (Padron) This article had been written for Jamaica, though it does not disclose her name. "*What its signature could not conceal, however,*" deplores Padron, "*was a humiliating surrender and a painful confession of Spanish political and military impotence at the time.*"

The dream of recapture lived on. In 1782, a Spanish engineer suggested landing 20,000 men to the various key points of the island to suffocate the enemy. Although very well detailed, it never went any further.

Towards a Civil Government
Following the ratification of the Treaty, Jamaica adopted a civil

government. On February 8, 1660, D'Oyley received a commission under the Great Seal of England, for the creation of a council of 12 members. The colony adopted the model of England: the Governor, representing the King and appointed by him, was to appoint and dismiss the members of the Council—or Upper House. The third political body was the Assembly, or Lower House, and it consisted in members elected by the landowners of each parish. Matters of sovereignty arose when Charles II, said by Edwards to be *inconsistent in this matter*, tried to impose a new body of law to Jamaica in 1678. It was directly inspired by the notorious Poyning Act, then applied in Ireland. So far, a law passed in Jamaica was adopted, and then submitted to the King—approved, it became official; else, it was declared obsolete. But suddenly, everything was called into question, and the colonists had to accept a new body of laws. *"The Assembly rejected the new constitution with indignation,"* explains Bryan Edwards. Colonel Samuel Long, ancestor of Edward Long, and member of the Council, fiercely opposed the King. Unable to quiet things down, D'Oyley was dismissed. "(He) *was a far better soldier than a civil administrator,"* says Clinton V. Black. He ended his career on an obscure affair of slave trafficking—called back to England, he died in London in 1675. His successor, the Earl of Carlisle, was sent to carry the Poyning Act into execution. He had Samuel Long arrested and carried a prisoner to England, where he successfully pleaded the cause of Jamaica in front of the Privy Council. But the contest between the colony and the King lasted for several years. *"The old story of revenue produced this inflexibility on the part of the government,"* underlines Edwards. Jamaica was the only colony to resist this new legislative system—but in 1728 the colonists eventually agreed to pay £8,000 annually to the King, thus settling the matter.

Meanwhile, the Assembly passed many bills regarding hunting, bridge building, and the development of agriculture. At the end of the 17th century, the island entered a period of plenty. Now aware of the importance of planting and divided into parishes, the colonists created a body of laws to protect the citizens, the planters against usurers and to encourage the coming of new colonists. This was the first golden age of Jamaica, when the island crumbled under the riches and the vices of her new hosts—soon her new masters—, the Buccaneers.

***

4

The *Maroons*, the Desultory Foes

T he Maroons were runaway slaves, who regrouped in the hills to fight for freedom. The phenomenon was not typically Jamaican; Maroons could have been found almost all over the New World. But in Jamaica, they put up incredible resistance against the English for over 50 years. The Assembly passed 44 bills and spent £250,000 to eradicate them—but in vain. The Marrons went barefooted, and fought with derisory means, yet constantly defeated their enemies until the treaty of 1739. Unfortunately, the said treaty cast an everlasting shadow on their achievements. Actually, the descendants of slaves in Jamaica are today equally proud and ashamed of the Maroons.

The wild-Negroes

Before the English captured Jamaica in 1655, there were 1,500 African slaves living in the island. The Spaniards allowed them to live among themselves in remote camps. Masters at hunting wild cows, they provided the Whites with meat and skins—the latter were sold to other colonies—, and enjoyed relative freedom. But when Penn and Venables invaded Jamaica, they became soldiers. The Spanish Governor Ysassi taught them to harass the enemy. In the meantime, they kept on providing the Spaniards with meat. Ysassi did his best to make sure they remained loyal—when they shifted allegiance, the Spaniards definitively lost Jamaica. But some of the Spanish slaves sided the invaders like Juan de bolas. Others took advantage of the chaotic situation to stay on their own; they started to roam the island in small groups, and, knowing no friends, attacked every one. They settled on the foothills of the Blue

Moutains and eventually became the Maroons. The name derives from the Spanish word *cimarron*—which translates to mean *untamed*. But at first, they were simply called the *wild-Negroes*. They planted corn and cocoa, and plundered the English settlements to improve their condition. Their camps became a refuge to runaway slaves, and a perpetual threat to the colonists. In the 18th century, the Whites lived in fear of an uprising. Probably because of the impressive amount of slaves on the island, and of the terrible tortures they inflicted on the Whites when they fell in their revengeful hands—also, as Carey Robinson suggests[*], is a result of a heavy feeling of guilt.

D'Oyley set up an expedition to eradicate the *wild-Negroes*, killing most of them. Those who surrendered had to prove their loyalty by tracking down their former friends into their most inaccessible hideouts. They killed many, offering the English a victory beyond their capacities. Leslie confirms: "*In such a sultry climate, the fatigue of climbing the precipices, and the very load of their arms was almost intolerable to an European constitution.*" D'Oyley was about to exterminate the last groups of them, but he did not. Was it because the project was not that easy? Or because 2 rebellious Colonels in his own army—who were executed shortly afterwards—, defied his authority at the time? The expedition was aborted and a few dozens of *wild-Negroes* were left alive. Within the next few years, they became deadly predators, shifting from the status of *wild-Negroes* to the one of *Maroons*. They became the plague and the nightmare of White Jamaica. Breastworks and forts were built in the plains. The expenditure was colossal, and the danger continuous. Furthermore, runaway slaves joined their ranks daily. "*Soon, the Africans left the plantations by the hundreds,*" writes Raynal, "*after they had slaughtered their masters and plundered their houses that they set afire. In vain were some active partisans used against them, who were promised £900 for each killed—that is for a severed head. This was useless, and the desertion became more general.*"

The Coromantyns

Slavery is an ancestral custom, but the triangular trade was exceptional in its proportions. More than 10 million people were deported over 400 years. Though such a figure might suggest a form of docility, the history of the New World is interspersed with slaves' revolts. History was written by the strong, who have not recorded all the acts of bravery of the weak—first to avoid the setting of bad examples, and then

---

[*] *The Fighting Maroons of Jamaica* (Jamaica, 1969).

to justify themselves. But the slaves rebelled so many times in Jamaica that it would have been impossible to conceal it. Yet, the colonists had an explanation. Jamaica, they said, was the slave drivers' first stop on their way to the continent, where they got rid of the most turbulent slaves. Among those slaves, bought in Senegal, or at Fort James on the Guinea River, were the Coromantyns. They were admired for their robustness and their determination, but they were also feared. Cudjoe, the historical leader of the Maroons, was a Coromantyn; so was Quao, or Tacky, the emblematic rebel of 1760 (see chapter 10). The historians praise their physical capacities, even those who disliked them like R.C. Dallas[†] or Bryan Edwards. The first says: *"Vigour appeared upon their muscles, and their motions displayed agility. Their eyes were quick, wild, and fiery (...). They possessed most, if not all, of the senses in a superior degree."* The latter goes on: *"Their mode of living and daily pursuits undoubtedly strengthened the frame, and served to exalt them to great bodily perfection.(...) The muscles (...) are very prominent, and strongly marked. Their sight withal is wonderfully acute, and their hearing remarkably quick."* They were responsible for most of the spontaneous and disordered revolts in the island. Although quickly suppressed, these uprisings remained scary, since they were unpredictable. Leslie tells about a specific one that took place on the estate of a planter who was *famous for his riches and justly valuable for his generous and hospitable disposition.* Our "rich and generous" man took in a slave whom he found dying on the roadside. He became his property. But punishing him one day for some fault, he made a deadly foe of him. The ungrateful creature soon assaulted his master's house with a bloodthirsty party, finding his benefactor lying in bed. The *wild-Negroes* tortured him to death with the rest of his family. *"All the barbarities that could either be invented by cruelty, or committed by rage and fury, were practised upon these unhappy men,"* says Leslie. *"Some of them were indeed dispatch'd in a minute. This was not owing to the mercy of the Negroes, but to the haste they were in. Others had a harder fate; for this resolute set of murderers took as much pleasure in torturing them, as well-disposed souls takes in acts of kindness and beneficence."* About the same story, Edward Long gives more details, calling the victim Mr B—, and stating: *"Being overpowered by numbers, and disabled by wounds, he fell at length a victim to their cruelty; they cut off his head, sawed his skull asunder, and made use of it as a punch-bowl."* The rebels then retreated into the hills of Lecuvard, where more runaway slaves regularly joined them—they became the terror of the North Coast.

---

† *The History of the Maroons* (London, 1803).

The First Maroon War

Following their many victories, the *wild-Negroes* grew confident and decided to take the island in 1690. This was the first Maroon war. In a concerted movement, several rebellious groups attacked various plantations all through the island. Governor Williams, second Count of Inchiquin, had just arrived in Jamaica. He sent his troops against the Maroons; but the latter refused to fight in the open, and hid in inexpungible caves instead, defeating their enemies in short but repeated skirmishes. The English troops came back, exhausted and disheartened. As a result, the slaves started to get nervous on the plantations. At Suttons Estate, in the parish of Clarendon, 400 of them assaulted their master's house. According to Leslie, they cut the throat of Mr Sutton and his family, but Long only tells about the murder of a white *Overseer*. They sacked the artillery, and then headed to the nearest plantation. From the neighbouring parishes, the English sent 50 men, horse and foot. Ill organised, giving way to panic, the rebels went back to Suttons Estate, from which they were dislodged the following day. "*The rebels withdrew to the cane pieces,*" writes Long, "*and set fire to them, in order to cover their retreat; but a detachment of the militia having fetched a little compass, found means to assault them on flank, while the rest advanced upon them in front; unable to withstand this double fire, the rebels immediately fled, but were so briskly pursued, that many were killed, and two hundred of them threw down their arms, and begged for mercy.*" The English confessed 16 dead—which is quite unlikely. Once identified, the leaders were hanged, but a handful of rebels got away and vanished in the hills of Clarendon. Among them was a short and stout Coromantyn, who went by the African name of Cudjoe. The English relations as well as the engraving joined to Dallas' book, represent Cudjoe as a hunchback—but this is doubtful. He might have been stout, but the way in which he led his troops in the steepest relief of the island proved that he suffered from no major physical disability.

As soon as 1656, Sedgwick was worried over these wandering Negroes, who refused to negotiate. Foretelling that they might become *thorns in the side* of the colony, he confesses his helplessness in a missive sent to Thurloe in England: "*Having no moral sense (...) and not understanding what the laws and customs of civil nations mean, we know not how to capitulate or treat with any of them (...) They must either be destroyed, or brought in upon come terms or other; or else they will prove a great discouragement to the settling of people.*" The colonists called upon the Mosquito Indians and their hunting dogs to dislodge them—

but in vain. Soon, it was impossible to circulate but on the perimeter of the island. The rest of the colony belonged *de facto* to these dreaded *wild-Negroes,* who, *by their barbarities and outrage, intimidated the Whites from venturing to any considerable distance from the sea-coast.* (Long) In 1660, Captain Ballard disbanded the troop of the Vermaholis Negroes. But this was a small victory. The helpless English promised to pardon every repentant *wild-Negro,* and to allot him a plot of land. None took the offer. Worse, Juan de Bolas, the former Spanish slave who had joined the English after the invasion of 1655, was ambushed and killed by a group of Maroons. Little has been written about these black troops that fought the Maroons. In Surinam (Dutch Guyana), they were called Rangers. At the end of the 18th century, John Stedman, a young English officer infatuated with the ideas of the *Lumières,* wonders about their motivations. *"What would men not do to be emancipated from so deplorable a state of subjection? (...) Having thus once engaged in this service, it is evident that they must be considered by the other party as apostates and traitors of the blackest dye; they must be convinced that defeat must not only expose them to death, but to the severest tortures; they were therefore fighting for something more than liberty and life: (...) miscarriage was to plunge them in the severest misery."* Stedman reports a discussion he overheard between some Maroons and some Rangers during an expedition: *"The former reproaching the rangers as poltroons and traitors to their countrymen, and challenging them next day to single combat (...). The rangers d—n'd the rebels for a parcel of pitiful skulking rascals, whom the would fight one to two in the open field if they dared but shew* (sic) *their ugly faces; swearing they had only deserted their masters because they were too lazy to work."* Stedman immortalized one of these Rangers with a wonderful drawing; he did the same with a Maroon (see illustration)—it is often used to illustrate the story of the Jamaican Maroons, as contemporary engravings are badly missed.

The English had to give up a vast part of Jamaica, but they never stopped trying to find a solution. Three expeditions were set up in 1730. The first one got lost in the morasses, where many soldiers drowned. The second one, though reinforced by a regiment from Gibraltar, underwent very important losses which forced it to turn back. The soldiers from the last one, after many days of a tedious walk and several inefficient skirmishes, realized that they were going nowhere fast. The Maroons of Winward and those of Clarendon had established a permanent and fleeting front as the threat was perpetual and unpredictable. The way the Maroons lived in their camps proved their determination. Always on the alert, deprived of commodity, and surviving through plundering and murders, they not only feared the English but also the traitors who would sell them out for a handful of pounds. This was a tough life. Their knowledge of the field and their speed of reaction allowed them to resist an ill-equipped and ill-adapted enemy. The *abengs*, those emptied cow horns used as trumpets by the sentinels, sounded the arrival of the English from hill to hill. They gave a powerful and modulating sound—the Maroons used it to coordinate their attacks or retreats. The only arms they had were taken to the enemies. They only fired when assured to hit their target, and thus became diabolically good shooters. They plundered isolated plantations for gunpowder. At first, the slaves supported them by letting them know of their masters' plans. They also used to give them a portion of their provisions. Some Maroons joined the crowd in Kingston, on market days, to buy a few bullets under the English's nose. On the battlefield, they proved to have been astonishing warriors. "*No sooner is their piece discharged, than they throw themselves into a thousand antic gestures, and tumble over and over, so as to elude the shot, as well as to deceive the aim of the adversaries, which their nimble and almost instantaneous change of position renders extremely uncertain,*" says Edward Long. Then he adds with contempt: "*In short, throughout their whole manoeuvres, they skip about like so many monkies* (sic)."

In 1730, the colony set up a militia dedicated to fight the Maroons exclusively. The Captain received £4 a month, excluding premiums. Indeed, he got £10 for each Maroon captured alive—the prisoners were then transported to another island—, and £40 for each severed head; the last option obviously offering more profits and less complications.

The Destruction of Nanny Town

Though indomitable, the Maroons remained in a precarious situation. Their war effort required many sacrifices. And they experienced a few backlashes, too, including the destruction of Nanny Town, in 1734. The name of this legendary Maroons' hideout in the Blue Mountains, derived from Nanny, the elusive female warrior—later raised to the rank of National Hero, she appears on the current $500 banknotes. She was allegedly Cudjoe's sister, or wife, and was said to have superpowers, such the highly symbolic capacity to catch the English bullets with her vagina, and then to fire them back at the enemy with her anus! The natural crucible formed at the confluence of the Nanny (or Macungo) and Stony rivers was continuously boiling; it was

Beside: a Maroon in Surinam, drawn by Stedman (end of the 18th century); in the background, a Ranger, or Maroon hunter, in Surinam (same source); map of Jamaica (Georg Ehret, 1750).

called Nanny's cauldron, and the Maroons claimed that any English who dared leaning over it, instantly suffocated to death. Nanny Town was the main settlement of the Maroons of Winward. Erected in a dreadful and magnificent place, on the brink of a vertiginous 900 feet precipice, it overhung the said cauldron, according to Robinson. Leslie reports that, in 1734, Captain Stoddart *got before the night to the foot of the hill* with a handful of men. They successfully hauled up some *field-pieces* onto the top of a nearby eminence, and *the pieces were loaded with musket-bullets, which killed and wounded a vast number of the rebels.* The assault did not last more than half an hour, but it was devastating; the town was set afire and all the Maroons who did not jump into the precipice were killed or taken prisoners. Leslie underlines that *they suffered more real hurt (...) on that day, than in 20 years before.* But there's something fishy about this story. How could Stoddart come so close without being spotted? Especially while hauling up some guns onto a hill. The oral history of the Maroons gives a different version. Alerted by the sentinels, the Maroons, it says, abandoned their town to the English, who, entering an empty place and being tired, decided to stay for the night. The Maroons had not gone far, and they returned to set their own town afire, forcing the English to jump into the precipice. The English historians themselves give contradictory information, including that about the name of the Captain in charge of the expedition. Anyway, the destruction of Nanny Town was a victory for the colonists. They destroyed more than a city, this very day—a symbol. Nanny was no longer invulnerable. The ruins of Nanny Town were abandoned to the *duppies*—ghosts—, and the place was never rebuilt. "*The spot is now, and has been ever since,*" says Gardner, "*a scene of superstitious awe to the Maroons; it is difficult, if not impossible, to persuade one to guide a traveller to the place.*"

This loss was a hard blow for the Maroons, but it did not discourage them. Near Bangels, they attacked a considerable English party, surprising Colonel Charleton and Captain Ivy, who were having dinner under their tent, almost killing them. At the same time, Spanish Town woke up in fear in the middle of the night, as a detachment of rebels had been spotted nearby—but they were disbanded by Captain Edmunds. Martial law was proclaimed at the early hours of the conflict and was kept for 9 months; but the problem was yet to be solved. "*From the commencement of the war (...),*" writes Long, "(the Maroons) *had not once ventured a pitched battle; but skulked about the skirts of remote plantations, surprising stragglers, and murdering the Whites by two or three at a time, or when they were too few to make any resistance.*" At night they stole things from the English settlements, setting fire to cane-pieces and outhouses, killing the cattle, and carrying off the slaves. "*By this dastardly method of conducting the war, they did infinite mischief to the Whites, without much exposing their own persons to danger,*" deplores Long. The Maroons were *desultory foes*, concludes the historian. They had nothing to lose, knew the field like the back of their hand, and could move their camps in the twinkle of an eye. "*Thus shall, sooner or later, triumph over the numerous armies (...) a people desperate at the atrocity of tyranny (...), if it choses hanger rather than the yoke,*" states Guillaume-Thomas Raynal. "*Such was the way these Negroes behaved with the English.*" As a matter of fact, no frontal attack could have broken their determination. It took the unexpected and almost unhoped-for conciliation of 1739 to turn Jamaica's worst enemies into her best allies.

1739 Peace Treaty

On March 11, 1739, Colonel Guthrie and Captain Sadler were sitting under a cotton tree in the Cockpit Country. Beside them was Cudjoe—stout, over 60 years of age but still alert, the historical chief of the black resistance was here to ratify a treaty with the English after 50 years of war. Cudjoe never surrendered. The treaty was offered to him by Governor Edward Trelawny, *a wise and probably human man*, says Raynal. The Maroons were granted their freedom, as well as a plot land of 1,500 acres. Apart from a few protected areas, they were also allowed to hunt all over the island. In return, they were to maintain roads from Trelawny Town (Cudjoe Town) to Westmoreland and St James, and to welcome 2 English superintendents among them on a permanent basis. These English were to *keep up friendly correspondence with the island* (Long), and, of course, an eye on their hosts. But the most controverted clauses of the treaty—clauses 7 and 9—stipulated that *the said Captain Cudjoe, and his successors, do use their best endeavours to take, kill, suppress, or destroy (...) all rebels wheresoever they be, throughout this island*; and *that if any Negroes shall hereafter run away from their masters or owners, and fall into Captain Cudjoe's hands, they shall immediately be sent back to the chief magistrate of the next parish (...); and those that bring them are to be satisfied for their trouble, as the legislature shall appoint.* (Dallas) In other words, the Maroons became runaway-slaves hunters—an irony that bordered on tragic. The historian Carey Robinson denounces the treaty as a *one-sided document*, and claims that the Maroons were probably ill prepared to fight the English on that ground; yet the Maroons apparently had no problem with these clauses, and complied willingly. For the English, the treaty had unexpectedly positive effects. *"This contest, which while it lasted, seemed to portend nothing less than the ruin of the whole colony, became productive of quite contrary effect in the end; insomuch that we may date the flourishing state of it from the ratification of the treaty,"* rejoices Long. Was Cudjoe the fool of the treaty? This intrepid warrior was an illiterate African, who had been taken from his native land, mistreated and hunted for dozens of years. In 1739, he was getting old—his exact age has never been displayed, but the plundering of the Sutton Estate had already taken place 49 years ago. Not to mention that the Maroons were slowly losing ground. The English called on the Mosquito Indians to hunt the Maroons with sniffing dogs; but the most important threat came from the young British officers. Unlike their predecessors, they did not care about engaging in allegedly "dishonouring" guerrilla warfare. On the contrary, they studied the tactics of their enemies, and copied them. As a result, the ambushes of the Maroons grew less efficient, and the reprisals more dangerous. Circled, Cudjoe had recently left Clarendon to move inland, on the banks of the Petty River Bottom—in the unfriendly Cockpit region. He had not heard from the Winward Maroons for a long time. Facing a shortage of provisions, he had to send his son Accompong to build a new settlement far from his. Cudjoe was in a delicate position, and he knew it. The treaty might have been insidious, but it remained an unbelievable achievement.

Cudjoe died just the way he had lived, free. We do not know about the precise circumstances of his death. Edward Long notices his presence at an official reception in 1764. *"By way of closing the ceremony, their leader, captain Cudjoe, in the name of all the rest, stood forth, and addressed his Excellency aloud, desiring the continuance of the great King George's favour and protection (...), according to the happy treaty and agreement subsisting between them and the white people of the island."* He was at least 90 years old.

Peace was completed a few months later, when Quao, the leader of the Winward Maroons, signed the treaty too. A former run-away, Quao had demonstrated his military skill after the destruction of Nanny Town, defeating the English troops sent after him in a masterful way. The trap that he gradually drove his pursuers in, is worthy to be taught in any guerrilla warfare school. This last victory definitely convinced the

Opposite: the Maroons throwing down their arms at the feet of the English; in the background, a war demonstration in Maroon Town (18th century).

Whites of the necessity to come to an agreement with these terrible enemies. As far as the Maroons were concerned, this treaty had to be signed. They could not have fought forever; the colony was becoming more populated each day, and better organized too. Yet, it was an abrupt breach in the black struggle. Giving the Maroons an official status, the English forced them to integrate a system. And when they turned against their owns, the Maroons partly lost their soul. Raynal judges them with severity: "*These coward Africans unworthy of the liberty they had regained, were not ashamed to sell the blood of their own brothers.*" In 1766, they intervened to suppress a revolt led by some Coromantyn slaves in Westmoreland; the House of Assembly officially thanked them for their help. The reconversion was probably not an easy task for these men, who had built their lives around war. But they apparently enjoyed hunting runaway slaves. Edwards did not like them, and denounces *their blood-thirstiness of disposition.*

He says: "*It is notoriously true that they wish for nothing more than a pretence to put the poor wretches to death (...), making the plea of resistance an excuse for their barbarity.*" Received every year in Spanish Town for an official ceremony, the Maroons now despised the slaves, whom they considered inferior. As a matter of fact, during the last Maroon War of 1795, the slaves refused to join them, and even fought against them alongside their masters. Worse, the Maroons themselves were now divided, and the Accompong ones helped the English so efficiently against those of Trelawny, that they were officially given a reward. This was quite a sad ending to such a glorious fight; and it still stains the story of these incredible men. Carey Robinson shows compassion: "*What* (their detractors) *fail to see is the savagery of the struggle which culminated in the treaties; the long, drawn-out sacrifices which the Maroons were called upon to make; their ridiculously small numbers, the scarcity of weapons, ammunition and food (...). They fail to understand that (...) they were in fact illiterate, unsophisticated people who were almost completely at the mercy of the colonial administrators when negotiating treaties.*"

The Last Battle

After 57 years of peace, the Maroons of Trelawny, probably excited by the nearby uprising of St-Domingue (see chapter 8), went to war in July 1795. It all started when 2 of them received 39 whiplashes in Montego Bay for stealing hogs. They went back home, *insulting every white person whom they met in the road*. (Edwards) In Trelawny, the Maroons then ordered the English superintendent to leave the place. According to Edwards, they did not contest their punishment, but the fact that it had been inflicted in front of some fugitives they had recently captured, and by the hand of a slave supervisor—this they perceived as an insult made to the sovereignty of the Maroon people.

They sought refuge near the historical hideout of Cudjoe, Little Bottom River, in the Cockpit, where they resisted the assaults of the regiment of Governor Blacarres. The first attacks were deadly for the English, but when the officer Walpole became in charge, everything changed. Walpole observed his enemies, and copied their tactics. He also cleared entire parts of the Cockpit, taught his men the art of camouflage; the morale of the troops improved as the losses grew thinner. Soon, Lieutenant-Colonel Quarrell came back for his mission in Cuba, bringing 40 hunters with their 140 dogs. Thanks to this new psychological ascendency, Walpole negotiated peace with favourable terms, having the Maroons down on one knee, begging for pardon.

Then, under the first pretence, he inflicted them the worst punishment, exile. Jamaica was like a feeding breast to the Maroons, who feared exile more than death. They had to leave, yet. On June 6, 1796, they headed to Halifax, Nova Scotia. But they soon demanded to be transported to a warmer country. Someone then remembered the utopian project of the English abolitionist Granville Sharp, who, in 1787, had sent back a group of freed slaves to Africa. The Sierra Leone Cie. that repatriated the freed slaves, picked up his idea 2 years later, building the town of Freetown —today's Sierra Leone's capital. But the experiment went sore, as the freed slaves rebelled and formed a small armed band to live out of plunders and exactions. The Maroons, sent there in 1800, put it back into order, forcing the rebels to implore the protection of the Europeans! Once more, the Maroons demonstrated their extraordinary fighting abilities.

History can be ironical. The first African slaves to return to Africa from Jamaica did so against their will. And many of their descendants, looking for their roots, went back to Jamaica dozens of years later! The Maroons who had remained in Jamaica went on chasing runaway slaves; they even intervened during the famous Morant Bay rebellion, in 1865. They were the ones who captured the leader of the revolt, Paul Bogle, who was hanged shortly afterwards—and made National Hero 100 years later.

***

5

The Buccaneers of Jamaica

D uring the second half of the 17th century, *a predatory tropical war* (Long) raged in the West Indies. It was led by battalions of Buccaneers, the warlike offspring of the French *Boucaniers*. It all started in 1630, when the Spaniards decided to remove the illegal settlers from Hispaniola. The latter came together to fight back, and ended up attacking the Spaniards on land or at sea, looting, raping and murdering. Their name alone made the Spaniards afraid, and they were rendered even more terrible by the dreadful sermons of the Spanish priests, who described them as an unstoppable God-sent plague. Used by nations at war, courted by the Governors of the New World—who would rather become their hosts than their victims—, the Buccaneers knew no master, hardly a god; pleasure and gain only motivated them. Their society was nonetheless ruled by precise codes. There were 4 branches among them: the Inhabitants, who planted; the *Bucaniers*, who hunted; the Servants, who served; and the Freebooters—later known as the Buccaneers—, who fought the *predatory tropical war*. The Buccaneers settled anywhere they were welcomed. Tortuga Island, off St-Domingue, and Port Royal, Jamaica, became their favourite resorts. Thus sheltered under the wings of crime and vice, Jamaica gained a crucial stand on the geopolitical scene of the New World.

The *Boucaniers*

In the beginning were the *Boucaniers* of Hispaniola. These nomadic adventurers, mostly French but also Dutch and English, settled there in 1630, after the Spaniards had chased them from St. Christopher—

today's St. Kitts. Isolated and living in small groups, they ended up forming a sort of society. Oliver-Alexander Esquemeling gives the most vivid description of them in *The Bucaniers of America*, which, 300 years later, remains the book of reference on the topic. Indeed, the author was a Buccaneer himself, and he partook in many bloody expeditions as a surgeon. He introduced himself as a Frenchman, and it is believed that he came to the West Indies when Louis XIV forbade all Protestants to practice surgery. He was broke, and had no choice but to engage as a *Servant*—or *engagé*, as they were called in the French colonies. As such, he endured the ferocity of a tyrannical master in Hispaniola, but soon passed to Jamaica, where he joined the Buccaneers of Henry Morgan. Taking for granted that *truth has the ability of making itself heard whenever uttered*, the French publisher of his relation gives very little pieces of information on his author. The book first came out in Dutch, in 1682, before being translated into English 2 years later. Henry Morgan sued it for libel and the *London Gazette* of June 8, 1685, reads: "*There have been lately printed and published two books, one by Will. Crook, the other by Thos. Malthus, both intitled (sic) THE HISTORY OF THE BUCANIERS: both which books contained many false, scandalous and malitious* (sic) *reflections on the life and actions of Sir Henry Morgan of Jamaica Kt. The said Sir Henry Morgan hath by judgement had in the King's-Bench-Court, recovered against the said libel £200 damages.*" Esquemeling was well-informed about the Buccaneers, and his work remains the most valuable testimony of a society he studied from the inside. The engravings joined to the French edition, stepping away from the warlike English ones, give a sociological dimension to the book. Thus, the 'plate of the Buccaneer' (see illustration) has captured the popular image of this fascinating character. But the French edition took many liberties with the original text, adding informative details, including the origins of the name *Boucanier*: "*Some native Indians from the Caribbean, called the Caribs, usually treated their enemies as such when made prisoners: they cut them into pieces and put the said pieces on a sort of grill, lighting a fire under them. They call these grills* barbocoas, *and the place they build them, a* boucan; *and the action,* boucaner *which means roasting and smoking at the same time—hence the name* Bucaniers." The engraving represents one of them, holding his famous rifle *made in France by one Brachie, in Dieppe, or one Gélin, in Nantes.* (Esquemeling, *French edition*). With these masterpieces, the best shooters could pick an apple off a tree at a distance of several dozens of metres, cutting the stalk without damaging the fruit. At his feet lay 2 dogs from his pack; he roamed the plains of

Hispaniola, hunting savage cows. The first time Esquemeling met a Buccaneer, it was off Tortuga Island—and he had a vivid memory of the moment. This scene, which allegedly took place just as Esquemeling arrived in Hispaniola, is missing from the English edition: "*A small boat came to us, loaded with six men, who astonished those among us who had never left France before. They wore a small linen blouse and short pants that covered only half of their legs. It was hard to say whether they were made of linen or not, as they were soaked in the blood of the game they usually carry around. Furthermore, they were tanned; some had their hair standing on end, others had tied them. They all wore beards, and they all had a sleeve made of crocodile's skin to the hip were they had stuck four knives and a bayonet. We learnt from those who had already been to the island that they were buccaneers.*" On the engraving, the Buccaneer wears handmade stockings, as well as a cap to protect him from the rain—he also smokes a pipe. Most of them lived as hermits, and slept in simple tents. To help ease their loneliness, they often went by 2, calling themselves *matelots*. They avoided the main settlements, and were plunged into a regressive way of life. "*The Boucaniers of St-Domingue,*" says La Harpe, "*were Christians, and lived among themselves. In less than thirty years, out of the lack of exercise or instruction, (...) they remembered nothing about their religion but baptism.*" These half-savages spread all over Hispaniola, sharing everything among them—including women, apparently. When 2 had a disagreement, they settled it with their rifles. Many were ex-convicts, or poor wretches, who had run away from the old Europe; others were mere adventurers. Hunting cows was their main occupation. When they caught one, they *bucaned* it—roasted it and smoked it—, and then shared it with their dogs.

The Buccaneers came to Hispaniola by various means, but almost all the French ones came from St. Christopher; they had captured the island with the English in 1625, but the Spaniards chased them out 5 years later. Charlevoix explains: "*Those from St. Christopher joined other English and French adventurers, approached Hispaniola and, on finding the North Coast almost deserted (...), decided to settle there. (...) They found themselves quite comfortable; as the Dutch later promised them never to let them starve, and to buy all the skins they would sell, they remained there. Most of these new colonists were from the French region of Normandie, they were called Boucaniers.*"

In 1632, the Buccaneers captured the island of Tortuga, off Hispaniola. The 25 Spaniards there in post, who *were bored stiff* (Charlevoix), jumped at the opportunity, and ran away. The body of

Adventurers developed from there. Those who decided to plant became Inhabitants; their role was less spectacular but crucial, since they also fought the Spanish militias on the land. The Buccaneers, for their part, were hunters; but some of them started to attack the Spaniards at sea. Their first expeditions were mediocre. They took some small Spanish barks, before returning in haste to the safe harbour of Tortuga. But their repeated successes made them bold. Many Servants sent by the merchants of Dieppe in France, joined their ranks—they signed a contract before a solicitor, engaging to serve an unknown master in the New World for *36 months*. In return, they did not have to pay for the crossing.

The Spaniards soon understood that these men represented a dormant threat, so they sent the General of the Galleons in the West Indies in 1638: "*Those who first fell into their hands were all put to the sword,*" explains Charlevoix. "*The others, who surrendered to save their lives, were hanged on the spot.*" Tortuga recaptured, remained the problem of the Buccaneers scattered all over Hispaniola. The General set up a body of 500 spearmen, which he divided into 5 groups. The Buccaneers called them the *Fifties*. Esquemeling confesses (French edition): "*They did not fail to kill many Buccaneers by surprise.*" The Massacre River, east of Bayaha, owns its name to the 30 Buccaneers who were ambushed by the *Fifties* and killed on the spot. One Charles Toré and his companions were also ambushed and killed in the area. Yet, the Spaniards' enemies were dangerous; sharp shooters, they feared nothing. The actions of the *Fifties* were too hazardous, so the Spaniards decided to starve their enemies by slaughtering the savage cows. "*Then the Buccaneers, finding no food to eat,*" underlines Charlevoix, "*were (...) forced to embrace a new way of life. Many turned Inhabitants.*" Others, *probably not the most honest among them,* (Charlevoix), became Freebooters. They rapidly spread to the Gulf of Mexico and alongside the coasts of South America; from Campeche to Yucatan, they learnt how to catch a new type of fish—the Spaniards. "*Talking about the Boucaniers,*" reads the French edition of Esquemeling's book, "*I meant to demonstrate that the most notorious Freebooters were bred among them; and we may say that they trained in the countryside, (...) with savage cows; and that they practiced at sea, and in the cities, with people.*" The society of the Freebooters (the name *Buccaneers* stuck; the English edition of Esquemeling spells it *Bucaniers*) was born. Raynal describes it as *the most singular ever*. He goes on: "*Without any system, any law, without subordination or means, they became the astonishment of their century—and probably of the ones to come. They would have conquered the Americas, if they had been as good conquerors as murderers.*"

Above: a Buccaneer and his rifle (Esquemeling, French edition); hunting a savage cow; way of life of the Buccaneers; the French part of the island of Santo Domingo (Bonne).

The Servants

They were called the *36 months* in the French colonies and Servants, in the English ones, and they were the white predecessors of slaves—and, later, their counterweight. Each Buccaneer had several Servants. Their condition was terrible. After the capture of St-Christopher, in 1625, Governor Desnambuc did his best to socialize his stubborn colonists. "*He (...) oblig'd (the colonists) to be mild and courteous one towards the other,*" writes* César de Rochefort, "*and that the stronger should not take advantage of the weaker. Thence it came that he made this commendable order, which is still in force in all those islands; to wit, that masters should not take Servants for any longer term then* (sic) *three years* (36 months—editor's note), *during which time they should be oblig'd to treat them with all gentleness and moderation, an exact of them only such servitude as were rational and answerable to their strength.*" In fact, they were treated no better than slaves—and sometimes worse. A handful of Servants disembarked in Jamaica the days following Charles Leslie's arrival. Some planters approached them: "*It was diverting (if such scenes can afford any) to see the shoal of buyers. The poor fellows were made pass in review before their future tyrants, and looked at, as if they had been a parcel of horses. (...) The Servants have a right of good usage, their masters pay their passage, and should they be maltreated, because they have obliged themselves (by contract) to serve a limited number of years?*" Well, yes—if we are to trust Esquemeling's dark testimony. He became himself a victim of a tyrannical master in St-Domingue, who almost drove him to death. When working in the field, *the master is here with a baton,* he writes. *If one of* (the Servants) *takes a look behind him or remains for a few moments without working, the master beats him, just like a convict on the galleys. And no matter if they're sick, they still have to work. I've seen more than one beaten so hard that they never recovered. They were thrown into a pit at the corner of the plantation, and nobody ever talked about them again.* The Servants were Whites of low birth, who could not afford the crossing to the New World—some never intended to come, in fact. "*Great numbers used formerly to be brought from Scotland,*" says Long, "*where they were actually kidnapped by some mantraders, in or near Glasgow, and shipped for this island to be sold for four or five years term of service.*" Father Labat visited Barbados at the turn of the 18th century, and he writes a few lines about the English Servants: "*Most of them are poor Irishmen, who were kidnapped, and who now lament over their hard servitude. They are supposed to serve seven*

---

* *The History of the Caribby-Island* (London, 1666).

years (the minors—editor's note) *or five years* (the adults—editor's note), *but their service is usually renewed under false pretences, which their masters are never short of.”* The Servants were a necessary counterpart to the growing population of black slaves. The planters had to own an amount of Servants proportionate to the number of their slaves. Those who failed were fined. But a Servant cost £14 plus a £35 salary. Taxes included, a slave was still cheaper, and submitted to less regulations. It was forbidden to whip a naked Servant, for example; or to get rid of him in case he became disabled. When he died, you could not bury him unless a justice or 2 neighbours had certified his death. Nonetheless, Long confesses that, in the 17th century, the Servants were neglected by their masters: *“They were allowed yearly three shirts, as many pairs of trousers, shoes and stockings, and a hat or a cap; which were probably of very wretched stuff, as the penalty for not making such an allowance was no more than forty shillings. Their subsistence was directed to be four pound weight of good flesh or fish per week, with a sufficient quantity of plantation provision, such as yams, &c.”* Trying to attract as many white settlers as possible, the Assembly exonerated taxes of the ships that disembarked at least 30 Servants. But they were from the rabble, and resumed their distorted way of life in the New World. Edward Long says they had *more vices and much fewer good qualities* than the slaves, whom they had to watch—and who despised them. The historian says they mingled with the most depraved among slaves, seducing their wives and creating disturbances, and eventually *bringing an odium upon the white people in general.* As soon as 1736, their condition improved. Better treated and paid, legally tried when opposed to their masters, they climbed the social ladder. But in the late 17th century, once their engagement was over, they usually joined the seadogs who sacked the Americas, becoming Buccaneers.

The Freebooters[†]

The French term of *flibustier*, says Charlevoix, *originated from the English* free-booter, *which means every man making war to loot.* Bruzen de la Martinière reminds us of the Dutch origins of the word: *“The word* vie-boot, *a sort of boat, is much older in Dutch than the French word* fribot, *which only derived from the mispronunciation of the former. We may say that the Dutch were responsible for providing the flibustiers with*

---

† The French make a difference between the *Boucaniers* (or bucaniers, or buccaneers) and the *Flibustiers.* The first ones were hunters in Hispaniola, and gave birth to the latter, who plundered the Spaniards at sea.

that type of boats—and that the name stuck to them. Vlie *and* Vlieland *are well-known places; and* boot *means bark, rowboat, etc."* They were said to be sometimes pious, but not that often; the Spaniards called them *the new Turks.* They respected the rules of their brotherhood only, the famous *brotherhood of the coastal brethren*—which happened to be so precise at times, that some historians see them as the sketch of an early libertarian constitution. But they were just meant to protect them as much as possible—and they are hardly evoked in contemporary writings. Boarding galleons was a risky occupation, and although they were incredibly bold people, the Buccaneers remained far-sighted. Esquemelin gives the terms of a *chasse-partie*, or preliminary agreement on a booty's share: "*A salary for the surgeon, and his chest of medicaments, which usually is rated at two hundred and fifty pieces of eight. Lastly* (we) *agree what rate each one ought to have that is either wounded or maimed in his body, suffering the loss of any limb; as for the loss of a right arm, six hundred pieces of eight, or six slaves; for the left arm, five hundred pieces of eight, or five slaves (...); for an eye, one hundred pieces, or one slave; for a finger, the same than for an eye."* The share thus obeyed certain rules. Each man had to swear on the Bible that he had not been hiding anything from others during the plundering; when caught in a lie, he was deprived of his goods, and then *marooned*—meaning abandoned on a desert island. The crew elected their captain, and could revoke him at any time. They were also free to leave the adventure at any time. "*Being bold and daring,*" reads the French edition of Esquemelin, "*they are stopped by no fatigue or danger; at the heart of the action, they focus on nothing but the enemies and the victory; most of the time, yet, they hope for gain, and not for glory (...). They resolve to work as easily as to pleasure, being equally used to both; and they go from opposite conditions in the twinkle of an eye: sometimes rich, sometimes poor, sometimes slaves or masters, they do not let hard times trouble them, or good times last.*"

Usually tracked down by the Spaniards, dying from hunger by Monday and sleeping upon a pile of gold by Thursday, they lived a life of uncompromised liberty. Many were animated by the thirst of adventure, and the taste of this rambling way of life, spending hard-gained fortunes in the arms of prostitutes or in the smoky taverns of Port Royal.

In 1708, Woodes Rogers circumnavigated the globe. He gives a less romantic portrait of the Buccaneers—but their golden era was already far behind: "*I must add concerning these Buccaneers, that they liv'd without government; so that when they met with purchase, they immediately squander'd it away, and when they got mony* (sic) *and liquor, they drank and gam'd till they spent all (...); and for any thing I could learn, they scarce shew'd one instance of true courage or conduct, tho* (sic) *they were accounted such fighting fellows at home."*

Just like ambushed predators, the Buccaneers set up expeditions to prey on the Spanish interests in the New World. When spotted, they could spend weeks on a lost islet, to eventually catch their enemies by surprise. To prevent their attacks at sea, the Spaniards formed huge and heavily armed fleets. The Buccaneers patiently followed them from a distance, sometimes up to the mouths of the Spanish rivers, hoping for an unfortunate ship to be isolated from the rest of the fleet by some storm. Europe soon resounded with the exploits of these new pagan warriors, and many young men rushed the West Indies to join them. They went to Tortuga or Port Royal by the hundreds. Consequently, the Spanish empire in America started to shake under their constant assaults. The maritime roads of their fleets were displayed, scrutinized, and infested by ambushed Buccaneers. The Gulf of Mexico had become unsafe, since Jamaica guarded its access—any ship sailing off Cuba could be spotted from there. At the end of the day, the Spaniards had to reduce their numbers of travels from the New World. Preventing the Buccaneers from hunting on their lands, they had forced them to attack them at sea; now reducing their numbers of ships, they forced them to plunder their cities.

Terrible people

The Buccaneers, though targeting the Spaniards in priority, attacked at random. Taken, they were hanged for piracy. To avoid this inconvenient, they sailed under *commisions*, or *Letters of Marque*. These official papers were issued by a governor, and gave the Buccaneers the right to attack the enemies of a said colony—they could not be treated as pirates. The Governors who issued *commissions* justified themselves by the necessity to protect their colony during on-going wars. The Buccaneers weakened their enemies, and thus secured the colony. Away from official conflicts, the Spaniards remained an all-time target, since they stubbornly refused to trade with other nations in the Americas. Sometimes, the Buccaneers attacked their settlements to force them to trade. But most of the times, they did it out of pure greed. They tortured their prisoners to make them say where they had hidden money or goods; women were raped; the Spaniards were suspended by their testicles, or violently thrown onto the ground; once a city taken, these festivities lasted for weeks. *"The indelible stain of pyracy* (sic) *sullies their great actions,"* says Leslie, *"and makes them look'd upon as disturbers of mankind and villains, who are only famous for murder and robbery.*" Among the most feared was L'Olonnois, a French Buccaneer based in Port Royal, whom an engraving from the English edition of Esquemelin's work represents tearing the heart from one of his victims' chest to force it into the mouth of another! Coming from Sables d'Olonne, France, he was shipped as a boy to the West Indies as a Servant. But later on, he took the lead of a small dirty bunch of murderers in Tortuga. In the region of the Darian, he made his name famous with bloody exploits; he's said to have cut off the heads of an entire crew, one by one, with his sword. In Nicaragua one day, *ill fortune assailed him*, says Esquemeling. *Here he met with both Spaniards and Indians, who jointly setting upon him and his companions, the greatest part of the pirates were killed on the place.* L'Olonnois escaped, though— but only for a time. He landed on the territory of the Indios Bravos shortly afterwards, who *within a few days after his arrival took him prisoner and tore him in pieces alive, throwing his body limb by limb into the fire, and his ashes into the air, that no trace or memory might remain of such an infamous inhuman creature.* According to the French edition, the Indians ate him up—this might have been tough meat to chew.

Roche Brasiliano was another Buccaneer to distinguish himself with wickedness. His nickname came from the fact that his family had to run away from Brazil when the Portuguese took it. Roche first went to Tortuga before ending up at Port Royal, Jamaica. "*He was of a manly look, and had a strong body,*" reports the French edition, probably describing the plate joined to the English edition, which gives no such description. "*He was of mediocre height, but firm and straight, with a face rather large than long.*" Esquemeling also says that *he had a great reputation at home, and though in his private affairs he governed himself very well, he would oftentimes appear brutal and foolish when in drink, running up and down the streets, beating or wounding those he met, no person daring to make any resistance.* Indeed, Roche was no poet. Almost all his prisoners were tortured to death. Esquemeling confirms: "*He commanded several to be roasted alive on wooden spits, for not showing him hog-yards, where he might steal wine.*" The Buccaneers were not only brutal, they were also courageous. Ten to 1 they triumphed, and could become ingenious when necessary. Taken prisoner at Campeche, Roche was to be hanged shortly. He wrote an anonymous letter to the Governor of the place, as if sent by a bunch of his accomplices, who declared themselves ready to burn down the city, if Roche was put to death. The prudent Governor spared Roche's life and sent him to Spain. From there, the Buccaneer returned to Jamaica, where he resumed his criminal life.

Reality

The French edition of Esquemeling's book reads: *"Just like the Spaniards have been, and still are, the curse of the Indians, we might say that the Buccaneers are, and will always be, the curse of the Spaniards."* This sentence illustrates the frontispieces of the Dutch and French editions, representing a Spaniard slaughtering an Indian before being slaughtered himself by a Buccaneer—a sort of just reward, so to speak; and a very convenient way to justify the cruelties imposed on the so-called selfish Spaniards. They *were always so jealous of this commerce,* writes Woodes Rogers, *that they wou'd never allow the least share of it to any other nation, but oppos'd them with force whenever they attempted it.* The Buccaneers were almost made the tools of the Lord's vengeance. Raynal states that, through them, *fortune, which hardly leaves crimes unpunished, expiated for the conquest of the New World, and the Indians were fully revenged.* As a matter of fact, when Las Casas, the Protector of the Indians, talked about his fellowmen, 100 years earlier, as being *for the major part idiots, cruel, avaritious* (sic), *infected and stained with all sorts of vices, and caring for gold only,* he might as well have talked about the Buccaneers. Their hate for the Spaniards even generated legendary figures such as Montbars the Exterminator, whose forged exploits were added to Esquemeling's relation by the French publisher. Outraged by the cruelties suffered by the Indians at the hands of the Spaniards, Montbars went to the West Indies to revenge them through a series of bold exploits worthy of the Iliad. Esquemeling's work was very successful, and many accounts of the type followed, mingling the truth and fictional facts. Woodes Rogers says that *'tis (...) a particular misfortune (...) that the buccaneers, to set off their own knight-errantry, and to make themselves pass for prodigies of courage and conduct, have given so much romantick* (sic) *accounts of their adventures and told such strange stories as make the voyages of those who come after (and cannot allow themselves the same liberty) to look flat and insipid to unthinking people.* Not to mention the apocryphal accounts of fake adventurers, built up from scratch by writers who had never left their library. Yet, the successful expeditions of Henry Morgan and the fairy tales about Port Royal, hid a rather dull reality. Many were attracted to the currents of fortune, who ended up in a bath of horror. Raveneau de Lussan was a young man when he made up his mind to join the Buccaneers; and he was not in want[‡]: *"I must confess I am not able to give an account of the*

[‡] Raveneau de Lussan's relation was usually added to Esquemeling's. Quoted edition: *The History of the Buccaneers of America* (Boston, 1856).

depth of my desires; and all that I can say, is, that I have always had a most passionate disposition for travel." He adds: "*This rambling sort of humour was accompanied with another, which I dare not dignifie* (sic) *with the name of a martial one, but was such as wrought in me an ardent desire to see some siege or battle.*" Notwithstanding the cries of his parents, he left in 1684 for the New World, where he joined the Buccaneers for an expedition to the South Sea that lasted until 1688. He came back traumatized: "*I had so little hopes of ever getting back, that I could not, for the space of fifteen days, take my return for any other than an illusion, and it proceeded so far with me, that I shunned sleep, for fear when I awaked, I should find my self again in those countries, out of which I was now safely delivered.*" His somewhat inconsequent character inspired Daniel Defoe for the main character of his novel *Robinson Crusoë*.

Woodes Rogers' expedition lasted 3 years, and he captured one ship only—a Spanish vessel taken off Mexico, which brought back considerable profits; in the course of his expedition, he had a heel torn off by a cannonball, his jaw and palate were broken with a musket shot, and he was so weak that it was necessary to use a winch to disembark him in England. As far as the legendary expedition of Captain Sharp is concerned, as related by Basil Ringrose and later added to Esquemeling's account, it was nothing but a terrible ordeal; as a matter of fact, the author was shot dead by a party of Spaniards.

The Buccaneers showed little compassion to each other. In 1669, Morgan's ship accidentally blown up off St-Domingue, causing the death of many Buccaneers—350 were on board, including Morgan, who escaped the tragedy. "*Captain Morgan commanded the bodies of the miserable wretches who were blown up to be searched for, as they floated on the sea,*" explains Esquemeling. "*Not to afford them Christian burial, but for their clothes and attire; and if any had gold rings on their fingers, these were cut off, leaving them exposed to the voracity of the monsters of the sea.*" Morgan also diverted a consequent share of the booty of Panama; he had just learnt that some of his men were plotting his death. In a word, *apart from a certain honesty that prevailed among them,* as underlined by Charlevoix, *and the human flesh, which they refused to eat, only a few of barbarians from the New World were as mean as they were; and a great number among the most ferocious were less from far.* Of all that was said or written about those people, the last word is left to the French publisher of Esquemeling, who ends up his book, reminding us that, at the end of the day, *the Buccaneers are terrible people.*

Jamaica and freebooting

The Spaniards considered the New World to be exclusively theirs, and took every foreign ship they came across; they also attacked every non-Spanish settlement. In the 16th century, they slaughtered the first French settlers in Florida, as well as those in Tortuga. Edward Long states, "*As the maritime powers in Europe were not disposed to acknowledge this pretended right of universal sovereignty in America; which the crown of Spain had arrogated; so this opposition gave rise to a sort of predatory Tropical war, which for many years subsisted previous to the conquest of Jamaica. It was chiefly conducted by private adventurers, French, English and other subjects; and gave no interruption to the peace in Europe between the respective nations and Spain. But many of these adventurers, if not most of them, were countenanced in these expeditions by their respective sovereigns, proved by their obtaining regular commissions; and the rest were not questioned for what they had done.*" The Americas became a sort of lawless area—a deed, whether legitimated by a *commission* or not, owned you the rope or the highest distinction. The European monarchs sent hordes of Buccaneers to assault the Spanish interests in America while signing peace treaties with Spain in Europe. Meanwhile, the interlop exchanges throve, as the colonies were in need of everything. Most of them established a regular trade with foreigners under false pretences. "*There was (...) a private trade by way of Jamaica to their coasts of the North Sea; which was carry'd on with great advantage to the few who thought fit to venture it, but was liable to very great dangers, because the Spanish guard-ships made prize of all they could, and our men were made prisoners, or rather slaves; and their own subjects, who treaded with us, were forc'd to do it by stealth, for fear of incurring the severe penalties of their own laws.*" Spain officially complained to other nations about the bloody exactions of their subjects in the West Indies—however, such was in vain. And Spain also knew how to bend the rules. Long says: "*In the reign of Charles I, and whilst a profound peace was observed in Europe, they attacked St. Christopher, Nevis, Providence, Santa Cruz, and some other insular settlements on which the English had planted themselves. They murdered or carry into slavery, most of the settlers; nor did the English ever receive from the crown of Spain the least reparation for these outrages.*" It was safer to act upon *commissions*; Jamaica, the most convenient place to obtain one in the late 17th century, became the hub of freebooting, especially when Spain and England went to war in 1655. "*When the war broke,*" writes Lediard, "*the King of Spain had all the goods belonging to the English, in all his dominions, seized; which was harmful to our nation.*" The identity of the first aggressor determined the legitimacy of the reprisals. The Spaniards considered that the capture of Jamaica was a rupture of the treaty of 1630. The said treaty stipulates that *from this day forward there shall be a good, sincere, true, firm, and perfect amity, league and peace to endure for ever, and inviolably to be observed and kept, as well by land as sea, and fresh water, betwixt the renowned king of Great Britain (..) and the most renowned king of Spain.* But Cromwell retorted the Spanish ambassador that, in contravention of these terms, the Spaniards had always treated the English as enemies in the West Indies. The take of Jamaica created a controversy. If the restored King considered Cromwell to be a usurper, then he could not consider the capture of Jamaica to be legitimate. The historian David Hume describes[§] the Western Design (see chapter 3) as *an unwarrantable violation of treaty*, quoting the names of several brave officers who refused to partake in this conflict. But Bryan Edwards castigates Hume. He saw things from a Jamaican point of view, just like his friend Edward Long. According to both of them, the initial Spaniards' behaviour in the New World was *a declaration of war to mankind*. War was actually permanent in the West Indies, and the Spaniards spared no one. The resentment was boundless: "*I do not undertake to excuse the cruelties which are said to have been sometimes practises on the Spaniards,*" declares Long. "*Both parties were embittered against each other by reciprocal injuries, in which the Spaniards had undoubtedly been the first aggressors.*" The colonists perceived the Western Design as an act of self-defence; and they could not justify their presence in Jamaica otherwise. At the time, Cromwell demanded free navigation in the West Indies to the Spaniards, as well as the withdrawal of the Inquisition from the New World. The Spanish ambassador retorted that it meant demanding *the two eyes of his monarch*—thus the war went on, and buccaneering throve.

The restoration of Charles II in 1660 questioned the decisions of Cromwell. The King even considered returning Jamaica to his new allies, but he changed his mind. Yet, wishing to facilitate the trade with the Spaniards in the West Indies, he put a crib on the activities of the Buccaneers. He sent Thomas Modyford to Jamaica, unaware that he would soon become the greatest support of buccaneering. Modyford was a lawyer by trade, who had sought refuge to Barbados after Cromwell's victory. His being appointed Governor of Jamaica was a reward for his loyalty—and he partly owned it to his powerful friend in England,

---

§The History of England (Montrose, 1796).

General Monk Duke of Albermale, a key figure of the restoration. In fact, they were relatives. Modyford's intentions were pure. He went to Jamaica with the firm intention to eradicate buccaneering, as ordered. Upon his arrival, he found a flourishing island nonetheless threatened by the proliferation of *commissions* issued by his predecessor Sir Charles Lyttleton, whom he described as *a weak man, and much led by mean fellows here.* (Cundall) Cundall explains: "*In June 1664, the King wrote to Modyford that he could not sufficiently express his dissatisfaction at the daily* (Spanish) *complaints of depredations done by ships said to belong to Jamaica.*" Modyford at once transferred the residence of the Governor from Port Royal, the headquarters of buccaneering, to Spanish Town. In February 1665, he even sent 14 pirates to the gallows, thus raising the discontent of the Buccaneers. *A fatal error*, he later confessed to Secretary of State Lord Arlington. Indeed, in Europe, England had just declared war to Holland, thus exposing the colony to the nearby Dutch islands in the Caribbean. Modyford feared a raid on Jamaica, and started to regret the Buccaneers—to tell the truth, he also feared their resentment; they knew the island like the back of their hand, its paths, its discreet harbours and its weaknesses. Should they turn against Jamaica, who could repel them? They were almost the only ones in Jamaica who could fight. Modyford was walking on thin ice; he asked for the authorization to grant *commissions* against the Dutch. Lord Arlington, who clearly did not like Modyford, carefully avoided answering him. But the Duke of Albermale told him to do whatever was necessary. *Alea jacta est,* Modyford called back the Buccaneers to Jamaica by granting his old friend Colonel Edward Morgan a *commission* against the Dutch islands of St Eustatius, Saba and Curaçao. But the expedition was chaotic. The vast majority of the 650 men who landed in St-Eustache were Freebooters recruited in the taverns of the Point—another name for Port Royal; and these men did not fight for glory's sake. Worse, Colonel Morgan died while taking the island. Modyford relates the circumstances of his death in his official report dated November 1665: "*The good old Colonel leaping out of the boat, and being a corpulent man got a strain, and his spirit being great he pursued over earnestly the enemy on a hot day, so that he surfeited and suddenly died, to almost the loss of the whole design.*" Modyford was losing a personal friend, who had been beside him since the days of hardship in Barbados. He died a poor man, leaving a large family behind him, including his eldest daughter, who fortunately married Sergeant Major Byndloss, member of the Council. Another daughter of his would soon find comfort in the arms of a Morgan, the nephew of the late Colonel, the famous Henry Morgan.

Following the Colonel's death, one Carey took the lead of the expedition, sending some troops to take Saba 3 weeks later. Nevertheless, the Buccaneers were delaying the attack on their priority target, the well-fortified Curaçao. It seemed to be a risky enterprise with little hope of gain. *"The project was too ambitious a one for so undisciplined a company,"* says Clinton V. Black. *"Quarrels over loot caused the rest of the project to fall through."* The Buccaneers, caring not about honour or recognition, hid their loot in the nearby harbours; and later returned for it, thus avoiding paying taxes to the Govenor. These bad troops were quick to dissension. At the end of the day, they decided to go back to Jamaica, leaving Curaçao in peace. They appeased Modyford's anger, promising to take the Dutch island as planned—but later. *"Some of the privateers are well bred,"* rejoices Modyford, *"and (I) hope with good handling to bring them to more humanity and good order."* Did he have the choice, anyway? He might not make these soldiers march in step, but he could use them punctually. He decided to keep them at hand. In February 1666, he declared in the Council that *the granting of said commissions did extraordinarily conduce to the strengthening, preservation, enriching, and advancing the settlement of this island.* And the Point became a nest of Buccaneers.

The Restoration plunged the island into turmoil. Cromwell's creatures were chased for the influent posts; but many had sought refuge to Jamaica, including some of the judges who had voted the execution of Charles I. Among the latter, Waite and Balgrave, *are said to have become peaceable settlers here, and to have remained after the Restoration unnoticed and unmolested.* (Edwards) Yet, the royal pardon granted to all by Charles II excluded the said judges. *"The culprits were almost all gutted alive by the executioner,"* writes Grégoire Léti. *"Only a few of them escaped their fate by running away."* In Jamaica, Modyford worried over the resentment of Cromwell's followers, who were soldiers. The Buccaneers became even more precious to him. First because they could resist the soldiers if necessary; second, because many of the Republicans decided to join their ranks rather than to create political disturbances. Both parties came together to fight the Spaniards, and Jamaica enjoyed peace. Furthermore, the Buccaneers also protected the colony from external threats.

Modyford multiplied the *commissions* but soon had to answer for the plundering of Porto-Bello, whence Henry Morgan triumphantly returned in 1668. Indeed, Morgan's *commission* gave him the right to attack the Spaniards at sea, not to plunder their settlements. The Governor justified the expedition, invoking the Spanish threat. According to him, the Buccaneers represented the only rampart of the colony against their enemies until Spain should recognize it as an English property—which it did, 2 years later, with the Treaty of Madrid. As a matter of fact, the expedition of 1670 and the plans of Ysassi, the former Spanish Govenor now residing in Cuba, proved that the Spaniards were still looking forward to reconquering the island. Edward Long is right, then, when stating in 1774: *"It is to the Bucaniers that we owe the possession of Jamaica at this hour."*

Sad Sir

Henry Morgan is an ambivalent historical figure, perceived as a hero by some, and as a villain by others. Francis Drake, who had to face the same critics in his time, had accomplished a few stainless exploits such as fighting the Invincible Armada or circumnavigating the globe. Morgan had earned his title of *Sir* by arming villains under suspicious *commissions* granted by a complacent Governor. Moreover, triumph without peril brings little glory. Though the cowardice of the Spaniards in the New World was obviously exaggerated, their main tactic still consisted in running away. Ravenau de Lussan explains that they placed sentinels along the rivers and the coasts so that they could flee to the hills with their riches whenever the enemy approached. The Buccaneers did not sail the Caribbean sea only; they went as far as the most remote Spanish settlements on the West coast of South America, and the Spanish empire soon suffocated under their constant attacks. Raynal describes their situation with contempt: *"They lived in terror. When the Buccaneers approached, fear drove them out of their minds, and made them flee without putting up a fight. They had been softened by luxury, weakened by the peaceful exercise of tyranny, and as befuddled as their slaves; they would not stand the fight unless twenty to one; and yet were defeated. Nothing was left of their noble and proud origins. They were so degenerated that the art of war was unknown to them, and they hardly know how to fire a musket. They were hardly superior to the Indians they had slaughtered. This weird phenomenon was amplified by the idea they had of their fierce aggressors. Their priests portrayed them as hideous devils straight out of hell."* This sounds a little bit exaggerated. The Spaniards were not that weak, as proven by their resistance in Jamaica. They organized and even recruited troops among the Freebooters, whom they paid very well. The Buccaneers called them *The Greeks*, and considered them *as the only enemies worthy of them in the West Indies.* (Charlevoix) The Greeks captured the fortress of Petit-Goâve, in St-Domingue, but were soon dislodged by the Inhabitants. They had no *commission*, so they were hanged on the spot. Little is known about these elite troops, which have operated as far as the South Sea. The exploits of these *new Greeks* remain to be told. But with or without them, the so-called coward Spaniards often forced the Buccaneers to flee in haste. Dampier, for example, had to walk across the Panama Isthmus with the Spaniards on his heels, leaving his injured men behind. The best weapon of the Spaniards was probably their net of communication, which they used to announce all over America the arrival of warlike boats. At the end of the day, buccaneering was a tedious occupation and the plundering of the Spanish Americas had nothing of an Iliad.

The panegyrists of Morgan say he was from the rabble—it's always a pleasure to have heroes who started from scratch. In fact, Morgan's origins remain obscure. He was born in Wales in

Opposite: Sir Henry Morgan; Monck, Duke of Albermale; view of Port Royal and Kingston in the 18th century (Long).

Port Royal

1735, most likely in a wealthy family of merchants. He went through Barbados before ending up in Jamaica, but the dates and his itinerary are still uncertain. In 1655, he married his cousin, the daughter of the late Colonel Morgan, joining a powerful family including Byndloss and Henry Archbould—the embryo of the *Morgan's clique*. When Modyford issued a new *commission* to attack the Dutch islands in 1666, the *ole pirate* (Esquemeling) Mansvelt was appointed Admiral and Henry Morgan Vice-Admiral of the fleet. This was quite a spectacular advancement for a man freshly disembarked. According to Esquemeling, Morgan had made a name for himself during several illegal expeditions, including one against Providence— today's Santa Catalina—, off Costa Rica. This island was a turntable of the Spanish trade, and Mansvelt captured it without *c o m m i s s i o n .*

Kingston

That's when Morgan allegedly earned his reputation. But there's no evidence of his being there at the time. As a matter of fact, this is precisely the part of Esquemeling's book that he sued—the publisher lost the case, which does not mean his author was wrong, just that he had no proof of what he had said. Esquemeling was not there, that's a fact—he was then in the hands of his tyrannical master in St Domingue, and only joined Morgan later on. But he sailed with Morgan, and spent a lot of time with his men in the taverns of The Point. So he knew about him: "*He trained at shooting, and was quite good at it*," reads the French edition. "*He was bold and determined; nothing could surprise him, since he expected anything; he was always confident in his enterprises, and it helped him to carry them out successfully.*" He was known as a formidable gambler, and respected for his thirst for gold. Thus, when the *ole pirate* Mansvelt allegedly died*, Morgan was appointed Admiral of the Buccaneers. During the 3 following years, he sailed the Gulf of Mexico, plundering Porto Principe, then Puerto Bello in 1668, as well as several Cuban settlements and Maracaibo, from where he brought more than 15,000 pieces of eight. The latter exploit put Modyford in a delicate position since the *commissions* he had issued did not regard settlements. Morgan had gone too far, and the Governor distanced himself, asking for a written justification, and blaming him in a missive sent to the King. In England, Morgan's testimony went unheeded. He bought a piece of land in Jamaica, and pretended to have become a farmer. The King of Spain was outraged. He demanded an exemplary punishment and the restitution of the booty. The King retorted that England knew no peace in the West Indies. Diplomacy now helpless, the Spaniards sent a declaration of war to all English subjects in the Americas, which was proclaimed at the sound of the drum in Cartagena. All English ships were seized. Three Spanish attacks were reported on the North Coast at the time. The threat was drawing closer, so the Council met in Spanish Town on June 29, 1670, and gave orders to Morgan to urgently gather a fleet. The Buccaneer was to secure the coasts of the island, *to fight with, take or destroy all the ships that* (he should) *meet with all the belongings to the subjects of His Catholic Majesty in the American seas*—the famous Panama commission. Morgan soon found himself at the head of 28 ships, plus 8 taken to the French, according to the French edition of Esquemeling's work: "*Morgan was on board of the* Cerf Volant, *a*

---

*Taken prisoner after the capture of Providence, he was seen in Puerto Bello by an English merchant in 1668. He was then chained in a Spanish vessel about to leave for Cuba, where he was executed in 1673.

Malouin ship armed with 24 canons (...). This ship had been confiscated by the Governor (...) and the Captain to whom she once belonged was glad he had been left alive." But the enemies seemed more determined than ever. A Spanish officer landed on the North Coast of Jamaica to pin a haughty warning on a tree: "*I, Captain Manuel Rivero Pardal, to the chief of the squadron of privateers in Jamaica. (...) (I) now am arrived to this coast, and have burnt it. And I am come to seek General Morgan (...) I crave he would come out upon the coast and seek me, that he might see the valour of the Spaniards. And because I had no time I did not come to the mouth of Port Royal to speak by word in the name of my King, whom God preserve.—dated the 5th of July, 1670."* (Cundall) Morgan sent John Morrice, one of his captains, who joined the arrogant Spaniard off Cuba, where he killed him with a bullet through the throat.

Morgan spread the word all through the Caribbean islands, exhorting all Freebooters to join him off the South Coast of St-Domingue, at the Isle la Vache. On December 2, he called a war council with his 37 Captains. They all agreed that the take of Panama *stands most for the good of Jamaica and safety of us all.* (Cundall) This attack was to become Morgan's masterpiece.

Isle la Vache

Departing from the Isle la Vache, several ships went to reconnoitre; meanwhile, Morgan refined his plan. In order to reach the beautiful Panama located on the shore of the South Sea—today's Pacific Ocean—, he did not want to round the dreaded Cape Horn; this was too long and tedious a journey. The Buccaneers agreed on sailing the Chagre River that ran through a part of the Isthmus of Panama instead, and then to walk to Panama. Morgan left a written relation of this long march—an 8 pages document he personally dictated to his secretary, and which he read in front of the Council. "*Understanding the castle of Chagraw* (sic) *blocked our way,*" he says, "*I called a council of all the chief captains, where it was determined that we should attack the castle of Chagraw* (sic)." Consequently, Captain Bradley and 470 men attacked the castle. The brave Spaniards refused quarter and fought till death—370 were killed according to the rules of war. "*Of our side,*" resumes the Admiral, "*was lost thirty out right one captain and one lieutenant, and 76 wounded, whereof the brave Bradley was one with two lieutenants, who died within ten days after of their wounds to the great grief of myself and all in general.*"

The plundering of Panama was an ambitious project. The city was the hub of the Spanish trade in the New World, and probably the richest city around. The French edition of Esquemeling's book reads: "*There were six or seven thousand houses in Panama, built of cedar wood; only a few were made of stone. The streets were beautiful and large, and the houses evenly built. This was where the riches from Peru arrived every year with a fleet loaded with bars of silver and gold (...) They had more than 2,000 mules to carry their gold (...) to Porto Bello, where it was loaded on the King's galleons.*" Thomas gage describes it 50 years earlier: "*The Spaniards are in this city much given to sin, looseness and venery especially, who make the Black-moors (who are many, rich and gallant) the chief objects of their lust. It is held to be one of the richest places in all America (...). It consisteh of some five thousand inhabitants, and maintaineth at least eight cloisters of nuns and fryers.*"

Morgan reached Chagre a few days after it was taken. Then, shouting *'Long live the King!'* with his 1,200 men, he started a 30 kilometres march through the Isthmus. The Spaniards fled, devastating the land behind them. Indeed, they knew that the Buccaneers usually carried no provisions with them, and fed on their takes. Soon, the invaders started to starve under the boiling sun. On January 14, the *wild bunch* stormed Santa Cruz, *a very fine village, and the place where they land and embark all the goods that comes and goes to Pennam* (sic). (Morgan) The Buccaneers were disappointed, as the Spaniards had left nothing behind them but a few meagre dogs and cats that were soon boiled and eaten. The march resumed. Some Indians faithful to the Spaniards floated in the surrounding forest, sometimes throwing a rain of arrows onto the Buccaneers, killing 1 or 2—but at the end of the day, they happened to be more annoying than dangerous. "*The 17th (...) about nine o'clock in the morning* (we) *saw that desired place, the South Seas and likewise a good parcel of cattle and horses.*" Esquemeling goes on: "*Here, while some killed and slayed cows, horses, bulls, and chiefly asses, of which there were most, others kindled fires, and got wood to roast them. (...) Such was their hunger, as they more resembled cannibals than Europeans, the blood many times running from their beards and their waists.*" Having eaten their fill, the Buccaneers pitched their camp within eyeshot of Panama. The trumpets and drums soon resounded in the air while the flags floated in the wind—Panama was about to be swarmed.

The Spanish army, *in battle array* (Esquemeling), *was ready to fight and so numerous that* (the pirates) *were surprised with fear, much doubting the fortune of the day.* (Esquemeling) Furthermore, the Spaniards had a secret weapon, a herd of bulls they intended to drive against the aggressors; but as soon as the battle started, *the wild cattle ran away, frighted* (sic) *with the noise of the battle*, says Esquemeling. *Only some few broke through the*

English companies, and only tore the colors in pieces, while the Buccaneers shot every one of them dead. The same author keeps on: "*The battle having continued two hours, the greatest part of the Spanish horse was ruined, and almost all killed; the rest fled, which the foot seeing, and that they could not possible prevail, they discharged the shot they had in their muskets, and throwing them down, fled away, every one as he could.*" In the city, the panic-stricken Spaniards ran away, but first destroyed their forts, *in such a haste*, notes Morgan, *that* (they) *blew up forty of* (their) *soldiers in it.* It only took Morgan a couple hours to take the mighty Panama.

Esquemeling then portrays Morgan as a tropical Nero, setting the city afire; yet the Admiral gives another version, claiming he had tried his best to reduce the fire said to be of unknown origins. A curious little book anonymously printed in France circa 1800 and entitled *Gramont le Grand, dernier chef des Flibustiers* (Tiger), relates the exploits of the famous French Buccaneer Gramont, who was part of the raid on Panama: "*Gramont, who feared the Spaniards might sneak upon his men at night, surreptitiously set fire to the city, spreading the words among the prisoners—and even his men—that the Spaniards were responsible for it. The fire spread so fast that before night, half of the town was already burnt down.*" Morgan concludes: "*Thus was consumed the famous and ancient city of Pennama* (sic), *which is the greatest mart of silver and gold in the whole world.*" In fact, the city alone was destroyed—not the suburbs. The biography of Gramont reads: "*The house of the President was spared, as it was standing aside, as well as five or six hundred houses of muleteers, and two cloisters.*" That was enough to have a good time. "*Herein this city, we stayed 28 days, making daily incursions upon the enemy by land for twenty leagues round about,*" tells Morgan. The Buccaneers sailed the Gulf of Panama everyday, looking for runaway Spaniards. They even found some of them at the bottom of wells—woe to those who were caught! "*It is but justice to Sir Henry Morgan,*" writes Edward Long, "(...) *to affirm, it does not appear that he ever encouraged or approved any such inhumanities.*" Indeed—but it's hard to imagine that he shed tears over the people of Panama. The French edition of Esquemeling's evokes his falling in love with a beautiful captive, who rejected him—an unlikely tropical version of *Beauty and the Beast.*

The hordes of Buccaneers eventually left Panama. They shared the booty—£443,200 according to Esquemeling—at Fort Chagre. But some Buccaneers were wolves to other Buccaneers, and some plotted against their Admiral, who double-crossed them by running away to Jamaica with an unknown part of the booty.

The Spaniards had saved the majority of their riches by loading them aboard 2 galleons before the Buccaneers reached Panama. Nonetheless, the take was tremendous. Clinton V. Black talks about 160 mules loaded with gold, silver and precious stones stolen from the churches, and of 600 prisoners, who were ransomed by their friends. Though welcomed as a hero in Port Royal and officially celebrated in the Council, Morgan was worried; and his old accomplice Thomas Modyford did not feel confortable either. Indeed, on July 8, 1670, just before Morgan's departure, England and Spain had signed the Treaty of Madrid, which put an end to the war. The Ambassador of Spain demanded a reparation for the sack of Panama. Morgan had acted on *commission*, indeed; but he was rumoured to have turned a deaf ear upon hearing about the peace truce on time. England wanted to preserve her commercial agreements with Spain in the West Indies, so the King had to keep up appearances. Thomas Modyford was removed from his position in June 1671, and replaced with Sir Thomas Lynch. The former Governor was sent to England and imprisoned in the London tower. This was a complacent punishment aiming at quelling the Spaniards. But it was not enough. Spain demanded the head of Henry Morgan himself. Thomas Lynch was reluctant to comply: "*And was afraid the sending home Morgan might make all the privateers apprehend they should be so dealt with, notwithstanding the King's proclamation of pardon,*" he justifies himself in a letter written to Secretary of State Lord Arlington. "*However shall send him home so as he shall not be much disgusted, yet the order obeyed, and the Spaniards satisfied. Could not do it now, for he's sick and there is no opportunity, but hopes the Welcome will be ready to bring him in six weeks. To speak the truth of him, he's an honest brave fellow, and had both Sir T. (homas) M.(odyford) and the Council's commission and instructions, which they thought he obeyed and followed so well that they gave him public thanks, which is recorded in the Council books. However, it must be confessed that the privateers did diver barbarous acts, which they lay to his Vice-Admiral's charge.*" (Cundall) As far as the 'nationalistic' writers such as Edward Long were concerned, Morgan was a hero, and the worthy instrument of the fair triumph of the English nation in Jamaica. "*Sir Henry Morgan,*" declares Long, "(...) *was equal to any* (of) *the most renowned warriors of historical fame, in valour, conduct, and success.*" Lynch eventually sent him home, where he remained for 3 years, unheard by justice. He drank his time away in the company of the late General Monck's son, the second Duke of Albermale. His new friends in London were powerful, yet his being cleared of disgrace took time. Edward Long laments that, meanwhile, the poor fellow had to spend all his fortune to sustain himself in London. But the wheel of fortune is whimsical; in 1674, Morgan was appointed Deputy-Governor of Jamaica. Since only people of quality could pretend to that type of function, Morgan was knighted—he became *Sir Henry*. The news hit the New World like a tornado: the Spaniards started to run up and down, they fortified their cities, raised troops, and got prepared for the worst. Indeed, the Buccaneer triumphantly returned to the West Indies alongside his faithful associate, Thomas Modyford—finally released from jail. Morgan even sailed before the ship of the new Governor, Lord Vaughan, anchoring for a while at the Isle Avache, from where he had launched the attack on Panama. A very bad omen for the Spaniards, who grew terrified; but they were wrong—Morgan had left as their worst enemy, only to come back as their best friend.

The Clique

In Jamaica, Morgan met again with his old friends: his brothers-in-law Byndloss and Archbould, as well as Captain Charles Morgan—his kinsman—, the hardcore of the *Morgan's clique*. Together they haunted the taverns of the Point at night, plotting illegal expeditions. Lord Vaughan never liked Morgan. He called him a *useless* officer, and claimed he should be recalled; he even suggested replacing him by Thomas Lynch, who was yet the object of an inquiry led by Morgan—regarding some illegal trade with the Spaniards. The complaints of Vaughan were not heard in England. Lynch was recalled, and the general situation in Jamaica worsened. The Governor suspected Morgan urged some Freebooters to sail under the *commissions* of the French Governor of St-Domingue—like James Browne, an English Buccaneer caught with a French *commission* and sentenced to death, since it was now forbidden to sail under foreign *commissions*. Browne's friends tried to intercede on his behalf but the Governor remained implacable.

Morgan fought the Governor on every occasion. "*I find Sir Henry,*" writes Vaughan to England, "*contrary to his duty and trust, endeavours to set up privateering, and has obstructed all my designs and purposes for the reducing of those that do use that curse of life.*" (Cundall) Morgan was not bothered. Lord Vaughan was not that much appreciated in Jamaica. People said he was haughty and venal. He clashed many times with the Council—especially with Samuel Long, the ancestor of Edward Long—and at the end of the day, the Crown enjoined him to settle the matter with Morgan without any further complications. Shortly afterwards, a slave rebellion broke out in St Mary. Vaughan had the island under martial law, and tried to implement the laws dedicated at reducing the number of slaves. The planters refused to comply, putting their benefits first. They vividly opposed Vaughan, as more slaves meant more riches—to hell with the revolts! Tired of so much opposition, Vaughan resigned and handed over to his enemy Henry Morgan. In 1678, Lord Carlisle arrived, but soon departed, handing over to Morgan again until 1680.

While in power, Morgan favoured the planters; the colony had now endeavour to produce sugar, the table had turned. Morgan fought against his former associates. Clinton V. Black states: "*Many (...) ended up with a rope around their necks at Gallows Point on the Palisadoes (often on Morgan's orders) because they would not give up their old way of life.*" Morgan proved merciless; he adapted to the tactics of his enemies, chasing them down into the smallest harbours, or sailing up the less deep rivers. In the meantime, he insisted on getting permanent revenue for the King, a favour Jamaica had always refused. This was a waste of time. Finally, the Crown sent a new Governor in 1682, Sir Thomas Lynch—an old acquaintance. Morgan waited for him, hoping to quickly get rid of him. In fact, he coveted Lynch's position, and he did all he could to put a spoke in his wheel. With his clique of *five or six little sycophants* (Lynch), they met at night in Port Royal to curse the Assembly and to plot illegal expeditions. Morgan was a cumbersome hero, whose ambitions were no mystery to Lynch. In order to thwart him, he obtained a dormant commission for Sir Hender Wolesworth Governor, in case he should resign. In October 1683, he charged Morgan and that *little, drunken, silly party of* (his) with *disorder, passions and miscarriages at Port Royal.*(Cundall) In fact, everything crashed for Morgan and his clique on October 2, 1683, when some loyal subjects of the King decided to celebrate a recent event that had taken place in England. Indeed, Charles II and

Opposite: details from the French edition of Esquemeling's work, showing America offering her riches, the Spaniards slaughtering the Indians before being themselves slaughtered by the Buccaneers; details of the map of the raid on Panama. (Esquemeling).

PUERTO BELLO

P. de Mancarilla
P. del Ponton
R. du Longolemo
Las Minas
de B. venture
le S. Hir
T. de
Philippe

C. d. Puerto Bello

Q. El Bujio

R. de Carcajal

V. de Boqueron

am Cerro Pelado

R. del Boqueron

O Fantaria
Cargado
T. de plata
Ceron
Cascajal
ico
ulla
va
nte

V. de Pequeni

R. de Pequeni

V. de Chaore

C. Parhama

R. de la Fuente

Hatto

R. de Chaore

cruzes

Cabicura
R. Chillbra

R. de las Laxas

Hatto

S. Joseph

ORIENT

CIUDAD DE PANAMA

Viate

ORIENT

Cervermilo

PAN

I. de

Playa

Perrico

C. de Pana

Perrico

I. Flamenca

his brother Duke of York, suspected of promoting Catholicism, had just escaped an assassination attempt planned by some Protestants from the Whigs party—the Rye House Plot. When the news reached Jamaica, a zealous royalist named Edward Halo headed to Port Royal to celebrate. He went to the tavern of Charles and Mary Barres, whom he knew as fervent royalists. He was sitting at the balcony of the tavern around 10 P.M, drinking to the King's health with Charles Morgan, Henry Archbould and the owners, when a set of guys arrived. A young Negro among them inadvertently threw a firecracker into the air, which exploded on the balcony. The explosion broke the glasses and stunned the group of friends for a short while. Recovering, Charles Morgan ran down the stairs with a gun in each hand, shouting: "*Who's the son of a bitch Whig who threw this firecracker?*" The ensuing fight almost turned to drama. Edward Halo was brutally beaten, another man had his jaw broken and several others were knocked down. The incident caused a scandal, and Lynch took advantage of it; he planned the disgrace of Morgan and his clique. The Council was called, and grievances poured like rain. It was underlined that during the incident at the Barres' tavern, Charles Morgan and his friends were the aggressors; furthermore, their victims were *sober and endeavoured to keep the peace*, reads the Minutes of the Council (Cundall), *and not Captain Morgan &c.* Captain Morgan was consequently dismissed from the captaincy of the Fort at Port Royal. Byndloss was not present that day, but was nonetheless turned off the Council as many other grievances were already held against him. It went the same with Sir Henry, absent that day; he had been overheard cursing the Assembly out loud one night, uttering the following gross sentence: "*God damn the Assembly!*" (Cundall) The Buccaneer did not really oppose the decision of the Council and stepped down without putting a fight. Thus ended his turbulent career in 1683, without glory or booty.

The Death of A Sir

Lynch deceased the following year, leaving Molewsworth in charge, as wished for. At the time, Jamaica faced serious problems. With the Buccaneers of St-Domingue, who were attacking the English fishermen; but also with the Spaniards from Cuba, who took all English ships and sent their crew to hard labour in the mines of the New World. But Henry Morgan did not care anymore. He had retired near Port Maria, where he was having some rest, drinking and talking with his former accomplices. He sued Esquemeling's book, but stayed far from business until the arrival of the new Governor. The latter was none but the second Duke of Albermale, with whom he had spent many white nights in London. Gardner does not show much respect to the heir of General Monck: "(He) *had not only wasted his fortune, but seriously impaired his health by vicious practices. A colonial government seemed the most convenient way of rescuing him from his distress, and James could hardly refuse this to the son of the man who had restored the Stuart dynasty to the throne.*" The Duke came alongside a young but famous botanist named Hans Sloane, here to take care of the Duchess, who suffered from mental disorder. Sloane spent 15 months in Jamaica, collecting yet identified species of plants all over the island. He brought more than 700 specimen, which later constituted the embryo of the British Museum collection. Sloane also discovered chocolate in Jamaica; deploring its uneasy digestion, he added milk to the beverage, and then applied for a patent for *milk chocolate* in Europe—the recipe earned him considerable profits.

Christopher Monk was appointed Governor in 1686, but he did not show up until December 1687. His real motivation was his being interested in a lucrative expedition orchestrated by the English Commissioner of Marine. In 1686, the latter sent a boat to lift the wreck of a rich Spanish vessel that had sunk 43 years earlier off St-Domingue. The operation was very lucrative and Albermale went to attend the share. He had not forgotten Morgan though—whom he endeavoured to have rehabilitated. The case was delicate, and it took long before Sir Henry was eventually readmitted to the Council in July 1688. He did not have much time to enjoy his new position. Two months later he got sick, and called upon every remedy in the island, including the powers of a black doctor, who plastered him with clay and water from head to toe—*and by it augmented his cough*, says Sloane. The naturalist attended Morgan, too, whom he described as *lean, fallow coloured, his eyes a little yellowish, and belly a little jetting out prominent*—a famous but alleged description. Indeed, Sloane only refers to this patient as *H.M*, and says he was about 45. Yet, Morgan died the following year, aged 53. His body was carried to Port Royal for a funeral Mass, and was buried nearby—all the ships in the port fired a salvo in his honour. Unfortunately, his tomb sunk into the sea during the terrible earthquake of 1692 (see chapter 6). "*I have enlarged upon this head, for the sake of doing some justice to a worthy character, and retrieving it from the prejudice it has received by being grouped with Teache* (sic), *alias Black-beard, and other lawless banditti by the learned compilers of their heroic deeds*," sates Edward Long. This is a straight reference to Esquemeling, who made himself a bad name among some English historians by attacking one of their historical icons. Frank

Cundall writes**: "*In justice to Morgan's memory, it may be said that some historians hold that Oexmelin's* (the French spelling of his name—editor's note) *account is a libel on Morgan, and that he was not nearly so black as he has been painted.*" Unfortunately, the state papers tell no better of him. The Duke of Albermale joined his friend in the grave in October. He had refused to pay attention to his friends who had warned him about the quality of the wine of Madeira he abused while in Jamaica—stronger than the French one, it rapidly drove him to the grave.

The Adventurers

To understand the role of Jamaica in buccaneering, it will not be useless to study the case of William Dampier, who published a relation of his many travels with the Buccaneers, including Captain Sharp—who might have then sailed under Morgan's secret orders. His testimony tells how easily a man could turn Buccaneer in Jamaica at the time. He went to the island with the intention to take care of the plantation of a wealthy planter. He tried for one year without success. At last, he resolved to come back home. "*I was just embarking myself for England when one Mr Hobby invited me to go first a short trading voyage to the country of the Mosquitos (…) Soon after our setting out we came to an anchor again in Negril Bay, at the West end of Jamaica; but finding there Captain Coxson, Sawkings, Sharp and other privateers, Mr Hobby's men all left him beside myself; and being thus left alone, after 3 or 4 days stay with Mr Hobby, I was the more easily persuaded to go with them too. It was shortly after Christmas, when we set out. The first expedition was to Portobel.*" The expedition lasted several years, and took him around the globe under various commandments, including Captain Reed's, who marooned—or abandoned—him on a desert island. Rescued by a passing ship, he headed back to England.

We commonly associate the end of buccaneering with the earthquake of 1692. Yet, buccaneering was already over at the time. *Commissions* had become very rare, and the Buccaneers who had not returned to civilian life had turned pirates. England now intended to develop her links with Spain, and Jamaica had nothing more to offer the Buccaneers but her threatening gallows. Trade is the master, underlines Thomas Raynal. Buccaneering was just an instrument in its march; when it became a burden, then it had to disappear.

** Historic Jamaica (The Institute of Jamaica, 1915).

6

Port Royal, Grandeur and Decacence

U ntil the end of the 17th century, most outsiders knew nothing about Jamaica except for the settlement of Port Royal. Conveniently located at the point of the long stretch of land that creates the bay—today's Kingston Bay—, it enabled the ships to unload directly on the wharf of its port, which plunged straight into the bay. The history of Port Royal, also referred to as the Point, started with the English invasion in 1655. Colonel Humphrey, who came with Sedgwick to Jamaica, noticed he could easily regulate access to the bay— and thus to Santiago de la Vega—from this point of land. He erected a fort there— called Fort Charles in 1660—, which attracted many English settlers, since many feared the attacks of the runaway Spaniards. Furthermore, the Council, wishing to promote the sales of imported royal Brandy—to insure consequent benefits to he King—, gave 40 taverns the permission to open in the Point in less than a month. With alcohol came debauchery. People went there to drink, to see prostitutes and to enjoy themselves. In the mean time, the settlement—first called *Cagway*—became the main trading place in the island, as almost all the goods sold in Jamaica passed through it. In 1659, Captain Myngs came back from a punitive expedition against the neighbouring Spanish islands, bringing back a consequent booty to Port Royal. Little by little, the Buccaneers, the prostitutes, easy money and the many taverns transformed the Point into *the most wicked and sinful city in the world*.

What's The Point?

A few streets, some paved; long wharves with tall storage buildings;

a fort and some houses, which betrayed the wealth of their owners—such was Port Royal at the end of the 17th century. It can be seen as a metaphor of the New World since luxury, progress, vice and corruption throve alongside hypocrisy, jubilation and disgust. *"There were more than two thousand perfectly well-built houses in Port Royal,"* reads *Le Voyageur François*, *"and the rents were as high as in London. There were so many people, that you would think it was a permanent fair, though there was not a single hut thirty years earlier. In a word, few cities in the world equalled it as far as trade, opulence, luxury and corruption were concerned."* This is quite a flattering description. Nonetheless, people started to get organised. Since the place was sandy and dry, several barks were going to and fro the opposite bank of the bay to collect fresh water, wood and provisions. Many adventurers were attracted to the port, where they could easily repair their ships, spend their booties, buy alcohol and spend some time with prostitutes. Some of them dilapidated fortunes in the glimpse of an eye. Esquemeling witnessed many of these pagan celebrations: *"I saw one of them giving a common strumpet five hundred pieces of eight to see her naked."* Fearing the threat of the nearby Dutch island during the Dutch war of 1655, Governor Modyford officially called upon the Buccaneers. Now celebrated as the defenders of the colony, they felt quite comfortable in Port Royal. There hung out the dreaded Roc the Brazilian or Mary Carleton. In 1671, Mary arrived from England, where she had been convicted for robbery. A former actress—her nickname, the *German Princess*, derived from he play she had played—she did not take long before becoming the main madam of the settlement. But she felt homesick, and went back to her motherland, where she was taken and hanged in 1673, far from the brothels of the Point. Sometimes, barrels of wine were drawn on the sidewalk, and the passers-by were sprinkled or forced to drink, while, inside the taverns, the girls sold their bodies for a few coins.

The Point was, of course, a highly symbolic place. In 1664, Modyford was sent with the mission to eradicate buccaneering. At once, he removed the residence of the Governor from the Point to the more respectable settlement of Spanish Town. Port Royal was also the core of the conflict that opposed the Buccaneers to the planters.

The planter John Style refused one day to contribute to the Church of his parish. Consequently, he was jailed in Spanish Town, from where he wrote to a former friend of his in England, Secretary of State Lord Arlington. Style had come to the island in 1665, where he had enjoyed 2 years of prosperity until the first Dutch War. Dreading an invasion from the nearby Dutch islands, the soldiers *who call themselves the conquerors of the land* (Style), enrolled all the colonists into the militia to watch the coast day and night. The small planters like Style had no choice but to leave their plantation in the hands of an *Overseer* or, most of the time, to sell it at a vile price to a big planter—the latter could afford to pay someone to serve in the militia in his stead. Style claims that this injustice was a plot to rob the small planters. There was also this on-going feud between the planters and the Buccaneers of the Point. Style saw them as devils in a nest of vices, *where the most savage heathens (...) might learn cruelty and oppression; the worst of Sodom or the Jews that crucified our Saviour might here behold themselves matched, if not outdone, in all evil and wickedness by those who call themselves Christians.* How, he wondered, could Jamaica be so complacent towards those drunkards, whose miserable trade hardly benefited the island? Indeed, he sums up their activities to a few exchanges with New England and Madeira. How beloved these rascals seemed to be in high places, while they gladly confessed the atrocities they had perpetuated upon the Spaniards. Meanwhile, the honest planters were harassed. Style writes: "*There is not now resident upon this place* (Port Royal), *ten men to every house that selleth strong liquors.*" He also underlines that *many sell their plantations, and either go out for privateers, or drinking themselves into debt, sell their bodies or are sold for prison fees.* The figure of 10 men to a tavern has lately been revised downwards, but alcohol was indeed at the very root of the Point.

Other testimonies draw a more exciting portrait of Port Royal. In the midst of perversion, ecumenism triumphed; there was a synagogue, an Anglican church and some meetings of Quakers. Provisions were abundant, and three daily markets provided the inhabitants with fresh products such as fruits, fishes or vegetables. Furthermore, trade was not as slow as stated by Style. "*The town of Port Royal, being as it were the store house or treasury of the West Indies, is always like a continual mart where all sorts of choice merchandises are daily imported, not only to furnish the island, but vast quantities are thence again transported to supply the Spaniards, Indians and other nations, who in exchange return us bars and cakes of gold, wedges and pigs of silver, pistoles, pieces of eight and several other coins of both metals,*" writes' Francis Hanson. "*In Port Royal, there is more plenty of running cash (proportionately to the number of its inhabitants) than is in London.*" The Buccaneers officially brought back 950,000 pieces of eight from the looting of Puerto del Principe, Puerta Vela, Maracaibo, Panama and Santa Cruz. Though the majority

---

* The Laws of Jamaica (London, 1683).

of the booty was directly transferred to England, this cash flow highly benefited Port Royal and the rest of the colony. At the height of its glory, the Point was then shining bright, casting its light on the West Indies. *"But at a time when the island was full of gay hopes, wallowing in riches, and abandoned to wickedness,"* says Leslie, *"the most dreadful calamity befel* (sic) *it, that ever happened to a people, and which many look upon as a tremendous judgement of the Almighty."*

1692, Beware, Jews or Gentiles

The *dreadful calamity* evoked by Leslie is the tremendous earthquake, which, on June 7, 1692, sent a part of Port Royal into the bay, and killed 2,000 in less than 2 minutes. This is a key event in the history of Jamaica, as it somewhat forced the colony to redeem itself. Left with nothing at all, mourning and suffering, the inhabitants of the island washed out a few of their sins in pain.

Before the drama, Jamaica lived under several threats. The 'Jewish one', to begin with—which was spreading, as stated by the Council. The history of the Jews in Jamaica goes back to the discovery of the New World. Harassed in Europe by the Inquisition since 1480, they were expelled from Spain in 1492—Marylin Delevante and A. Alberg talk[†] about 300,000 exiled. Those who remained had to embrace Christianity, and were called *conversos*—pigs. The *conversos* became the favourite target of the Inquisition; when accused of hypocrisy, they were tortured, and sometimes burnt alive. Many sought refuge to Portugal, where the Inquisition caught up with them in 1539. Then, many fled to the Portuguese colony of Brazil. *"When the Inquisition visited Brazil in 1580, some fleeing Jews ended up in Jamaica,"* write Delevante and Alberga. The on-going legal feud opposing the Columbus family to the Crown of Spain had put Jamaica under a private status that prevented the Inquisition to settle in the island. The English conquest of 1655 was another landmark in the history of the Jews in Jamaica, as they were then granted free practise of their religion. The Portuguese Jews, according to the same authors, even helped the English to capture the island. They obtained the right to build some Synagogues, including in Port Royal; but they were still denied the rights to vote or to become civil servants—these restrictions were repelled in 1831. If Jamaica had then become a refuge against anti-Semitism and persecution, the Jews were hardly tolerated. The merchants relentlessly complained about them to England, arguing that, far from remaining in the fields of

---

† *The Island of One People* (Ian Randle, Kingston, 2008).

agriculture and settling as expected, they had taken over the trade in Port Royal: "*For want of this the Jews eat us and our children out of the trade.*" (Cundall) On the contrary, the authors of *The Island of One People* consider that the Jews played no crucial part in the economical life of the island, and amounted their population to 100 or 150 families only, in 1686. Port Royal also lived under the threat of earthquakes, as it was mostly erected on a bank of sand. Of course, the island had already shaken; in 1687 for example—but people just lived with the idea. Especially since a new threat was on their minds, the French of St-Domingue. Indeed, England and France being at war, the French came to Jamaica on May 28. The martial law was proclaimed, and some credits granted to the refurnishing of the guns of Fort Charles. Port Royal, Spanish Town and Liguaena (Kingston) were under alert. A few days later, in the middle of preparations, the earth shook. *Le Voyageur François* published the testimony of a witness:

> June 7, between 11 a.m. and noon, the house where we were staying started to shake, and we saw the pavement of the room rising. At the same time, we heard some terrible cries from outside, and as we rushed outside, we found many people stretching their hands towards the heavens to implore mercy. We walked alongside the street, where we saw several houses crumbling down or being swallowed by the earth. The sand was swallowing under our feet just like sea waves, unbalancing people; then deep crevices appeared. Soon, a deluge of water took away numerous of unfortunate, who unsuccessfully tried to grab the joists of the disembowelled houses to save their lives. Others were suddenly buried under the sand, and their arms only stuck out of the ground. I had fortunately sought refuge with fifteen or sixteen people on a solid ground. As soon as this violent quake had vanished, everyone started to look for his or her belongings and families.

Our narrator then jumped on a bark, and found his wife, who had been miraculously spared. He goes on:

> Opening on several occasions, the earth has devoured many inhabitants, whom she threw up in other places. More than two thousand acres of land have sunk. There's not one

standing
house in the
whole   peninsula.

The two main mountains that
were at the entry fell into theopen space between them (...)
and dried the river for more than one day (...). Another
mountain split up (...) and killed many colonists[‡]. Several
ships were totally wrecked, and others have sunk. A frigate[§],
was carried by the unpredictable flood (...), and landed on
the top of some destroyed houses, thus saving many lives.
Meanwhile, the Minister exhorted the people to pray, and
some Jews were seen kneeling down with Christians; in the
excess of their fear, they even invoked Jesus' name out loud
(...). Others were looting the houses that were still standing,
though sunk up to the balconies. It's true, yet, that a second
earthquake made them all perish. In some places, some
dreadful crevices disappeared as fast as they had opened; an
infinity of people were seen falling into some of them; a
tremendous flood of water sprang from the others, throwing
away many corpses that had previously been swallowed up.
Here, some men trapped into crevices by the middle had
been deadly crushed; there, only the heads were still visible.

---

‡ Near Yellons.
§ The famous *Swan*.

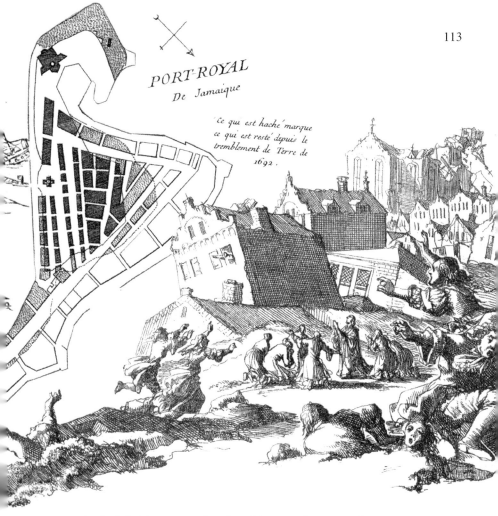

PORT-ROYAL
De Jamaique

Ce qui est haché marque
ce qui est resté depuis le
tremblement de Terre de
1692.

And while Nature was thus horribly convulsing, people were
running up and down, pale and trembling (...), with the idea
that the whole world was coming to an end (...). Six thousand
people are said to have perished[¶]. Those who escaped the great
earthquake sought refuge on board of the ships, where they
remained until the end of the earthquakes.

[¶] The earthquakes, that lasted for more than a month, and the ensuing diseases cost the
lives of 5,000 people.

**Above: detail of the engraving illustrating the relation of the earthquake
published in *The Gentleman's Magazine* (1755); detail of a map of Port Royal
(1755); detail of an engraving of the 18th century.**

In *Histoire abrégée des Voyages*, by La Harpe (1759), we find another interesting account: "*I've lost my wife, my kids, my sister, my daughters, my knaves and servants (...). I had gone fishing in the morning with one of my sons in Liguaena; the earthquake hit us on our way back, and we were almost gulped down by the waves, which impetuously rolled towards us six feet above the surface without any gale. At Liguaena, where we had to go back, we found all the houses destroyed and no other shelter than the huts of the Negroes.*" In the small cemetery close to St Peter's church, in Port Royal, lays the tomb of Lewis Galdy—it used to be at Green Bay, on the other side of the harbour, but was taken there for the official visit of Queen Elizabeth II in 1953, probably to make Port Royal more picturesque. The engraved tombstone tells the story of its host: "*Dieu sur tout* (God above all things)—*Here lyes the body of Lewis Galdy, Esq, who departed this life at Port Royal the 22nd, December 1739, aged 80. He was born at Montpellier in France but left that country for his religion and came to settle in this island where he was swallowed up in the great earthquake in the year 1692. And by the providence of God was by another shock thrown into the sea and miraculously saved by swimming until a boat took him up. He lived many years after in great reputation, beloved by all that knew him and much lamented in his death.*" According to some sources, he and his brother Laurent were pirates; and his was in jail when the earthquake happened. But Gardner gives a few more, and contradictory, details about him: "*After this he flourished as a merchant in Port Royal, represented four parishes in successive assemblies, and seems to have been generally loved and respected.*"

The most famous testimony of the great earthquake was given by Dr Heath, then Rector of Port Royal, and published in London in *The Gentleman's Magazine* (1755) under the title of *A Full Account of the Late Dreadful Earthquake at Port Royal*:

On Wednesday the 7th of June I had been at Church reading prayers which I did every day since I was rector of Port Royal to keep up some show of religion among a most ungodly and debauched people, and was gone to a place hard by the church, where the merchants used to meet, and where the President of the Council **(...) engaged me to take a glass with him; upon which he lighted a pipe of tobacco which he was pretty long in taking; and not being willing to leave him before it was all out, this detained me from going to dinner

---

** Governor John Whyte.

to one Captain Ruden's where I was to dine; whose house, upon the first concussion, sunk first into the earth, and then into the sea, with his wife and family, and some that were come to dine with him; had I been there, I had been lost. But to return to the President, and his pipe of tobacco; before that was out, I found the ground rolling and moving under my feet; upon which I said to him, 'Lord, Sir, what is this?' He replyed being a very grave man, 'It is an earthquake; be not afraid, it will soon be over.' But it increased and we heard the Church and Tower fall, upon which we ran to save ourselves; I quickly lost him and made towards Morgan's Fort, because being a wide open place, I thought to be there the securest from the falling houses; but as I made towards it, I saw the earth open and swallow up a multitude of people; and the sea mounting in upon us over the fortifications."

Dr Heath was later taken on board *a ship called the Siam-Merchant, where I found the President safe, who was overjoyed to see me: there I continued that night, but could not sleep for the returns of the earthquake almost every hour, which made all the guns in the ship to jarr* (sic) *and rattle.* Did offended God hear the cry of Port Royal just like He had heard Sodom's and Gomorrah's at the time? The historians rather traced a parallel with the Apocalypse, in fact. Hence the panicked Jews converting to Christianity in the midst of chaos—indeed, the Apocalypse theologically depends on their conversion. Some even described a red sky—a detail that seems quite improbable. As a matter of fact, Bryan Edwards writes, in 1794: *"I'm inclined therefore to suspect that the description of the shock is much exaggerated."*

Kingston Was Born

The earthquake shook the entire island. Some mountains inland split up, the wells had overflown, the Rio Cobre dried for a few days; and changed its course. Leslie explains that some slaves ran away to the hills in the middle of chaos. But they returned running, terrified by raging Nature! Others tried to take advantage of the situation. *"Your heart would abhor to hear of the depredations, robberies, and violences that were in an instant committed upon the place, by the vilest and basest of the people,"* writes the Council to the King. *"No man could call anything his own, for they that were strongest and most wicked seized what they please and whose they pleased, and where they pleased without any regard to propriety. Gold and silver, jewels, plates or goods, was all their own that they could or would lay hands on (...). Even the very slaves thought it their time of liberty, wherein they committed many barbarous insolencies* (sic) *and robberies, till they were suppressed by the death of some, and punishment of others. (...) We have in the midst of this confusion apply'd our selves with all the vigor to the restoreing* (sic) *of things, we have taken into their Majesties service the Richard and Sarah, a mercht. ship where tho to our great loss in the neglect of our private affairs we sit (...) in Council (...), preventing robbery and stealing amongst the ruins decideing* (sic) *controversies and punishing quarrells* (sic), *(...) taking care of the sick and wounded, lastly (...) feeding and sustaining the necessitous wch. must now be done out of ye country stock, all kinde* (sic) *of stores being lost in the ruin of Port Royal.*" (Cundall) During the several months of chaos that ensued, the English still found the necessary strength to fight back a group of 80 French, who had landed on the North Coast, hoping to take advantage of their enemies' misfortune. Repelled by a dozen of English, who killed 10 of them, the French hastily re-embarked in their boat while fired at. According to the Council, 30 French drowned, losing a first ship and sacrificing a second one to retreat to St-Domingue—a complete victory.

The earthquake had thrown many survivors on the shore opposite to Port Royal, on the Liguaena plain, where it was decided to erect new houses close to the few existing ones. On the map of *The English Pilot* of 1689 (Cundall), we count 7 of them. An earlier map of 1683 reads: "*At Liguania, the inside of the harbour, opposite to Port Royal, about two leagues is several houses, some of them very handsome, and well built, which place in time is like to become a pretty town.*" (Cundall) The events hurried its birth. The Council bought the land to Sir William Beeston for £1,000. The new town was officially baptized Kingston on July 21, 1692. It was erected according to the already existing plan drawn by Colonel Lilly, *an experienced engineer,* underlines Long; *in propriety of design it is, perhaps, not excelled by any town in the world. The plan is a parallelogram, one mile in length by half a mile in breadth, regularly traversed by streets and lanes, alternately crossing each other at right angles, except in the upper part where a large square is left.* Cundall claims it was built in *the chessboard fashion of all Spanish cities in the New World.* All the slaves from the parish of St Andrew were called upon to build it; the parcels of land were rented, and the inhabitant had the obligation to build a house upon theirs, within 3 years' time; the survivors of 1692 were favoured. A fort was erected and the merchants soon settled there. The first hours were harsh ones, nonetheless. Sickness killed as many people as the earthquake did—the victims are said to amount 3,000, including Governor Whyte, who died on August 22. A letter sent from Port Royal and dated July 3, 1693, reads: *"Others went to the place called Kingston (or by others Killcown) where from the first clearing of the ground, and from bad accommodations, then huts built with boughs, and not sufficient to keep out rain, which in great and unusual manner followed the earthquake, lying wet, and wanting medicines, and all conveniences, etc., they died miserably in heaps. Indeed, there was a general sickness (supposed to proceed from the hurtful vapours belch'd from the many openings of the earth) all over the island so general that few escaped being sick; and 'tis thought it swept away in all parts of the island 3,000 souls; the greatest part from Kingston only, yet an unhealthy place."* (Cundall) But Kingston had a strategic location compared to Spanish Town, which stood far from the shore and was indefensible. Kingston was surrounded by swamps, laid against the mountains and protected in the East, from 1694 onward, by the Rock Fort. Gardner says that in the middle of the 18th century, two thirds of the civil cases originated in Kingston, where half of the jurors lived. *"In fact, Kingston, and not Spanish Town, was the proper place,"* he goes on. *"(Governor) Knowles gave his assent to the bill on the 7th of May, 1755."* Kingston then became the capital of Jamaica.

From 1692 onward, the destiny of the town of Port Royal is reminiscent of the myth of Sisyphus. Divine plagues kept on falling upon this small piece of land that men stubbornly tried to inhabit. It had not yet been fully recovered from the earthquake when a fire devastated it in 1700; excited by the narrowness of the lanes and the flammable beams imported from America, the flames totally destroyed the city, sparing Fort Charles only. Disheartened, the members of the Council officially forbade anyone to settle in Port Royal anymore, urging the survivors to settle in Kingston instead. But Kingston had some disadvantages too. First, it was open to the winds that carried the pestilent smells from the nearby swamps; then, too many people died from sickness in Kingston. During the rainy season, floods of mud also came running down the mountains and entirely covered the streets for weeks, carrying a terrible smell—assimilated with diseases at the time. At the end of the 18th century, Long notes that since the creation of the city, a full street had been gained over the sea out of these regular floods of mud.

Eight months after the fire, 300 families had already returned to Port Royal; there was already a butcher, 5 taverns—though alcohol was

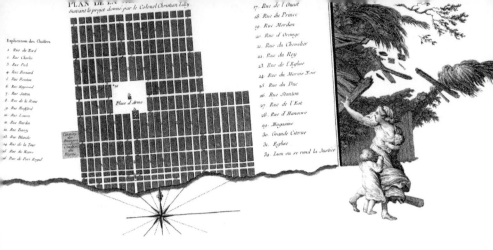

officially banned—as well as 50 houses. The Council eventually repealed the bill and Port Royal officially revived. The city got over the 1712 storm, but suffered badly from the 1722 one—as well as from the 1726, 1744 and 1751 ones. As if doomed by gods, the little city went through fire and rain until it became the headquarters of the English marine in the 18th century. *"Though Port Royal is not half what it used to be,"* reads *Le Voyageur François* in 1777, *"it's still quite a lovely place defended by Fort Charles (...). The harbour is still among the most beautiful and the surest in the world, where a thousand vessels (...) can anchor, being there protected from all disgraces."* In 1793, Edwards draws a more contrasted portrait of the city: *"Port Royal, once a place of the greatest wealth and importance in the West-Indies, is now reduced, by repeated calamities, to three streets and about two hundred houses. It contains, however, the royal navy yard, (...) the navy hospital and barracks for a regiment of soldiers. The fortifications are kept in excellent order, and vie in strength, as I am told, with any fortress in the king's dominions."*

***

Above: the map of Kingston (Bellin, 1758); detail of en engraving representing a hurricane in the West Indies (Raynal, 18th century).

7

Pirates of the Caribbean

D escribed as *the enemies of humanity* by Cicero, the pirates existed long before the discovery of the New World. However they multiplied in the Caribbean at the turn of the 18th century. The difference between the pirates and the Buccaneers is subtle; but it mainly lies in the fact that the former acted without *commissions*. The Pirates preyed on any ship, regardless of her nationality, shooting, killing and looting indiscriminately. They had nothing to lose since they were hanged when caught. But many pirates were former Buccaneers. During the war of the Spanish succession (1702-1713), the European nations turned their Buccaneers into royal soldiers to fight in the Caribbean. But once the war was over, only a few returned to civilian life. The others went back to their old ways. Now without *commissions*, they risked everything. "*The pyrates (sic) in the West-Indies have been so formidable and numerous*," writes* William Defoe, "*that they have interrupted the trade of Europe in those parts; and our English merchants, in particular, have suffered more by their depredations, than by the united force of France and Spain, in the late war.*" Pirates were now *thorns in the side* of merchants, it was just a matter of time before they were eradicated. Despite their warlike exploits and their outstanding number, they couldn't stand the joined operations of the reconciled nations dedicated to their ruin. You cannot teach an old dog new tricks.

Woodes Rogers and the pirates
William Defoe lists 3 reasons to explain the proliferation of pirates

---

* A General History of the Pyrates (London, 1724).

in the Caribbean. First, plenty uninhabited islands and *keys* provided them with very convenient shelters—many are to be found all around Jamaica, for instance. And it was particularly hard to chase their small boats among the *small inlets, lagoons and harbours* of the region. Second, the *great commerce* in the area assured them many booties. But the real reason why they throve so much was the corruption of the institutions in the New World. *"The rise of these rovers,"* Defoe goes on, *"since the peace of Utrecht* (1713—editor's note), *or at least the great increase of them, may justly be imputed to the Spanish settlements in the West-Indies; the Governors of which, being often some hungry courtiers, sent thither to repair or make a fortune, generally countenance all proceedings that bring in profit. They grant commissions to great numbers of vessels of war, on pretence of preventing an interloping trade."* Edward Teach, better known as Blackbeard, had the unconditional

Above : detail of a boarding of pirates in the moonlight (English engraving from the early 19th century); Mary Read kills a man in duel after he had defied her lover (same source); map of the Bahamas (18th century).

support of Charles Eden, the Governor of North Carolina. The latter, being interested in Blackbeard's takes, made sure he acted in impunity while plundering so much as to interrupt the trade of settlements such as Charles-Town. The upset inhabitants had to call upon the Governor of Virginia to put a reward on the pirate's head. But following the war of the Spanish succession, complacency was out of fashion. The royal pardon offered to all repenting pirate in 1717 was the last opportunity for them to avoid the rope. Many seized it—some just to gain time.

At the time, the pirates had long deserted Port Royal for the keys of the Bahamas, off Florida—especially the island of Providence. The French and the Spaniards captured this former English settlement in 1700, but were driven away by a bunch of pirates 5 years later. *"Then 'twas found absolutely necessary, in order to dislodge that troublesome colony,"* writes Defoe. In 1716, the King stated over the fate of Providence, coming to the conclusion that *unless some effectual means be used, the whole trade from Great-Britain to those parts, will not only be obstructed but in imminent danger of being lost.* The official statement specifies: *"His Majesty has (...) been pleased (...) to order a proper force to be employed for the suppressing of the said pirates."* A fleet was immediately put together, and entrusted to Captain Rogers, a well-known privateer. He was ordered to issue the offer of the royal pardon in the West Indies: *"Whereas we have received information that several persons, subjects of Great Britain, have since the 24th day of June, in the year of our Lord, 1715, committed divers piracies and robberies upon the high seas, in the West Indies (...) which has and may occasion great damage to the merchants of Great-Britain (...) we have thought fit, by and with the advice of our Privy Council, to issue this our Royal Proclamation; and we do hereby promise, and declare, that in case any of the said pirates, shall on, or before, the 5th of September, in the year of our Lord, 1719, surrender him or themselves (...) shall have our gracious pardon."* Upon the arrival of Woodes Rogers, the pirate Charles Vane sailed away. But the majority of the other pirates, including the famous Jenings, embraced the royal pardon. Among those was the notorious Blackbeard. But his repentance *wasn't sincere*, notes Defoe. He soon resumed his criminal activities, and was eventually caught by Lieutenant Maynard, who beheaded him and triumphantly sailed back to Charles-Town, exhibiting his morbid trophy.

The pirates of the Caribbean were living their last days. Some made their mark in the history of Jamaica before going down. Jack Rackam was one of them, who, on November 16, 1720, was tried in Spanish Town with his *men*—well, so to speak. Indeed, all of a sudden, upon hearing their death sentence, 2 pirates stood up and declared being women; and pregnant.

John Rackam

Jamaica was less concerned with piracy than it had been with buccaneering; yet, many pirates were English Freebooters, who had learnt their trade sailing under Jamaican *commissions* during the war of the Spanish succession. Blackbeard, among others, had sailed numerous times with the Freebooters of Jamaica during the latest war, according to Defoe. But the history of Jamaica was particularly marked by the story of a love triangle composed of Jack Rackam, Mary Reid and Ann Bonny.

On November 1, 1720, Captain Barnet sailed to Negril to arrest Jack Rackam. Since the month of August, the pirate had been active on the North Coast. He was a dangerous man, who had sailed alongside Charles Vane—the same who fled from Providence upon Woodes Rogers' arrival. When his crew finally repealed Vane, Rackam was made Captain of a brigantine. He despised the royal pardon and roamed the West Indies. After escaping an ambush set up by the Spaniards by stealing a gorgeous boat from them, he went to Jamaica *scouring the harbours and inlets of the north and the west parts of Jamaica.* (Defoe) His small crew restricted him to small preys only. He went to St-Domingue then back to Jamaica, where he took a boat in Port Mary and a rowboat in Dry Harbour; he was then seen near Ocho Rios. Captain Barnet eventually joined him in Negril. He *gave them chase, and, having the advantage of little breeze of wind, which blew off the land, came up with* (Rackam's boat), *and brought her to Port Royal, in Jamaica,* Defoe says. Tried 2 weeks later, the pirates were all hanged, except Mary Read and Bonny, who revealed their being pregnant women to escape death. They stand among the most fascinating personalities of piracy. And their stories were quite peculiar.

Ann and Mary

To become a pirate, Mary Read pretended to be a man; a habit she had developed since her childhood days, in England. Her mother had married a sailor, who disappeared at sea as she had just given him a son. Depending on the care of her mother-in-law, she hid her second pregnancy—from another man—from her late husband's mother, and secretly gave birth to a girl, Mary. When her son died soon after, she replaced the deceased boy with Mary, in order to keep the financial support of her mother-in-law. Later on, having developed a masculine character, Mary joined the army, still pretending to be a young man, but she fell in love with another soldier to whom she soon revealed her secret. After the war, the couple opened an inn near Breda, but the husband died shortly afterwards. Mary then left for the West Indies dressed as a boy; when some pirates intercepted her ship, she decided to join them. She followed them to New Providence, where the whole crew embraced the royal pardon to join the troops enrolled by Woodes Rogers to chase the remaining pirates. "*Scarcely had the ships sailed,*" writes Defoe, "*when some of their crews mutinied, and run off with the ships, to pursue their former mode of life. Among these was Mary Read.*" Thus she roamed the Caribbean alongside Rackam, until a young sailor with a heavy secret courted her. Indeed, this young boy happened to be... a young girl! She was Ann Bonny, and she had fallen in love with Mary Reid, whom she had mistaken with a young man.

Ann Bonny's story was also quite novelistic. Her mother was a maid in Ireland. She got pregnant with her master, who wanted to keep his illegitimate daughter close to him. He thus disguised her as a boy, introducing her to his wife as a friend's son, whom he had promised to take care of. The forgery was soon revealed, and the husband, who had no personal fortune, was chased from his household with his daughter. He left for the New World with her. The trial revealed that she was already a fiery woman, who had shot dead a Servant and bitten a suitor so hard that he was left disabled for several weeks. Despite her father becoming a successful lawyer in the West Indies, Mary married a sailor from the rabble, whom she followed to Providence. There she met John Rackam who became her lover. Women were not allowed to sail, so she dressed as a boy to follow Rackam; she even secretly gave birth to a child in Cuba.

Were these 2 women pregnant when they went to trial? This is doubtful. But which magistrate would take the risk of killing an innocent creature in the bosom of its mother? The death penalty, while applied the morrow to the rest of the pirates, was postponed in the cases of Ann and Mary. They were locked down in Spanish Town instead. Their personalities fascinated. Mary claimed to be a virtuous wife, who had never been with a man but the father of her children—he was indeed her legitimate husband. She pretended to be a weak woman, who had been dragged into this misadventure against her will, and who hated this lifestyle forced upon her. Yet she stood among the fiercest fighters of the crew. She was the only one to resist arrest, as a matter of fact. Upset at the coward men who surrendered without resistance, Mary had opened fire on them, killing one and wounding several. In court, she declared: "*As to hanging, she thought it no great hardship, for were it not for that, every cowardly fellow would turn pirate, and so infest the seas; and men of courage would starve.*" (Defoe) Sentenced by the court, she got sick in her jail, and died shortly afterwards.

Ann Bonny avoided the gallows. "*Her father was known to a great many gentlemen planters of Jamaica, who had dealt with him, and among whom he had a good reputation (...); wherefore they were enclined* (sic) *to shew* (sic) *her favour,*" explains Defoe. This might explain why she was surreptitiously taken out of jail. She went to join her father, and was never heard of ever after. Yet, her fiery temper was revealed during her last meeting with Rackam, as the pirate was about to go to the gallows. Far from pitying him, she said: "*If you had fought like a man, you need not have been hang'd like a dog.*"

***

8

Wars with Tropical France

The relationship between Jamaica and the French in the New World dates from the beginning of the 16th century; and it was not exactly friendly. *"The French pirates, allured by the opulence and blind avarice of the improvident Spaniards,"* writes Bridges, *"had already commenced that desultory species of warfare which was afterwards carried on by them under the name of Flibustiers; and the northern coast of Jamaica afforded frequent spoil to this bold band of corsairs. The consequence was, that the settlement of Oristan was destroyed in its infancy; Melilla was abandoned almost as soon as built; and the capital itself became the repeated prey of a lawless banditti."* But Nueva Sevilla was not abandoned instantaneously, and it was still populated, when, in 1554, according to some relations—questioned by Padron—, it was hit by a last bloody raid of French pirates. *"Bare walls and sculptured archways alone survived the loss of the inhabitants,"* says Bridges, *"affording shelter to a few fishermen, and a convenient resort to the corsairs of Tortue."* Two years later, a French ship anchored for 3 weeks in the harbour of Caguaya (Kingston), firing the Spanish defences and kidnapping 2 inhabitants of Santiago de la Vega. But 20 ambushed Spaniards jumped on the French bark that had ventured too close to the shore, killing 4 and taking 11 prisoners—the latter were exchanged for the kidnapped Spaniards. The ship then sailed away. A few months later, another French ship entered the bay, dragging a captured Spanish vessel behind her. The French demanded a ransom, but the Spaniards, considering that a part of the crew had landed, went to capture the ship in the middle of the bay. Not too bad for people described as *indolent* (see chapter 2).

The relationship between the French and Jamaica became much more significant once the island was captured by the English in 1655. The 2 nations reproduced their stormy relationship in the New World. Yet, they had settled in the Caribbean in a joined operation in 1625, sharing the island of St-Christopher. Rochefort writes: "*How the island was to be divided between the two nations had been defign'd before that voyage; but the particular articles of the division were solemnly agreed to and concluded on the 13th of May, in the said year, M. DC. XXVI (1627).*" As long as it benefited both parties, the *entente cordiale* lasted; but tensions often led to conflicts. Around 1630, the French chased from St. Christophe by the Spaniards, went to settle in the western part of Hispaniola, which they renamed St-Domingue—today's Haiti—, 160 km west of Jamaica. The Tortue Island (or Tortuga), on the northern coast, soon became a nest of Buccaneers; just like Port Royal in Jamaica. As a matter of fact, the English coveted Tortue, and the Freebooter Willis had it under English dominion until the French took it back in 1660. But the Buccaneers used to go to and fro between Tortue and Port Royal, according to their interests and the policies of their respective Governors. The Buccaneers thus drew a solid bridge between the 2 nations. Charlevoix even claims that the Buccaneers of St-Domingue actively partook in the capture of Jamaica in 1655. This assertion is confirmed by no other writing. Yet, the same author underlines the decisive actions taken by the French during the "*Spanish wars of Jamaica*" (see chapter 3): "*The Spaniards were hiding in the hills and the forests, which they knew like the back of their hand, to resist their enemies. To solve the problem, the English put a price on the heads of the Spaniards, and let it be known to the French buccaneers, who, being accustomed to hunting wild animals in the most remote places, appeared to be the most qualified to chase the Spaniards up to their hiding places. The buccaneers rushed in number to Jamaica and slaughtered so many Spaniards so rapidly that the rest had no choice but to negotiate with the English, and to leave the island.*"

The Buccaneers

The Governors of Jamaica and St-Domingue both tried to attract the Buccaneers to their respective colonies. They quickly understood the interest of having them around. Not only did they protect the colony as well as spending their riches there, but they could also, when settling down, become Inhabitants and help at populating their young colonies. Trade was at the heart of the relationship between the 2 islands. When

France forbade all exchange with foreign colonies in the New World, the French Governor d'Ogeron wrote to the King that most of the Buccaneers were now leaving for Jamaica, where they found more affordable commodity. Orgeron knew Jamaica well, he even tried to settle there at one point. But in 1655, he was taken for a ride over a shipment of brandy, by some commissioners he hardly knew, and who *did not leave him with a dime.* (La Harpe) Ruined, he came back to France but soon returned to St-Domingue to start a plantation in St-Margot. "*Notwithstanding the disgrace he had suffered in Jamaica,*" resumes La Harpe, "*he had developed an inclination for the English, which, added to the advice of a man he respected—Father Du Tertre, a Jacobin and author of a* Histoire des Antilles*, who boasted of this story without telling us why he gave him such a weird piece of advice—, led him to start a new habitation in this island. He worked at it with all his care; but far from making profits, he lost eight to ten thousand pounds. Such was his situation when the company of the West Indies thought about him to administer the French colony.*" Appointed Governor, Ogeron kept an eye on Jamaica. He tried to revive Tortue, populated with 400 men only upon his arrival. Four years later, he wrote to the Court that it counted 1,500 men. He described it as a key piece on the political chessboard. Did not it breed determined and disciplined men? It also kept the English away, discouraging them from attacking the colony, and insured the French sovereignty in the Caribbean. "*During the last war,*" he recalls, "*the Governor of Jamaica apologized for not being able to send reinforcements to Nevis, as he feared to face the force of Tortue. He even doubled the watch. He fortified his places and his ports; and he recently offered perpetual neutrality to me, regardless of the wars going on in Europe, which he had previously refused (...). The English have nothing to gain with us, who are living in the woods; and must fear us.*" And they'd better to, if we believe the French Governor: "*I had gathered five hundred men at Tortue during a full month, who were ready to raid Port Royal; I would have taken it without a doubt, if the powder I was expected had reached on time.*" Thus, swearing to maintain perpetual neutrality, each side did its best to hurt the other. When the French colonists were about to rebel against their Governor in 1671, Charlevoix blamed the influence of Jamaica—one Suzanne, he says, based in the island, allegedly promised the rebels to buy all their goods in case of conflict; consequently they became *quite insolent.* In 1682, a note was found in a Spanish rowboat. "*The Governor of Jamaica had written it from Havana, and it detailed the project of a union between the* (English and Spanish) *nations, aiming at chasing the French from St-*

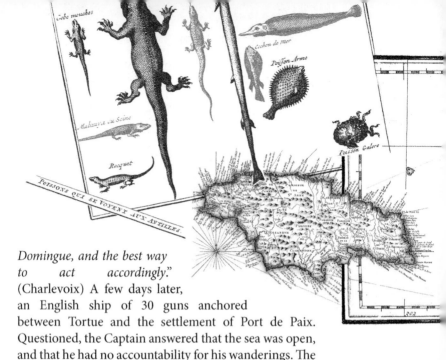

Domingue, and the best way to act accordingly." (Charlevoix) A few days later, an English ship of 30 guns anchored between Tortue and the settlement of Port de Paix. Questioned, the Captain answered that the sea was open, and that he had no accountability for his wanderings. The French did not like his answer, and sent a rowboat full of Buccaneers to board the ship. After a violent fight, the English sailed away. The French Governor sent the famous Gramont after the ship. The bold adventurer soon joined her, and *put the whole crew to the sword.* (Charlevoix) In Jamaica, the French were not liked, who kept on raiding the North Coast to kidnap slaves—they nicknamed the North Coast of Jamaica *Little Guinea*, a malicious reference to the African country where many slaves were bought. The French Governor Du Casse, quoted by Philippe Hrodej, reckons that in the early 1690s, the French had kidnapped 800 to 900 slaves. And when the mother countries went to war with each other, things got even more serious. In 1692, just before the dreadful earthquake (see Chapter 6), a small group of warlike French landed near St Ann.

The Daviot Shake

In 1688, as Jamaica was fighting against buccaneering in order to enter a new era of prosperity, some major political events agitated

Above: details from an engraving of the 18th century, representing some animals from the West Indies; details of a map (Bellin, 18th century) showing the distance between Jamaica and St-Domingue.

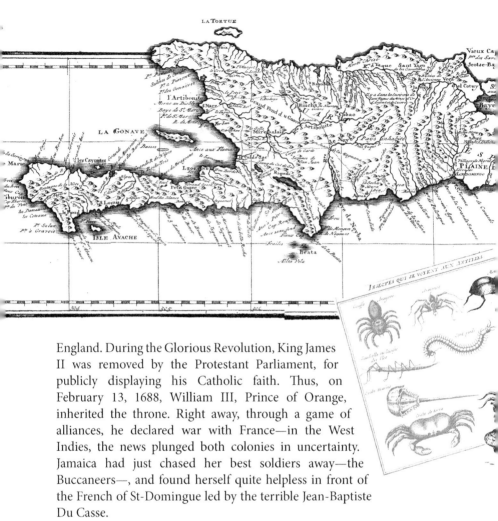

England. During the Glorious Revolution, King James II was removed by the Protestant Parliament, for publicly displaying his Catholic faith. Thus, on February 13, 1688, William III, Prince of Orange, inherited the throne. Right away, through a game of alliances, he declared war with France—in the West Indies, the news plunged both colonies in uncertainty. Jamaica had just chased her best soldiers away—the Buccaneers—, and found herself quite helpless in front of the French of St-Domingue led by the terrible Jean-Baptiste Du Casse.

Du Casse first went to the colony as the representative of the *Compagnie Négrière du Sénégal,* but his eloquence and his ability to lead people, including the Buccaneers, owned him the position of Governor in 1691. He had become rich selling slaves, had many powerful political acquaintances, and knew the West Indies pretty well. Upon his arrival, he found a dull colony; one that was ill populated, ill organized, and suffocating under taxes. The tobacco planters were so heavily taxed that they ended up revolting. After several years of uncertainty, St-Domingue started to become productive thanks to the trade of indigo; soon becoming considerable, *it brought a lot of money, and enabled many individuals to build sugar factories*, explains La Harpe. Sugar factories were the key to prosperity for any West Indian colony. Du Casse knew it, so he did all he could to provide the colonists with some; at the expense of Jamaica.

The colonies were not as reactive as the mother countries. The war broke in 1688 in Europe but the West Indian colonists took time to make a move. In Jamaica, people feared the attack of their turbulent neighbours. The Governor declared martial law, and Port Royal was hastily fortified. They tried to seduce the Buccaneers, promising the royal pardon to any one who would fight for the King. The old *Swan*, anchored at Port Royal, was refurbished to serve as a fire ship. Governor John Whyte was responsible for the safety of the colony, since Inchiquin had passed on January 16, 1962. Whyte, who had been living in Jamaica since 1671, had occupied several important positions in the colony— appointed judge of the Admiralty by Henry Morgan in 1680, he was revoked 8 years later for wrongdoing. In a letter he wrote just before his death, Inchiquin describes him as *a honest gentleman*, and then appoints him as his successor. Finally, with the French of St-Domingue not showing up, martial law was repealed in March.

But the French still had Jamaica on their minds. Early in June, the famous corsair Daviot sailed from Petit Goave with a fleet of 32 ships and 285 Buccaneers. He landed 35 of them on the North Coast of Jamaica, near St Ann. "*Our men caused absolute carnage and took away 52 slaves,*" rejoices Charlevoix. But as they were still ashore, a storm forced the ships to sail away. They started to panic. "*Some were stubborn enough to try to sail a rowboat—they drowned,*" laments Charlevoix. Aware of the French presence, the English arrived, and engaged in combat with their outnumbered enemies. The latter resisted for 15 days, until the earth shook. Charlevoix gives a crucial account of the way the earthquake manifested on the North Coast. The English historians hardly quote it: "*The buccaneers, now reduced to 115, (...) had some 40 prisoners with them (...). As soon as they felt the earth shaking under their feet, they took on board their rowboats but, overturning them in their haste, were glad enough to reach back the shore. They decided to flee inland, and started to run. (...) But the sea, which had just overflown with a dreadful roar, (...) soon caught up with them. Several were swallowed by the waves, some fell into the crevices that opened suddenly under their feet; the rest climbed the trees. With some of these trees being wiped out by the waves, they had the presence of mind to tie themselves to the higher branches, and stood the falling of the trees. There were still a lot of them on rowboats; the ebb carried them away. But the sea, now rising at an incredible speed, they had to row with all their might not to wreck on the coast. But they held on strong, and although the sea went up and down six times in five hours' time, they refused to leave their shelter from the wrath of the trembling earth."*

Though severely affected by the earthquake, the English set up 2 expeditions against the French intruders. The first one, led by Captain Wheeler, went after Daviot's ships, and joined them off Cuba. The fight cost several English their lives, but Daviot's ship exploded, after the powder was touched by fire. Wheeler came back victorious, with 21 prisoners. The second expedition targeted the 80 French who had remained ashore. Located by the smoke of their fire, they surrendered, *except a small group of the bravest*, underlines Charlevoix. This was a hard blow for Du Casse, who was losing here some of his best men just when a joined attack of the Spaniards and the English on St-Domingue was rumoured. The 2 nations had the colony in a stranglehold. Yet, he soon learnt about the miserable state of the Spanish settlements, and knew he had little to fear from the recovering Jamaica. As a matter of fact, Du Casse had very relevant information about what was going on in the island. His biographer Hrodej quotes Governor Beeston, who, in April 1694, reports about the questioning of an English subject by Du Casse: "*Du Casse told him he would not ask anything about internal affairs of Jamaica, as he doubted he knew better than him. He added that he obtained daily or weekly reports about us, and that he knew about our forces and our positions.*" In fact, he was in touch with some English renegades and some Irish deserters who were said to be naturally inclined to help their Catholic peers. Du Casse, excited by the misfortune of the English, was impatiently clamouring for reinforcements; on May 4, 1693, he wrote to Minister De Pontchartrain, in France, to remind him of the necessariness of an operation against Jamaica, and how it would easily be carried out. He offered to conquer it, *as soon as the Buccaneers return, if only you might provide us with a few ships*. He set up 3 expeditions against Jamaica in 1694. The first one came back with 350 slaves; *a petty theft*, he said, to leave the enemies in suspense. The second one was more consistent; with 400 Buccaneers, including his second Beauregard, Du Casse sneaked along the coasts of Jamaica, capturing *The Falcon*, a coast guard ship, and killing 8 English. But this was just the prelude to the real attack, the third expedition.

John Baptist Dou Cass

Described by Hrodej as *a man of war above all*, Du Casse did not raid Jamaica on a whim. He was obsessed with the conquest of the Spanish part of St-Domingue, and knew that he had to get rid of the English first. He says to Pontchartrain: "*Sir, I shall always remind you of the importance of plundering this island, the most considerable of all those belonging to the English, thanks to its location and the furtive commerce that they make in the Spanish Indies (...). Should His Majesty ruined this colony, the English would have none left in the Gulf of Mexico, and they could not replace it by Barbados.*" (Hrodej) Du Casse wanted to destroy Jamaica to control the Spanish trade in the West Indies. It's quite significant that, although the war raged on, Du Casse engaged in dialogue with the Governor of Cuba, to whom he sent some prisoners, exhorting him to do the same. Usually, both nations sent their prisoners in exile, or used them on their warships. Du Casse even appealed to his Catholic feelings, as the English were Protestant. Du Casse would have loved to conquer Jamaica, but as it was beyond his current strength; he had to satisfy himself with a more realistic option. He decided to loot the Jamaican plantations in order to steal the required equipment to exploit sugar canes in St-Domingue. When the war broke, *Jamaica had all the luck*, says Hrodej. *The colony was rich thanks to her plantations and the Spanish trade (...). She was strong, populated, far better fortified than St-Domingue.* The French colony, remote from the 'lesser islands' in the Caribbean (Guadeloupe, Martinique), hardly interested the French Governor General of the Islands, who saw it as a tank of *Flibustiers*, good enough to complete his fleet in wartime. St-Domingue had not been bought by the King, but colonized by a vile spawn of adventurers with no ambition, who survived by looting and stealing. "*The French,*" confirms Governor Beeston, "*do not trade, they live out of what they steal from their neighbours.*" (Hrodej) Du Casse agreed. In 1684, he portrayed the settlement of Petit Goave as *a nest of corsairs, who live a dreadful life, unfitted to the rest of mankind.* (Hrodej) He yet intended to turn this cutthroat into a rich sugar colony. But it was very expensive to exploit sugar canes, mostly because of the required material. But Jamaica had plenty.

On May 31, 1694, 3 exhausted English reached Jamaica on a makeshift rowboat. They were Captain Elliott and 2 soldiers, freshly escaped from the jails of Petit Goâve, St-Domingue. Upon arrival, Elliott asked for an immediate interview with the Governor, as he had learnt that Du Casse was about to swarm Jamaica with 20 ships and 1,000 men! Martial law was decreed at once, a fort was built on Parade, and some fresh troops were sent to Rock Fort. People in Carlisle Bay and Old

Harbour expected the worse—and they were right. Jean-Baptiste Du Casse, though feverish, reached Jamaica on June 27, alongside the terror of the Spaniards, the Buccaneer De Graff. Officers Du Rollon de Lesquiniou and Beauregard were there too. The French divided their forces. Beauregard was dispatched to Port Morant, in the East, while De Graff disembarked 800 men in Cow Bay, East of Kingston. Beeston writes: *"They looted, burnt and destroyed everything in their way (...). Some scattered people were left behind, who were tortured, especially two of them, murdered in cold blood. They desecrated the tombs and committed other inhuman barbarities never committed by the Turks or the infidels."* (Hrodej) Beauregard joined De Graff's troops by land, burning everything on his way. But upon reaching Port Morant, he realized that the English had sabotaged their guns, before seeking refuge in fortified places. He remained there until July 26; meanwhile, Beauregard and 200 men plundered the North coast.

For his part, isolated from the fleet by a storm, Du Rollon sailed alongside the Jamaican coasts for several days, looking for Du Casse; at Carlisle, the English fired him, but he left to reconnoitre Port Royal. He was soon forced to go for some water nearby a place that Charlevoix calls *Brusselt*—he phonetically translates all English terms and names, turning Cow Bay into *Coubé*, etc.—, where he came under attack. The French, says Charlevoix, gloriously repealed the attackers regardless of their inferiority in numbers. However, when Du Rollon saw a cavalry brigade coming, he ordered his men to re-embark and sailed off. Sickness spread among the crew, forcing Du Rollon to make a stop at St-Domingue; but he went back to Morant Bay right away, where he eventually joined the rest of the fleet. On July 26, the fleet sailed towards Cow Bay, where some troops were landed, ready to march towards Port Royal. *"Though Du Casse intended to give a false alarm to attract the English troops and militia,"* says Father Labat, *"the men, carried away by their courage, landed, having scattered with a surprising valour the great numbers of troops and militia that had tried to repel them. They immediately set the place on fire, and then, having re-embarked during the night, went to anchor at Ouatiou."* Beeston feared an attack on Kingston, and he had already sent reinforcements to Winward Road. That is when the ardour of the French seemed to cool down. They remained for 3 hours in good order—contrary to Labat's nationalistic relation, unless he only means a few skirmishes—, but eventually made up their minds to go for the real target of the expedition—at least a priority one—, Carlisle Bay. On July 27, De Graff set sail with 14 ships to anchor at *Ouatirou*. This name of *Ouatirou*, used in several French relations, including Hrodej's in 1999, is quite mysterious. Indeed, it corresponds to no place in Jamaica, neither near Carlisle nor elsewhere. Charlevoix says it stood *17 leagues East of Coubé*; but he was obviously mistaken, as *Coubé* is the phonetic French translation of Cow Bay, which stands 7 leagues East Port Royal. It seems logical to say that *Ouatirou* is the phonetic French translation of a place in Jamaica—it was indeed a common practice. Bryan Edwards' book, for instance, was published in 1812 under the name of *Bryand Edouard*. Thus, the place near Carlisle Bay, which name comes closer to *Ouatirou*—or *Ouatiou*, as written by Father Labat—was Withy Wood; called Wither Wood on the English map of Jamaica drawn by Blome in 1670. This phonetic translation is disturbing since it implies a wrong pronunciation of the English name. The French mistook *whity* with *withy*, translating the name as *bois blanc* instead of *bois sec*. *"The lower district of this parish* (Vere—editor's note)," explains Long, *"called Withywood, took its name from its having been formerly overspread with woods and withes when the English first settled upon it."* In fact, the French probably landed at the mouth of Rio Minho—called Salt River on Blome's map—, where Long locates the town of Carlisle now vanished.

Du Casse did not pick up his target at random. Upon the extremely fertile soil of Withy Wood, the English had started many plantations of indigo, but also built many sugar-works. *"The opulence of* (these) *owners is spoken of by several writers; and though it has been called in question by some,"* says Long, *"yet it is very certain, that more carriages of pleasure were at one time kept here, than in all the rest of the island, Spanish Town only excepted."* When the French arrived, the colonists of Withy Wood set a slave ship afire so that it would not be taken—they also fired the invaders, in vain. The following day, 1,000 French set foot safely on the shore. Here, the relations diverge according to the nationality of their respective authors. The French explain that De Graff and Beauregard overtook 3 English entrenchments defended by a contingent of 700 or 1,400—depending on the sources—English. They says that the English lost 360 men, and the French only 22. For their parts, the English talk about a heroic resistance of 250 compatriots, entrenched in a small breastwork and fighting against 2,000 enemies. One thing is for sure, the English ended up running away alongside the Rino Minho, *where many drowned.* (Hrodej) *"In the mean time five companies of foot and some horse advanced against the French,"* explains Leslie. *"They were so spirited against them, that tho' they had marched all night, they not only put a stop to their pursuit of the English, who had quitted the breast-works, but attack'd them in so gallant a manner, that they made them retreat very precipitately."*

According to the French historian Charlevoix, De Graff heard about 200 horses coming from Spanish Town to reinforce the enemies, met them, and defeated them after a tough fight. Father Labat also relates the glorious French deeds. He claims that De Graff faced not less than 700 English, an important squadron of horses and 12 guns. *"Our people chased them, sword in hand, scattered them, took the fort, settled inside; and for eight days, remained there, while our troops, continuously roaming the battlefield, beat our enemies, plundered, looted and burnt the whole country 4 to 5 miles around; so that we had burnt more settlements and villages in Jamaica than the English and the Spaniards had burnt in St Domingue* (during retaliation, see below)." For several days, both factions engaged each other in small skirmishes until the French endeavoured to take the nearby house of one Mr Hubbard, who was garrisoned inside with 20 men. The fight, during which the entrenched received the help of a providential detachment from the bay, was terrible. *"The French, finding that they had lost so many of their officers and men, and that they could not penetrate farther into the country, contenting themselves with firing the small town of Carlisle (...), and then retreated to their ships,"* says Cundall. Thus, just as Governor Beeston expected a massive attack, the enemies retreated. Mr Hubbard's house, which played such an important part in the fight, was still standing in the early 19th century: *"The brick house (...) remains with the shot visible in its walls,"* tells Bridges in 1828. Charlevoix seems to think that many houses in Carlisle were built that way: *"What saved Jamaica (...) was a precaution taken by the inhabitants of Ouatirou. Each individual built his house upon a sort of fort where they locked up all their belongings; (...) The buccaneers (...) did not expect to be stopped by these forts, which walls were too tall to be climbed;* (they even) *had to step away from them, as the English fired at them from cover; Captain Le Sage and fifty of his men were killed while trying to take one of them."* Charles Leslie considers that this failed attempt at Mr Hubbard's house forced the French to flee disorderly, but Charlevoix gives another version of their departing. According to him, Du Casse took all his time to loot the place; a Capucin monk even sang a Mass before the town was burnt down, and the guns destroyed. Finally, he says, Du Casse left the place on August 3, and reached Petit Goave on the 14. Labat also talks about a retreat in order, and then adds: *"Sieur Du Casse made a prodigious booty in slaves, money, silverware, furniture, sugar works and merchandise. He took his time to*

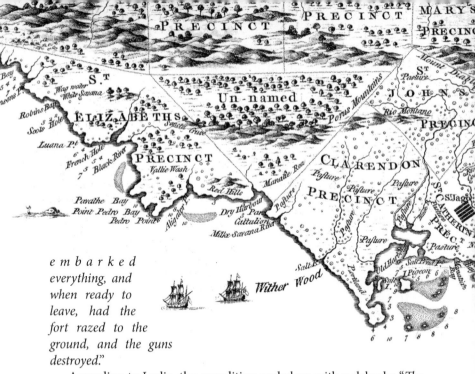

embarked everything, and when ready to leave, had the fort razed to the ground, and the guns destroyed."

According to Leslie, the expedition ended up with a debacle: "*The French lost upwards 700 men in this expedition. On the side of the English, there was only killed about 100;* " And guess what? "*Most of these were Jews and Negroes.*" The English celebrated, rewarding Captain Elliott, who had escaped his jail in St-Domingue to warn the colony; but the losses were important. "*Fifty sugar-works were destroyed,*" reminds Cundall, "*and many plantations burnt, and about thirteen hundred Negroes carried off. Du Casse received for this undertaking a pension of one hundred pistoles per annum.*" Charlevoix comments the overenthusiastic official relation of the expedition sent to France by Du Rollon: "*Nothing was gained but Negroes, around 3,000 of them; the cities that were plundered were very rich but I'm afraid there's a lot of exaggeration in what Mr Du Rollon said.*" Du Casse intended to ruin the commerce of Jamaica—he ended up far from it. The booty he brought back was so ridiculous, that some believed he had kept a large part to himself. "*But,*" says Father Lepers, who witnessed the events, and upon whose notes Charlevoix wrote his *Histoire de S. Domingue*, "*we'll accuse him not, as he was not convicted.*" (Hrodej) Du Casse might have been

Above: detail of the map of Jamaica drawn by Blome en 1670, showing the settlement of Wither Wood (aka *Ouatirou*).

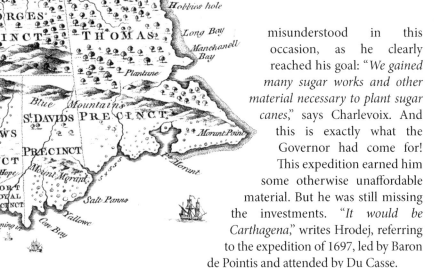

misunderstood in this occasion, as he clearly reached his goal: "*We gained many sugar works and other material necessary to plant sugar canes*," says Charlevoix. And this is exactly what the Governor had come for! This expedition earned him some otherwise unaffordable material. But he was still missing the investments. "*It would be Carthagena*," writes Hrodej, referring to the expedition of 1697, led by Baron de Pointis and attended by Du Casse.

At the end of the day, the expedition met with a limited success. Du Casse was rewarded, but had lost many men—mostly out of sickness. The Court let him know that he would not get any more reinforcements from France, unless he should pay for them. Cundall concludes: "*And thus ended the most serious attempt at the capture of Jamaica* (which, in fact, was not one—editor's note) *ever made upon its shores during the English occupation*."

Retaliation

The English did not wait for reinforcements to retaliate; and their celerity caught Du Casse off guard. On October 11, 3 English warships, a fire ship and 2 rowboats anchored in front of Léogane—today's Port-au-Prince—, in St-Domingue. In the 18th century, the place is described by La Harpe as *a* (small) *plain (...) bordered on one side by the sea, and on the other one by a chain of mountains. There are 200 inhabitants, who are said to be the wealthier of the whole colony*. From 8 a.m. until 3 p.m., the English fired the place, and then headed towards their true target, Petit Goave. 40 French followed them on the shore, ready to welcome them ashore. Petit Goave, accroding to the same author, then sheltered 60 inhabitants, *which is too much; the air is bad, the soil is even worst; yet, the town is well-built, and the port excellent*. Finding the French quite determined, the English simply fired the place before sailing off to Isle Avache (or Isle-À-Vache), south of the island. "*There they burnt one or two huts*," giggles Charlevoix, "*but seven or eight inhabitants, alerted by the noise, fought back, killing two and forcing the rest to re-embark."* This expedition did not go any further—yet, it worried Du Casse. His informers in Jamaica told him about a gathering of 2,000 men ready to join the Spaniards for a joined raid on St-Domingue. A few months later, on January 22, 1695, Captain Robert Wilmott left Plymouth, England, with 5 warships and 2 fire ships. His orders exhorted him to call a war council with the Governor of Jamaica, and, if necessary, to plunder Petit Goave. The official instructions, transcribed by Lediard, even specifies that he should capture the place, and harass the French of St-Domingue to insure the safety of Jamaica. But this expedition resembled the Western Design. Indeed, Wilmott and Colonel Lillingston were at odds. The latter eventually contested Burchett's official relation of the plundering of Cap François and Fort de Paix, accusing Wilmott of having endangered his troops and spoiled their Spanish allies to make more profits. Of course, the *entente cordiale* with the Spaniards was not perfect; but their combined actions earned them a few success. In fact, aware of his weak position, Du Casse abandoned his colony to the enemies, ordering his men not to fight in the open, but to favour skirmishes instead—guerrilla style. The famous Buccaneer Laurencillo de Graff, whom Du Casse *had never trusted* (Hrodej), was to lead this manoeuvre of retreat punctuated by a series of ambushes. However, things never occurred as expected. Father Lepers writes: *"No one had ever been as worried as De Gaff in this occasion (...); as he feared (...) to be captured by the Spaniards, he headed into the woods with a few men, refusing to sleep twice at the same place, deeply disadvantaged in his movements by the Dutch corpulence of his, that not so sedentary a life and the abuse of good beer had made even worse (...). Everybody wondered where the brave Laurencillo, former terror of the Spaniards, had gone? No matter how hard we searched, we could not find him in himself."*

This expedition twice benefited Jamaica. First, Wilmott left 4 ships in Port Royal before taking leave, which insured the safety of the island. Then, it weakened St-Domingue. Quoted by Lediard, Lillingston considers that he had *destroyed the entire colony, leaving the enemies hidden in caves, and the Spaniards masters of the place.* Charlevoix puts things into (French) perspective, reducing the expedition to the loss of *a few huts and two small towns made of small houses.* A few fowls, a handful of slaves and 200 dead? *"A storm that breaks out with a lot of noise,"* says our author, *"but leaves things almost untouched."* Wilmott reached Jamaica in July, where he sold his booty for a very good price, then headed back to England on September 3; the journey, because of diseases and damages, was terrible. Wilmott and several of his officers miserably perished on board.

Pointis attacks

The relationship between England and France deteriorated in Europe, especially after the assassination attempt on William of Orange, seen as a plot orchestrated by the French, who supported James II, exiled in France since his disgrace. Then, a consequent fleet led by De Pointis left France for the West Indies. In Jamaica, the word was going around that some former colonists informed the French. When the fleet reached St-Domingue on February 28, the English started to panic. They evacuated the women and the children from Port Royal, fortified their houses and stocked provisions in Kingston and Spanish Town. According to Leslie, these preparations dissuaded De Pointis from attacking Jamaica. But if the French, who had carefully planned this expedition for 3 years, had considered taking Jamaica at one point, they had changed their mind for Cartagena long before De Pointis reached the West Indies. Consequently, the fleet, joined by Du Casse and 1,000 Buccaneers from St-Domingue, by-passed Port Royal a few days later.

Upon confirmation that Pointis had just left Petit Goave, Vice-Admiral Nevil, stationed in Barbados, headed to Jamaica to meet him. He then did his best to join the French fleet but could not reach Cartagena before the town was plundered. This was quite an inglorious feat of arms, very much stained with acts of barbarity. Among the victims stood Du Rollon; following an injury, he had a leg amputated, and did not survive the surgery.

Admiral Nevil still intercepted a part of the fleet on its way back, and captured a ship worth £20,000. Lediard reports: *"Knight Beeston, Governor of Jamaica, having given advice to the Vice-Admiral on June 22nd, that he would serve the interests of Jamaica by destroying Petit Goave, he sent Rear-Admiral Meeze with 8 ships."* On the returning Buccaneers' heels, the English reached Petit Goave on July 8, landing by night, and swarming the little town at dawn. Du Casse, awaken by the shotguns, looked in the street and saw that the place and the houses were surrounded by enemies, *who fired the doors and the windows,* says Charlevoix. He jumped out of an opposite window and followed the hedges to a hill, a quarter mile away. Wearing a simple nightgown, the Governor rallied a handful of men, and led the counter-attack alongside Beauregard. In town, Du Casse came across an impressive number of English—900 had landed! Scared, his troops disbanded; and he was left with 8 men only. "*Running the risk to be taken*," Charlevoix goes on, "*he jumped into a yard, reached the church and soon sprang out of it with a few men to attack the other side of the entrenchment.*" Meanwhile, on the seashore, the French Captain Godefroi, also dressed in nightgown, repelled an important contingent of English. Du Casse had the lead in this fight—a miracle. According to what their prisoners had told them, the English did not expect to find more than 40 men in Petit Goave. The bold resistance of the place destabilized them. Fearing that the enemies might be much more numerous, and knowing them as fearless Buccaneers, they decided to retreat. Yet, this expedition was a hard blow to the colony, which had already lost many men during the expedition on Cartagena. Thus, it secured Jamaica until September 20, when England, Spain and Holland signed the Treaty of Ryswick with France. The lull did not last. In 1702, war broke out again, and the West Indies plunged back into chaos.

The War of the Spanish Succession

In November 1700, Duke Philip of Anjou, a grandson of Louis XIV, succeeded Charles II to the throne of Spain. The reunion of these 2 super-powers threatened the neighbouring countries, which united their forces. In England, when William of Orange passed away—March 1702—, Queen Ann succeeded him, stating that she would *carry out all the preparations undertaken to oppose the great power of France.* (Lediard) Finally, England and Holland declared war on France and Spain in May 1702. The battles, a vast majority maritime, took place mainly on the European seas. But a few took place in the West Indies, and they proved *how advantageously* (Jamaica) *is situate, for annoying both French and Spaniards, in case of a war.* (Leslie) This was a privateers' war from the start. The English Lords sent a letter to the Queen, stating: "*As the preparations of the enemies of Her Majesty indicated their intention to make a corsairs' war (...), the Lords think it would be advantageous (...) to encourage Her Majesty's subjects to equip and arm warships at their own expenses, and to their private benefits.*" Any privateer or soldier could charter a ship, chase the enemies with a *commission* and get rich with his captures. This kind of war suited the colonists of Jamaica perfectly, who, if we believe Leslie, made considerable profits during the war: "*Not a day passed, but rich prizes were brought in.*" Then he adds: "*The island became richer than it had been since Morgan's days.*" But Jamaica still feared the dreadful Du Casse—after a short stay in France, the French Governor had come back among his Bbuccaneers, who were as dangerous and undisciplined as ever. Not to mention the impressive fleet of Count Château-Renault, spotted in Martinique in March 1702. The French had sent it to protect the galleons of their new Spanish allies, not to raid Jamaica. Furthermore, 15 English warships were anchored in Port Royal since December 1701, under the commandment of Vice-Admiral John Benbow. The war went on as planned, a succession of punctual 'courses', of lightning strikes and other aggressions carried out from the American colonies. The Governor of the Massachusetts Bay set up victorious 'courses' against the French interests, so did the privateers of Barbados, Nevis and Antigua.

In May 1702, the word spread that *Du Casse was expected in Port Louis (...) with four warships, to destroy the Negroes trade of England and Holland.* (Lediard) Wishing to confront the French Governor, Admiral Benbow sent Rear-Admiral Whestone to intercept him—in vain. "*In July 1702,*" says Charlevoix, "*the English of Jamaica were informed of the declaration of war, the Vice-Admirals Wetchstou* (Whestone) *and Bembou* (Benbow) *were already at sea with strong fleets and seemed to threaten our southern and western coasts (...); they really meant to loot, as they could hardly do anything more, having almost no troops to disembark. But they were mostly embittered towards Du Casse.*" In July, Benbow went to Léogane after Du Casse, forcing a ship to wreck, sinking and capturing a few others. As Du Casse did not show up, Benbow sailed back to Port Royal. When Whestone came back, he was free to go after Du Casse again. "*He sailed southwards,*" writes Hrodej, "*straight to St. Marthe; he knew he could not miss his prey.*" Hi ship, the *Breda*, indeed joined Du Casse off Colombia on August 19. The Governor's fleet was 12 ships strong, some armed with 30 or 40 guns. Benbow started a six-day long battle. "*But 3 or 4 of his ships remained behind and did not come forward, though ordered to do so,*" underlines the English historian Oldmixon. This particular quote is translated from a 1716 French book entitled *La Vie d'Anne Stuart* (Amsterdam). In another book, written in English and entitled *Lives of the Admirals*, the same historian coyly describes the scene: "(Benbow) *fought (...) bravely for five days; which not only demonstrates the courage and conduct of this gallant seaman, but the fidelity and affection of his own ship's company; since, it is impossible, he could, in such circumstances, have maintained the engagement so long.*" Benbow's determination in this occasion earned him eternal respect from his nation. But on 24, at 2 a.m. he reached the last ship of the enemy's fleet and fired her; the ship fired back and, at 3 a.m., *a chain-cannonball broke the Admiral's leg*, goes on Lediard. The aforementioned book attributed to Oldmixon goes on: "*Not being embarrassed, he order his bed to be carried upon the deck, and gave his orders so well that he saved his ship.*" At the end of the day, dropped by his war council, injured and disheartened, Benbow came back to Port Royal. "*The French accounts,*" goes on Oldmixon in *The Lives of the Admirals,* "*indeed, represent the whole affair to their own advantage; but M. Du Casse, who was a brave man, and withal the best judge of this matter, has put the thing out of dispute, by the following short letter, written by him immediately after his arrival at Carthagena.*" The Jamaican historian Clinton V. Black reproduces the said letter, which, he said, was still in the hands of Benbow's family in the early part of the 20th century:

> Sir, I had little hopes on Monday, but to have supped in your cabbin (sic): but it pleased God to order it otherwise. I am thankful for it. As for those cowardly captains who deserted you, hang them up; for, by _____, they deserve it.

This message seems to be a forgery. Charlevoix's account is one of those chastised by Oldmixon. It reads: "(Benbow) *joined* (Du Casse) *at last, on August 30, 12 leagues off St. Marthe, and despite having 4 ships only, Mr Du Casse did not refuse to fight. The battle went on for five days, and on the sixth one (...), Bembou* (Benbow) *sailed backward and got back to Jamaica. A broken leg caused his death shortly afterwards. Most of his ships could not take the sea any more, and he had lost half of his crew. Mr Du Casse only had one ship damaged, and twenty men dead or injured. Yet, he did not chase Bembou* (Benbow); *maybe he did not realize that he was in such a perilous situation; he sailed on towards Cartagena.*" Du Casse, in the account he published in the *Mercure Galant,* far from praising Benbow, does not pay the English officer much respect; he fought, he says, *as a haggler and a fox.* (Hrodej) The bravery of Benbow was reinforced by the cowardice of his officers. Two of them were tried off Port Royal, and then executed on board the *Bristol,* off Plymouth, England. Though Benbow died from his injuries, the English had the last word since they caught up the Spanish galleons at Vigo, off Italy, and partially looted them.

Du Casse died on June 25, 1751, in France, from the injuries received during the siege of Barcelona a few months earlier. In Port Royal, Vice-Admiral Groydon succeeded Benbow, but before his arrival, Captain Whetstone made a successful expedition, taking and destroying a great amount of French and Spanish ships in their very harbours, and bringing away 120 prisoners, with a very considerable booty. Diseases killed most of the 2,000 men that had come with Groydon. The latter, said to be brutal and disdainful, gathered the English forces scattered in various colonies to plunder Plaisance, and to deprive the French from the trade of Terre-Neuve. For his part, Whetstone left in February 1703 for 5 weeks of skirmishes alongside the coasts of St-Domingue. The merchants of Port Royal did not remain inactive, funding some privateers' expeditions. After several months spent at sea, Groydon came back to Jamaica where, says Burnett, *he behaved so harshly that it seemed he had come to spread terror rather than to fight it.* He eventually set sail for England, leaving a few ships to protect Jamaica until the peace of Utrecht, signed in April 1713. Among several advantages, England was awarded the Spanish trade in the West Indies, including the profitable Contract, or *Assiento*, previously held by France, regarding the supply of slaves. "*Jamaica* (benefited it) *most of all*," explains Clinton V. Black, "*for the island became the distribution centre for the trade, the majority of the slaves being shipped from here to Spanish ports in vessels locally owned and manned.*" The island entered its most prosper era—the days of plantations. But the French were not done with Jamaica yet; and they came back for more in 1782.

The Battle of the Saintes

The second to last confrontation opposing 'Tropical France' to Jamaica took place in 1782. Just like England, destabilized by the American war of independence and under attack of the French, the Dutch and the Spaniards were seemingly about to crumble down. Jamaica seriously suffered from the trade restrictions imposed by her mother country—mostly on North America, but also on the French and Dutch dominions in the West Indies. Running short of flour and corn, the island suffered from famine, and 15,000 slaves died from hunger between 1780 and 1787. The planters diversified their productions to survive, cultivating ackee—a fruit originated in West Africa—, mangos—the English got their first plants from a French ship captured by William Rodney—, or coffee.

France supported the American rebels, and the impressive fleet of Count d'Estaing that reached St-Domingue in 1779, deeply worried Jamaica. Recently promoted commandant of a frigate, which he was then awaiting at Port Royal, the young Horatio Nelson was pacing up and down the quarterdeck of the fort of Port Royal—today's *Nelson's Quarterdeck.* Worried, the 20-year-old officer, who, following many injuries and a glorious death in Trafalgar, would become *the greatest of all British naval heroes,* (Black) was scrutinizing the horizon, fearing the coming of the French forces he knew the island could not resist. "*I think you must not be surprise to hear of my learning to speak French*," he writes to a friend (Cundall). But the French invasion was not to be; indeed, the Count d'Estaing sailed directly to America, and some English reinforcements reached Jamaica soon afterwards.

Aiming at cutting off all communication between the diverse Spanish colonies of the continent, Nelson sailed to the Lake of Nicaragua. But the disease stroke the crew, including Nelson himself, and forced the fleet to come back to Jamaica. He recovered until March 1780, when he was succeeded by Admiral George Rodney. In between, he partook in the arrest of Lewis Hutchinson, the first serial killer in the history of Jamaica, who committed dozens of murders in the parish of St Ann; unmasked, he tried to escape by sea, but was quickly caught up by a ship sent after him by Nelson. Tried in Spanish Town, Hutchinson was hanged. In the first months of his turn, Rodney had several skirmishes with the French fleet of De Guichen; then he spent the hurricane season near the coast of America, escaping one of the most devastating calamities to hit the island ever. Governor John Dalling officially reported to London about the event (Black):

> On Monday the 2nd (...) the weather being very close, the sky on a sudden became very much overcast, and an uncommon elevation of the sea immediately followed—whilst the unhappy settlers at Savanna-la-Mar were observing this extraordinary phenomenon, the sea broke suddenly upon the town, and on its retreat swept everything away with it, so as not to leave the smallest vestige of man, beast or house behind—This most dreadful catastrophe was succeeded by the most terrible hurricane that ever was felt in this country with repeated shocks of an earthquake, which was almost totally demolished every building in the parishes of Westmoreland, Hanover, part of St James's and some part of St Elizabeth.

The same hurricane killed 7,000 people in Martinique and over 4,000 in Barbados. The following year, the bold Rodney patrolled the Caribbean, taking St Eustach from the Dutch—the French De Bouillé soon recaptured the island—, then Demerara and Berbice (English Guyana). But in October 1781, the English General Cornwallis surrendered to General Washington in Yorktown, Virginia, thus signifying the independence of America. The English empire seemed to fall apart. De Grasse tried to take advantage of the situation by planning the capture of Jamaica. In the island, fear led to panic; the inhabitants even accidentally set fire to a part of Kingston while trying to fortify it. Meanwhile, off the islands of the Saintes (located between Dominica and Guadeloupe), Rodney engaged De Grasse's fleet, and changed the course of history.

The French despising the manoeuvre of Rodney, did not even bother evacuating the living cattle from their decks—the provisions. Thus, when the English Vice-Admiral broke the enemy's line, the terrified animal broke loose, adding to the general confusion. Taken off-guard, the French were unable to take control of the situation. "*At sunset, De Grasse struck his flag,*" says Black, "*The day was won and the threatened invasion of Jamaica prevented.*" Back to Port Royal, Rodney showed off his takes, the majestic *Ville de Paris* of over 100 guns—a jewel of the French fleet—, as well as Admiral De Grasse himself. Grateful, the Jamaicans ordered the sculptor John Bacon to immortalize the hero through a life-size statue erected in the square of Spanish Town, where it still stands today, surrounded by 2 gorgeous guns from *Ville de Paris*. The famous English writer Matthew G. Lewis —author of the masterpiece *The Monk*, published in 1797—was in Jamaica in 1815. He gives[*] a critical description of the grandiloquent monument: "*The old Admiral is most absurdly dressed in the habit of a Roman General, and furnished with buskins and a truncheon. The temple itself is quite in opposition with good taste.*" It takes nothing away from him, or his victory, still praised today as a turning point in the history of the island. "*Rodney's victory,*" claims Black, "*—the only gleam of sunshine in the whole miserable war—not only saved Jamaica from invasion and almost certain capture, but restored British prestige, badly lowered by the success of the American revolution, and enabled Britain to secure more favourable terms under the Treaty of Versailles, which formally brought the war to an end in September, 1783.*"

Tropical Revolution

The next conflict was quite peculiar, as friends and foes blended together in the middle of the black tornado that transformed St-Domingue into the first independent black Republic, Haiti. The historian Bryan Edwards, then on site, witnessed the event. "*About nine miles from the city, upon a plantation called Noé, the rebellion commenced. In*

---

[*] *Journal of A West India Proprietor* (London, 1834).

the middle of the night twelve or thirteen of the ringleaders advanced to
the sugar-house, and dragging a young man, an apprentice to the refiner,
they cut him into pieces with their cutlasses in front of the dwelling-house.
The overseer awakened, and alarmed with his woeful cries, amid the
agonies of such cruelty, went to his assistance, and was shot upon the spot."
In fact, it started long before that—and far from the West Indies. Indeed,
the insurrection was rooted in the French revolution. When La Bastille
was taken, on July 14, 1789, the revolt had been raging for a while. As
soon as December 1788, the *Etats Généraux* feverishly gathered, and the
planter of St-Domingue forced their way into the debate. The humanist
and abolitionist movements that had spread over Europe for a few
decades had created a general hostility towards the planters—they were
seen as exploiters. Based on the English abolitionist societies, the *Société*
des Amis des Noirs—Society of the Negroes' Friends—, published
pamphlets against slavery, actively trying to destabilize the planters—
including by talking in the free Mulattoes who lived in France. In the
West Indies, the freshly disembarked slaves enjoyed less consideration
than the Creoles, born there; and the Creoles themselves enjoyed less
consideration than the Mulattoes, who could boast of some white
ancestors in their linage. Following the *Déclaration des Droits de*
l'Homme (Declaration of the Rights of Man) in 1789, the *Amis des Noirs*
tried to spread the revolt to the colonies through the Mullatoes, who, as
underlined by Edwards, did not remain idle at the time: "*Informed of the*
favourable sentiments of the French nation concerning them, and at the
same time instructed in their rights, became very tumultuous, and
imperiously demanded instant emancipation. They even assembled in vast
number in arms; but not acting in concert, they were soon vanquished."
Denouncing the hostility of the Assembly, the planters threatened to
voluntarily place their island under the yoke of a foreign nation,
England. They started to organize, calling to arms through various
provincial assemblies, and eventually publishing the famous decree of
May 28, 1790. Questioning the authority of the National Assembly, they
plunged the colony into a foretold civil war. Right in the middle of
chaos, where many decision-makers played all sides, suddenly appeared
Jacques Ogé. The son of a free mulatto, owner of a coffee plantation and
born from a white father, Ogé grew up in Paris. While in his thirties, he
was introduced to the meetings of the *Amis des Noirs, under the*
patronage of Grégoire, Brissot, La Fayette, and Robespierre, the leading
members of that society. (Edwards) Ogé soon found himself entrusted
with a mission of saving his brothers in St-Domingue. Logistically

supported by the *Amis des Noirs*, he bought some weapons in New England in June 1790, and then secretly landed in St-Domingue. He demanded at once the extension of the privileges enjoyed by the Whites to all in the island. But after several weeks spent clandestinely in the island, Ogé realized that the Mullatoes were not as ready as his friends from the *Amis des Noirs* had told him; he had hardly enrolled 200 men, most of them, according to Edwards, being *raw undisciplined youth, and totally averse to all kind of subordination and order*. They slaughtered a few Whites, indeed, as well as a handful of Mulattoes who had refused to join them, but Ogé's men were soon disbanded by a troop of French soldiers. They sought refuge to the Spanish part of the island, but the Spaniards captured them and handed them to the French authorities in late December. In March of the following year, 20 were hanged. "*A more cruel and terrible death was reserved for Ogé, and Chevane the lieutenant,*" says Edwards. "*They were adjudged to be broken alive upon the wheel; and in that woeful condition they were left to linger until dead.*" Ogé allegedly lost all composure, trying to escape death by all means—in vain. His terrible fate only hardened the feelings between the Whites and the Mulattoes in the island. In Paris, the *Amis des Noirs* staged a tragedy relating his story, which exacerbated the animosity towards the planters, now *held in universal detestation and daring not venture their persons in the streets of Paris*. (Edwards) Whereas the English abolitionists first contented themselves with putting a stop to the slave trade—without freeing the Blacks currently held as slaves—, the French revolutionaries did not care about endangering civil peace. *Perish our colonies rather than one principle,* claimed Robespierre. On May 15, 1791, a decreed published in France declared that any Black born out of free parents in the colonies was now considered as a free man; enjoying the same rights and privileges than any French citizen, he could even apply to a position in the assemblies. The reaction in St-Domingue was terrible. The colonists rejected the decree, and formed a General Assembly of their own. Seeing that the Whites wanted to deprive them from their rights, the Mulattoes gathered in armed groups. The slaves were active too and, on August 23, 1791, early in the morning, St-Domingue caught fire! The slaves rebelled in a general movement, setting dozens of plantations on fire all through the island, inflicting the most dreadful torments to the Whites they caught. "*Shocking even so much as to mention! the young women were barbarously treated, and often immediately after murdered; and sometimes only reserved to future barbarity,*" deplores Edwards. The White believed they could bring things under control—they were wrong. More than 12,000 people—including 2,000 Whites—died during the first 2 months of the revolt. 180 plantations were ravaged; the inferno was so huge that the ashes were allegedly carried as far as Jamaica! St-Domingue was torn apart. As a matter of fact, the island never recovered, but died in the middle of the torments to reborn with a new face, black and triumphant, and bearing her ancient name of free land, Haiti.

In Jamaica, the planters feared contagion; and kept a close watch on the events, rescuing the French colonists who came begging for help. The government granted them a modest sum of money, but the merchants, for their parts, gave them considerable credit. Major-General Adam Williamson, then Governor of Jamaica, sent a ship to pick up refugees at Cap François—the historian Bryan Edwards was part of the expedition. Jamaica tried to keep away from the conflict, but remained focused. Some French revolutionaries, it was said, had secretly come to Jamaica to exhort the slaves to rebel. The role of these agitators was thoroughly researched during the last upheaval of the Maroons in 1794 (see chapter 4). "*However,*" concedes Black, "(...) *the majority of the St Domingue refugees who remained on the island settled satisfactorily into the community, the government and the people subscribing generously towards their support. Nor did their arrival bring gloom only; a few of them were actors and professional entertainers who helped to brighten life by their performances at the Kingston Theatre—like Monsieur du Mulin, for example, whose main act was a dance on the tight rope with two children tied to his feet!*" Among theses new hosts was also M. de Charmilly, a wealthy planter from St-Domingue, who had not passed to Jamaica to go to the theatre—but to turn St-Domingue over to the English, providing they saved the planters from their current miseries. At first, Jamaica seemed hesitant—but in Europe, things sped up. Louis XVI was executed in 1793, and all the European kingdoms came together to fight the regicide republic. Revolutionary armies were formed, and the French Assembly declared war to Great Britain, plunging Jamaica into her last conflict with St-Domingue. Thus, as the northern province was occupied by dozens of thousands of armed slaves, Jamaica accepted M. de Charmilly's offer. "*Accordingly, in the summer of 1793,*" writes Edwards, "*planters received dispatches to General Williamson (...), with instructions to repair, with the troops which could be spared, and accept terms of capitulation, and take under his protection all those who were willing to surrender themselves.*" But the republican Commissioners sent from France to fight both the Mulattoes and the slaves, had no intention to surrender the island to the English; upon the imminent arrival of the enemy, they took a historic decision, they declared free all Negroe slaves willing to fight for the republic.

The English expedition happened to be more difficult than expected. The whole island had become a battlefield, where several factions fought one another. Edwards claims that 40,000 rebels were located in the northern parts, ready to *rush down* everybody. The support received by the English from the French colonists was also quite timid—Edwards claimed that only 2,000 of them joined the English troops. In fact, the exiled planters supported the English, as their last hope to ever recover their belongings. But those who had remained, had already annexed their former neighbours' properties, and they did not welcome the English—Edwards accuses them of taking advantage of chaos. Not to mention that, despite the critical situation, many French simply refused to surrender to the English. Williamson received a lukewarm welcome, and his 870 men were far from enough to cope with the situation. The inhabitants of Jérémie officially surrendered, and the English settled there on September 10, raising the British flag. Fort St-Nicolas surrendered 12 days later. Consequently, Colonel Whitelocke, leading the operation, grew optimistic. Until he arrived in the Tiburon Bay on October 4, where he was bitterly repelled by the enemy. Soon, sickness appeared among the exhausted soldiers. Williamson sent 800 men from Jamaica, weakening his own colony but impressing the French planters. At once, the parishes of Jean-Rabel, St-Marc and Arcahaye, submitted to the invaders, who still brooded over their failure at Tiburon. Several weeks passed, and the English returned to Tiburon. Despite the bravery of a group of French, they eventually took possession of the place. Now controlling Léogane, the English started to look upon a successful outcome. On February 19, they even took Port au Prince. But the more the English expanded their territory, the quicker they reached the limits of their forces. *"About this time,"* says Edwards, *"upwards of two thousand of the most desperate negroes attacked our troops who kept the garrison of Cape Tiburon, who were repulsed with great slaughter; but the signalled victory was procured with the loss and wounding of many of our men."* How many assaults could they stand? The country was so vast, and the enemies so numerous! Even their former allies turned against them. Jean-Rabel, which had submitted to the English, now hosted many hostile planters. And it only took them a short insurrection to recapture the place. Eight months after their arrival, the English were about to lose all they had gained so far—but reinforcements of 1,465 men led by Commodore Ford and General Whyte arrived from England! They decided to take Port-au-

Prince, where richly loaded French vessels were rumoured to anchor. Some 300 men landed while the fleet fired the forts of the port—a handful of soldiers made their way into Fort Bizotton under a hail of bullets. *"The capture of* (the fort) *decided the fate of the capital,"* states Edwards, *"which was evacuated on the 4th of June."* Thus, by June, the English were in Port-au-Prince.

Like Leaves In Autumn

The French who were chased from Port-au-Prince retreated on the nearby heights, organizing the counter-offensive while the conquerors fortified the place—a tedious work, mostly for men who had remained confined on board of a ship for 6 months. Disease stroke once again. The yellow fever decimated the enemy. *"The gallant troops dropt* (sic) *like the leaves in autumn,"* deplores Edwards. The reinforcements sent from Guadeloupe, far from relieving them, made things even worse, as the plague came during their journey, killing 100. *"And the wretched remains,"* states Edwards, *"upon their landing, seemed in a state nothing better than those they came to relieve."* Sick, Whyte left for Europe, and was succeeded by Brigadier-General Horneck, who had passed to Jamaica with 50 men in September. For 7 months, without any reinforcement or provisions, Horneck held his position, yet unable to prevent the Mulattoes from recapturing Léogane. Only one English triumphed, Lieutenant-Colonel Birsbane, who submitted the plain of Artibonite, defeating some rebellious Negroes and some republican troops, even sending 10,000 slaves back to their plantations. But the island was too vast. Victorious here, vanquished there at the same time, the English were slowly losing ground. The French Commissioners convinced the Mullatoes of St Marc to rebel against the invader, forcing Brisbane to abandon his position on the plain to intervene. At once, the rebellious Negroes put themselves together, forgetting about their promises.

The northern province was under control of the troops of François-Dominique Toussaint, nicknamed L'Ouverture, or The Breech—following a brilliant military manoeuvre—*one of the most outstanding black men who ever lived*, says Black. His action against the English was decisive. *"The Negroes led by Toussaint and his Lieutenant Rigaud,"* confesses M. de Marlès, *"restlessly held the* (English) *in check."* After several years of a restless war, the English came to the conclusion that they were going nowhere fast. Brigadier-General Thomas Maitland, then in charge of the troops, pressed from all parts, and foretelling a deadly ending, decided to negotiate with Toussaintt L'Ouverture. These discussions led to the definitive retreat of the English troops from the island in 1798.

Toussaint was the son of 2 slaves from the *Breda* plantation. First a herdsman, he joined the Spanish army for a while, and then the French one at the dawn of the insurrection. Thanks to the situation, he quickly evolved until he eventually became Chief-General of the republican army in 1796. *"He got rid of all who could have impeached him,"* affirms Marlès, *"and thus governed the colony until Leclerc arrived."* But Premier Consul Bonaparte did not send the famous Leclerc until 1802. In between, Toussaint set up a fair government, protecting the Negroes as well as the Whites, and passing intelligent laws that restored peace. *"He used his power to maintain social peace,"* claims Marlès—the calm before the storm.

Leclerc and Toussaint

At the end of 1801, the European wars being over, Premier Consul Bonaparte sent 25,000 men to restore order in St-Domingue. He appointed his brother-in-law, General Charles Leclerc, head of the expedition. *"Such was the confidence of its success,"* reports Rainsford, *"that he was accompanied by his lady, and her young brother, Jerome Bonaparté."* He carried a letter with him that the Premier Consul had written for Toussaint: *"We have conceived for you esteem, (...) and we wish to recognize and proclaim the great services you have rendered to the French people; if their colours fly on St. Domingo, it is to you, and your brave blacks, that we owe it."* But Leclerc had landed as a conqueror; he raided Cap François, intending to submit Toussaint and his army of Negroes. His true instructions were to subjugate the Negroes and to conquer the rest of the island. He wrote to Admiral Duckworth in Jamaica upon landing: *"One of the ministers of his Britannic Majesty has said, that the peace just concluded was not an ordinary peace, but a sincere reconciliation of the two greatest nations in the world. If it depends on me, Sir, this happy prognostic will certainly be verified, at least I am pleased to imagine, that our pacific communications will be worthy of* (our) *two nations."* He even enclosed *a faithful statement* of his forces in St-Domingue. Upon understanding his secret intention, Toussaint and several generals took arms against Leclerc, and the colony witnessed new terrible scenes of war. *"An infinite number of Blacks and Mulattoes perished in torments,"* writes Marlès, *"all those who were suspected of having partaken in the slaughtering of white people were mercilessly put to death."* Rainsford, who witnessed many exactions, gives striking accounts—he even illustrated some of them with blood-curdling

engravings. The French had their dogs
tearing people to pieces, breaking their skulls
and devouring their entrails. Rainsford was
deeply affected by what he saw, and he quotes
M. de Charmilly, the French emissary in Jamaica,
on the title-page of his work: "*One would speak the
truth by saying that only a few of these horrors could
be blamed on the Blacks.*" Charmilly's book was, as a
matter of fact, an answer to Edwards'—here quoted—,
which he denounces as partial.

   The troops of Leclerc gained ground rapidly,
forcing many black generals to get into line. At the end

of the day, they all surrendered, including Toussaint, who retired and went to live on his own plantation in Gonaïves, *L'ouverture*. But Leclerc was no man of his word. Early in June, 2 French frigates discreetly landed in Gonaïves, and circled Toussaint's house. The black General was sent to France, where he died in 1803, at Fort de Joux, in the province of Doubs. "*Toussaint L'Ouverture is dead*," reads the *Times*. "*He died, according to letters from Besançon, a few days ago. The fate of this man has been singularly unfortunate, and his treatment most cruel. He died, we believe, without a friend to close his eyes.*" On June 22, 1802, endorsing the title of General-in-chief, which he had taken from a man he described as *treacherous and hypocrite and responsible for so many losses in our ranks,* Leclerc published a decree reinforcing martial law. In Jamaica, Admiral Duckworth congratulated him on his success.

The Tropical 'der des ders'

The English had not said their last word. They were rumoured to provide the rebels with guns while sending Leclerc deferential missives. In St-Domingue, things were getting from bad to worse. Diseases killed thousands in the army, including officers. Leclerc himself got sick. Meanwhile, the black forces organized on the North coast; a few legendary fighters such as the elusive Sans Souci, fed the rebels with hope, and the exactions committed by the French only exacerbated the hatred of their enemies. Rainsford reminds us that General Dugua, Chief of Staff, joined a conjuration after he was *sickened by the inconceivable tortures inflicted to the black leader Charles Bellair and his Amazonian wife.* (Rainsford) The French army, losing its balance, tried to establish equilibrium of terror. "*In attempting to disarm the black troops which had been incorporated with the French, the necessity whereof was discovered too late,*" says Rainsford, "*the most barbarous methods were practised, ship-loads were collected, and suffocated in the holes (...) In one instance, six hundred being surrounded, and attempting a resistance, were massacred on the spot; and such slaughters daily took place in the vicinity of Cape François, that the air became tainted by the putrefaction of the bodies.*" The deathblow came with Leclerc's death on November 1, 1802, when General Rochambeau succeeded him. "*The way the new man in charge behaved,*" explains Marlès, "*upset everyone, and led the Negroes to rebellion.*" Dessalines took the lead of this new uprising; he

Opposite: the French white soldiers get rid of the French black soldiers; *Toussaint Louverture (detail, 19ᵗʰ century).*

was a former allied of Toussaint, and *his courage was boundless*, says Marlès; *yet, he was bloody, fierce and perverse*. His military actions brought the French army to a breaking point, and cornered Rochambeau and his last languishing forces in the Cape. But in May 1803, the Treaty of Amiens was broken in Europe, and war broke again between France and England. At once, the English of Jamaica headed to St-Domingue.

Dessalines considered using the English against the French, and got in touch with Commodore Loring; they agreed to pressure the Cape from both sides. "*Pressed (...) almost to death by absolute famine, and after waiting for a considerable time, wretchedly appeasing the desperate calls of hunger by feeding on our horses, mules, asses, and even dogs,*" relates Rochambeau, "*we had no way to escape the poignards of the enraged negroes, but by trusting our fate to the sea.*" (Rainsford) He negotiated with Dessalines, obtaining a delay of 10 days to leave the island. Loring, for his part, refused Rochambeau the privilege to repatriate 500 French to Europe. Rochambeau had to surrender unconditionally. The French hesitated; but the black troops were triumphing all over the island, proclaiming general freedom. Loring lost patience, and decided to raid the Cape. At the last instant, Rochambeau agreed to surrender, provided that he could sail the bay waving the French flag and have a broadside, before surrendering. "*The force being taken possession of by Commodore Loring, comprizing* (sic) *eight thousand men, with the shipping, consisting of three frigates, and seventeen merchantmen, were conveyed to Jamaica, from whence Admiral Duckworth immediately dispatched General Rochambeau, and the officers particularly in his confidence, to England,*" states Rainsford. But this victory was all the English could hope for; the rest of the island being well armed and galvanized by Dessalines, they had to give up all dream of conquest. They left. "*The enemy, not that generous,*" rages Marlès, "*consoled himself by perpetuating evil deeds.*"

Soon after, Dessalines became the first Emperor of Haiti to the sound of the guns. A *Te Deum* was sung in church to celebrate, and the day concluded by public rejoicings, *apparently the most sincere that ever greeted a similar occasion*, rejoices Rainsford. Marlès, being more critical, comments: "(Dessalines) *took the title of Emperor, as the one of king was not enough; his despotism spread all through his empire, and soon alienating the hearts of his subjects.*" Now free and masters of their destiny, the Blacks in Haiti engaged with confidence on a painful path. However, Bonaparte was already digging a pit for them. But this is another (sad) story.

9

Sugar and Slaves

Slavery was not born with the discovery of the New World, but it exponentially developed with its conquest, until it became an essential part of it. From the start, the Spaniards saw it as the solution to the shortage of their labour supply. They first exploited the Indians, who happened to be weak and easily subjugated—at least in the Caribbean islands. They used every excuse to enslave them. The Caribbean Indians, convinced of cannibalism, lost the chance to redeem themselves while those who rebelled lost their lives. The *repartimientos*—or repartitions—of Indians, which were left to the discretion of the Governors, were at the heart of the development of the settlements in the New World. But the Indians were poor slaves—too quickly exhausted, buried, and decimated by the sword or diseases. Despite the protestations of Las Casas or Queen Isabella, the genocide was soon completed. Upset, the Spaniards turned to the Portuguese. Edwards retraces the beginnings of the Slave Trade: "*Under the celebrated Prince Henry of Portugal (see chapter 1), in 1442, the first African slaves were carried from home by Europeans. Anthony Gonzales had captured two Moors near Cape Bojador, and brought them home; but being ordered by his Prince to restore them to Africa, he sold them at Rio del Ora, and received from the Moors ten Blacks and some gold dust. The avarice of the Portuguese was awakened by this successful exchange, and a traffic was begun on a large scale.*" The 18th century historian De Paw underlines that the Portuguese acted accordingly to a Papal bull of 1440. "*The Infant (Prince Henry) was the first Christian to use Negro slaves,*" he writes. "*Ferdinand the Catholic then sent a few in America, for his personal benefit, as soon as 1510."* Edwards goes on: *"In 1481, the Portuguese built a fort on the Gold Coast; another, some time afterwards, on the island of Arguin; and a third at Loango Saint Paul's on the coast of Angola; and the king of Portugal took the title of Lord of the Guiney."* A slave market was held in Lisbon as soon as 1539. A document from the time unveiled by De Paw reads: *"The Africans well deserved to be treated as beasts, since they spoke Arab and were circumcised."* Taking their neighbours as a model, the Spaniards soon sent some Africans to the West Indies—but the trade was only progressively set up.

Oranges of the New World

"By a royal ordinance of 1501," explains Washington Irving, *"negro slaves were permitted to be taken (to the New World) provided they had been born among Christians* (in Spain—editor's note). *(...) In 1510, king Ferdinand, being informed of the physical weakness of the Indians, ordered fifty Africans to be sent from Seville to labor in the mine. In 1511, he ordered that a great number should be procured from Guinea, and transported to Hispaniola, understanding that one Negro could perform the work of four Indians."* But the African slaves, who first arrived in the colonies in 1501, worried the Spaniards. And, in 1516, Cardinal Ximénes, regent for Charles Quint, put a ban on the trade by royal decree—the Governor of Hispaniola, Ovando, feared they might rebel and take control of the colony. Concerned by the fate of *his dear Indians* (Raynal), Las Casas had the ban lifted in 1517. *"Las Casas,"* notes De Paw more than 250 years later, *"through the most bizarre mindset, wrote many memoirs to denounce the conquest of America as unjust and atrocious, but, at the same time, envisaged enslaving the Africans."* To their greatest misfortune, the African perfectly acclimated to these new regions. Charlevoix rejoices: *"Apart from the fact that a Negro can perform the work of six Indians, they acclimated far better to the yoke, and it seems they were born to endure it; there are not that easily upset, and do not need much to survive, being strong although barely eating."* At the time, many reckoned that the Africans were bound to be slaves. Furthermore, they were more docile than expected. *"The Negroes have pride, of course,"* Charlevoix says. *"But it only required a little bit more to tame them, and to remind them who are the masters with the whip."*

The Europeans tried to justify the trade, stating that these wretched creatures, being bought from Muslim masters, could only live happier under the kindly yoke of Christians. As a matter of fact, they prospered in the tropics—to such an extent, it seemed they could not die. *"Just like oranges,"* underlines Herrera, *"they found their ideal soil in Hispaniola."* Thus, the Spaniards solved their problem of labour supply, benefiting from the unexpected support of Las Casas, who later repented. *"His reasoning, however fallacious it may be,"* specifies Irving, *"was considered satisfactory and human by some of the most learned and benevolent men of the age."*

The English soon got involved in the trade. The terrible John Hawkins set the trend in 1562, getting rich by selling 300 Africans in Hispaniola. But the French and the Portuguese were already quite active by 1564, while the English were slow to imitate them. James I granted an exclusive chart to a few Londoner merchants in 1618, but the Royal African Company did not see the light before 1672—it enjoyed exclusivity until 1688. The following year, the English and the Spaniards agreed upon commercial terms, which turned the former into the most active slave traders in the world. Of course, many of these slaves were sent to Jamaica. In 1658, 3 years after the island was taken over from the Spaniards, there were 400 slaves and 4,000 colonists in Jamaica; by 1775, there were 200,000 slaves and 8,000 colonists. This 'demographical' reversal was due to the development of agriculture, which had transformed sugar canes into gold.

Sugar and Blood

The fate of the Jamaican slaves was intimately linked to sugar canes, which, by the end of the 17th century, had become the true wealth of the island. Originating from the Pacific, and introduced to Europe by the Indians, the plant arrived in the New World in the hold of Columbus' ship, according to Edwards. In his *Histoire naturelle et morale des Indes* (1588-90), Joseph Acosta says it was already successfully cultivated in 1590: *"We earn considerable profits with sugar, as it is commonly used in the Indies, and exported to Spain (...). We build sugar-houses in the islands, in Mexico, in Peru and elsewhere, and we earn considerable profits from it. (...) Sugar is the main source of revenues in these islands, as men are so fond of it."* In 1640, the English started the systematic plantation of canes in Barbados, where it revealed *so profitable (...) that within ten years the wealth of the planters had multiplied twenty times.* (Black) Edward Long says there were some cane plantations in Jamaica under the Spaniards, but that the sugar production was then limited to the local market. The colonists of Nevis, who had come to Jamaica with Brayne in 1656, were the first to seriously plant it; several officers who later became planters followed them, including Colonel Barrington. But the first shoots gave a grainless black sugar. The industry did not developed until Modyford took over in 1664. That is when the sugar price skyrocketed in England. Some finely selected shoots were imported from Barbados, where so-called cane specialists were hired at a high price. Leslie gives the following description of the plant: "*Sugar grows in a long stalk, which we call a cane, full of joints, two, three, four or five inches asunder, and about six foot high, the sprouts and leaves at the top rising up so high, as may make it near eight foot in all. The body of the cane is about an inch diameter, seldom more. The colour of the cane-tops is a pure grass-green; the cane itself is yellowish when ripe; 'Tis covered with a thin skin or bark, somewhat hard on the inside, being of a white spungy* (sic) *substance, full of juice, which the Servants and others suck, and eat great quantities of without injuring their health. Nothing is pleasanter than this sap, when the cane is ripe (...); and this sweetness as far exceeds that of honey, as a Pippen does a crab.*" It was planted during the rainy season, from August to December, and it took 15 to 18 months to reach maturity. The planters dug some furrows, 20 centimetres deep, to lay two canes side by side; this method did not come naturally to them. At first, they would stick the canes vertically into the ground. Each cane was thus growing one plant only, furthermore they were fragile. Lying, the cane grew a plant at each of its joints! In the 18th century, when everything went philosophical, planting canes generated societies of intellectuals. "*In the year 1767,*" says Long, "*a plan was formed here, for establishing a patriotic society; for improving the productions and commerce of the island, and extending the cultivation of its lands.*" Learned men from Europe, motivated by the works of naturalists, published treatises on agriculture. Soon, the young shoots were surrounded with manure; a long and tedious operation, which kept busy two-thirds of the slaves. The canes were then cut off one by one, and then transported as bundles to the mills. The mills were activated by beasts of burden—the first windmills appeared early in the 18th century on the estate of Governor Ascough. Inside, a female slave slipped the canes one by one into rollers that squeeze them completely dry. The juice thus extracted was then boiled and clarified. Some white lime in powder was then added to the juice, *to get rid of the superabundant acid*, explains Edwards; and this *is the great difficulty in sugar-making*, he adds. Following a few more complicated operations, the final juice was poured into conic containers where it hardened to become sugar. This commodity became a craze all over Europe; it could be found in almost all islands in the West Indies, but the Jamaican sugar was renowned for its purity. Said to gleam more, the Jamaican grain became more expensive than the one from Barbados. By 1670, there were more than 600 windmills in the island, and ten times more in 1730. Jamaica now counted 430 plantations, owned by rich planters. These planters became so powerful, that the 'sugar colonies', as these islands came to be called, *were the most valuable possessions of any empire, fiercely fought over in every war that broke out in Europe and as fiercely bargained for at every peace conference*, says Black. *Their importance in the eyes of governments was out of all proportion to their size; indeed, the British West Indians had more political influence with the government in England than did all thirteen American mainland colonies. Their indignation at the favour shown to these islands was one of the grievances (...) that led them to revolt against British rule and become an independent republic.* Thus Jamaica, at first a mere consolation prize for the Western Design, became the richest possession of the British in the New World; a status she owned to her slaves. This is what Voltaire reminds his contemporaries of in *Candid* (London, 1759). Two characters come across a mutilated slave in Surinames: "*When we work at the sugar-canes, and the mill snatches hold of a finger, they cut off our hand ; and when we attempt to run away, they cut off our leg: both cases happened to me. It is at this expense of ours that you eat sugar in Europe.*" A speech relayed by Montesquieu in *The Spirit of Laws*: "*Sugar would be too expensive if the plant producing it were not cultivated by slaves.*" Charlevoix confesses that without their slaves, *the best established colonies (...) would be of little value.*

Slave Code

At the turn of the 18th century, plantations spread as far as the eyes could see. The big planters slowly put the small ones out of business, and the number of slaves considerably augmented. Indeed, many slaves were required to run a plantation. In Jamaica, the Royal African Company brought in dozens of thousands of them—it is believed than more than 2 million slaves were carried to the English colonies in the West Indies alone between 1680 and 1786. Slaves were bought on the African shores, but not for money. "*Except the Portuguese,*" explains Raynal, "*all nations roughly trade them for the same things such as swords, rifles, canon powder, steel, brandy, hardware, carpets, glass jewellery.*" Embarked on slave ships, the slaves crossed the ocean—the Middle Passage—under terrible conditions. It is believed that a third of the slaves died at sea during the first decades of the trade. Step by step, regulations were imposed to the transporters, who more or less complied. It was then fashionable to condemn, among the 'enlightened planters', the *inexcusable avarice* of some slave drivers as well as *a destruction of the human species on which it is impossible to reflect without indignation and horror!* (Edwards) For the sake of profitability on one hand, and the pressure of the abolitionist societies on the other hand, some fundamentals were soon required. First, every slave ship had to be equipped with fans, so that the slaves would not suffocate in the hold; then, the 1794 regulations made compulsory the presence of a doctor on board, as well as a vital space for provisions and a maximum countenance of 5 slaves per ton.

At the end of the crossing, the ships anchored off the island for a while. Edwards, who witnessed several sales of slaves, relates: *"The arrival of a Guinea ship in the West Indies is announced by public*

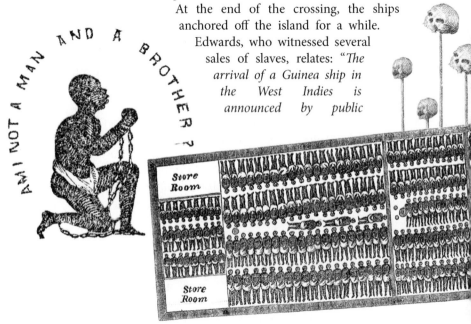

advertisement, specifying the number of Negroes imported, the country from whence, and day of sale. It was the practice until of late, to open the sale on shipboard (...); but, as visitors were admitted without hesitation or inquiry, it frequently happened (...) that such crowds of people went on board, and began so disgraceful a scramble, as to terrify the poor ignorant Africans with a notion that they were seized on by a herd of cannibals, and speedily to be devoured. The wisdom of the legislature of Jamaica has corrected this enormity in that island, by enacting that the sales shall be conducted on shore, and that care shall be taken not to separate different

Opposite: logo of
the abolitionist;
the cross section
of a slave ship (19th
century); a slave in
Surinam, hung to a
hook (18th century,
Stedman); detail of
a map of Guinea, Africa
(Bonne, 18th century).

branches of the same family. I'm afraid it hath been found difficult, in all cases, to enforce this latter regulation." The masters then branded their slaves on the spot. Edwards gives a bucolic description of the operation: *"It is the custom among some of the planters in Jamaica, to mark their initials of their name on the shoulder or breast of each newly-purchased Negro, by means of a small silver brand heated in the flame of spirits (...). But it is growing into disuse."* Edwards then disserts over the price of slaves, varying upon age and physical condition. In 1791, a planter paid £150 for man in the prime of his life, £149 for a woman, and £147 for a teen-ager. Children were sold for £40 or £45, exclusive of the colonial and importation taxes. The labour supply represented the main investment for the planters, and required considerable sums of money that they borrowed from usurers—hence the frequent bankruptcies.

In Jamaica, slaves were perceived as a necessary evil. Their workforce was essential, but the Whites lived in perpetual fear of their insurrections. Was not it true that these people feared not death, and that they even saw it as a deliverance? It came, they said, to free them from slavery, and to take them back to Africa among their relatives. *"They look on death as a blessing,"* confirms Leslie. Some relations even state that it was quite frequent for them to cut their own throats, so to haste their return to Africa. How could such men be subjugated? As far as Edwards was concerned, this belief is, *like other European notions concerning the Negroes, (...) the dream of poetry; the sympathetic effusion of a fanciful or too credulous an imagination.* In fact, the masters knew little about their slaves; they cared mostly about keeping them under their strict and repressive rules. The first written laws related to slaves did not appear in Jamaica before 1696. There were 7 of them, and they composed the infamous Slave Code—deriving from the same code in force in Barbados, itself inspired by the French Code Noir.

1°. Straggling slaves, apprehended without a ticket (or pass), are to be punished with moderate whipping.

2°. Striking or doing violence to a white person (except by command of their master or employer, or in defence of his person or goods), punishable at discretion of two justices and three freeholders, according to circumstances.

3°. Stolen goods found in the custody of a slave—such slave on conviction of receiving, knowing them to have been stolen, to suffer death, transportation, dismembering, or other punishment, at the discretion of two justices and three freeholders.

4°. Wilfully returning from transportation, death.

5°. Compassing or imagining the death of a white person, and being attained thereof by open deed (or covert act), before two justices and three freeholders, death.

6°. On complaint made to a justice of any felony, burglary, robbery, burning houses, canes; rebellions; conspiracies; or other capital offences; the justice is to issue his warrant to apprehend the offenders, and for summoning the evidence before him. The evidence of one slave to be admitted against another slave; (...) if upon full and due hearing of the matter (the freeholders being first sworn , by the justices, to judge uprightly, and according to the evidence), they deem the culprits guilty, the judgement is then forthwith to be given of death, transportation, or other punishment, as they, in their judgement, shall think meet to inflict.

7°. All *petit* crimes, trespasses, and injuries, committed by a slave, are to be heard and determined by any of his majesty's justices within the island.

"*The free use of the whip was perfectly legal,*" comments Gardner in 1873. "*The slave code was cruel in the extreme; it gave the master almost unlimited power, and sanctioned some of the most horrid enormities ever tolerated by law.*" The condition of the slaves evolved as time went by, and the punishments here evoked appeared very cruel a century later. In 1774, the brave Edward Long makes it clear that dismembering, evoked in the third article, was by then obsolete; it was even, he adds, prohibited by a law passed in 1735. Gardner contradicts him: "*Reference to the records of the slave courts of St. Ann's Bay, and of St. Thomas in the East, proved that it was not so. Such punishments were inflicted while Mr. Long was in the island, and for a quarter of century later.*" The same Gardner then lists the tortures suffered by the slaves: ears and legs cut off, nose split or other wise mutilated, flogging, branding on the cheeks. One slave, he says, was put to death *by a mode of torture too horrible to relate or to read without a shudder*; record of which, he adds, was almost erased on purpose later on. He also told the story of *poor Priscilla*, who tried to run away in 1783; she had her both ears cut off and received 39 lashes once a month for a whole year.

The slave code of 1696 was rooted into the *villeinage* laws of the middle age, when these punishments were inflicted by the English Lords onto their serfs. The fact that it was so tough testifies that the masters were deeply afraid of their slaves. "*The Africans, first imported, were wild and savage to an extreme,*" deplores Long. "*Their intractable and ferocious tempers naturally provoked their masters to rule them with a rod of iron; and the earliest laws (...) are therefore rigid and inclement, even to a degree of inhumanity."* He adds: *"Among men of so savage a disposition, as they scarcely differ from the wild beasts of the wood in the ferocity of their manners, we must not think of introducing (...) polished rules and refinements. (...) Such men must be managed at first as if they were beasts; they must be tamed before they can be treated like men."* It is probably no coincidence that these laws were passed a few years after Cudjoe's upheaval (see chapter 4). Long wonders: *"Perhaps the depravity of their nature, much more than their colour, gave rise to a belief of their inferiority of intellect; and it became an established principle to treat those as brute beasts, who had so little pretentions to claim kindred with the human race, except in the shape of their bodies, and their walking upon two legs instead of four. However, it might be, certain it is, that the planters of that age thought it no greater crime to kill a Negroe, than to knock a monkey on the head."* Witnessing the condition of the slaves in Jamaica in the early 18th century, Leslie states: *"No country excels* (it) *in a barbarous treatment of slaves, or in the cruel methods they put them to death."* Rebellious Negroes were tied on their bellies on the place of execution, and then slowly burnt alive, starting by the feet. Others were left to starve to death in front of a loath of bread: *"I have seen these unfortunate wretches gnaw the flesh off their own shoulder,"* says Leslie. Then he goes on: *"The most trivial escape is punished with a terrible whipping. I have seen some of them treat in that cruel manner, for no other reason, but to satisfy the brutish pleasure of an overseer, who has their punishment mostly at his direction. I have seen their bodies all in a gore of blood, the skin tore off their backs with the cruel whip; beat pepper and salt rubbed in the wounds and a large stick of sealing was dropped leisurely upon them. It is no wonder, if the horrid pain of such tortures, incline them to rebel; at the same time, it must be confessed, they are generally very perverse."* Your slaves are mean? *"Not mean enough with you!"* rages Diderot.

Loved and treated humanly

During the Age of the Enlightment, the debate raged on. In the name of which principle did the Europeans hold Africans captive? The duty of any Christian should be, on the contrary, to insure his brothers' liberty—*all* his brothers. In order to treat Africans as beasts, some claimed they were no men. They compared their hair to the wool of the sheep, laughed at their savage manners, and at their lack of common sense—did not they sell slaves for glass jewellery? Such creatures should rejoice to pass under the yoke of Christians, anyway. In France, Montesquieu answers the last argument: "*It is impossible for us to assume that these people are men because if we assume they were men one would begin to believe that we ourselves are not Christians.*" But it was not enough to convince Mr Long, who claims that under Christian masters, *who, I venture to say, are not such tyrants as the African slaveholders, they enjoy indulgence.* According to the partisans of the slave trade, to own slaves made you an instrument of God's will. "*In the distribution of our gratitude,*" Long says, "*we are bound to bestow some share on those, whom God has ordained to labour. The just subordination, within the line of which our Negroes must be kept, does by no means dispense with our loving, and treated them humanly.*" Diderot answers Long and his friends: "*Your Negroes are narrow-minded because slavery would break every soul. (...) They are treacherous because truth is never owned to a tyrant (...). You have almost succeeded in making them believe that they are from a singular race, born to be abject and dependent, to work and to be punished. You spared nothing to degrade them, and then you accuse them of being vile.*" As a matter of fact, some doubted that the Africans benefited from their closeness to whites. Leslie testifies: "*When they first arrive, 'tis observed they are simple and very innocent creatures, but they soon turn to be roguish enough: And when they come to be whipt, urge the example of the Whites for an excuse.*" Not to mention the depraved Whites, usually some ignorant ex-convicts, who, once in the colonies, mingled with the slaves to satisfy their vices, offering quite a poor picture of Christians. In fact, the real reasons behind so much cruelty were a part of obvious sadism, and a so-called necessity. Leslie reflects upon the matter: "*Perhaps, indeed, such severities may in some shape be excused, when we consider the state of the country, and how impossible it were to live amidst such numbers of slaves, without (...) punishing their faults with the utmost severity.*"

At the dawn of abolition, the planters considered themselves prisoners of a system, which could not be reformed without ruining the colonies—and they were not that wrong. Edwards, a planter himself, describes his peers as innocent people for the most part. Among them was the famous writer Matthew G. Lewis, who inherited 2 plantations in Jamaica in the early 19th century. The young and educated man, who later became slave owner, went twice to Jamaica, in 1815 and 1817, keeping a fascinating diary of his stays. Published posthumously, it reveals a 'humanist' approach of slavery. Lewis admits that *every man of humanity must wish that slavery, even in its best and most mitigated form, had never found a legal sanction, and must regret that its system is now so incorporated with the welfare of Great Britain as well as of Jamaica, as to make its extirpation an absolute impossibility, without the certainty of producing worse mischiefs than the one which we annihilate.* Indeed, without causing a blood bath like in St-Domingue, the abolition of slavery tolled the end of prosperity in Jamaica.

Both for Reason and Self-interest

Raynal was a radical philosopher, dedicated to the demolition of the *Ancien Régime*; as such, he gives a partial vision of the condition of the slaves in the New World, which he saw as *the most terrible one*. But a close analysis reveals some subtleties Raynal did not care about—he did not intend to stick to a so-called historical truth, but to awaken political consciousness. To start with, slavery in Jamaica lasted for several centuries; it is quite difficult to compare the condition of the slaves in 1696 with the condition of those living on one of Lewis' plantations in 1815. Some of them, says the writer, pretended to be sick every now and then, so they could spend a day or two resting at the hospital. Others would run away for a few days before coming back to work. All proprietors were not as comprehensive as Lewis, of course; but the law was more and more demanding. As soon as 1696, the slave code was divided into 2 parts; the first one dealt with the rights of the masters; the second one with their duties. They had to cloth their slaves, giving each of them a jacket and a pair of trousers—or a petticoat for women—, each year. They also had to grant them an acre of land, so they might provide for themselves—if not, they were charged of 40 shillings for each missing piece of land. Slaves who captured one of their runaway peers were rewarded; those killing, or taking, a Maroon were given a coat with a red cross on it, and a reward of £10. A pregnant woman could not be put to death before she had delivered her child, and the justices granted the slaves holy days at Christmas, Easter and Pentecost. The planters were also required to elevate the souls of their slaves, as specified in article 8: "*All masters, mistresses, owners, employers, &c. are to endeavour, as much as possible, the instruction of*

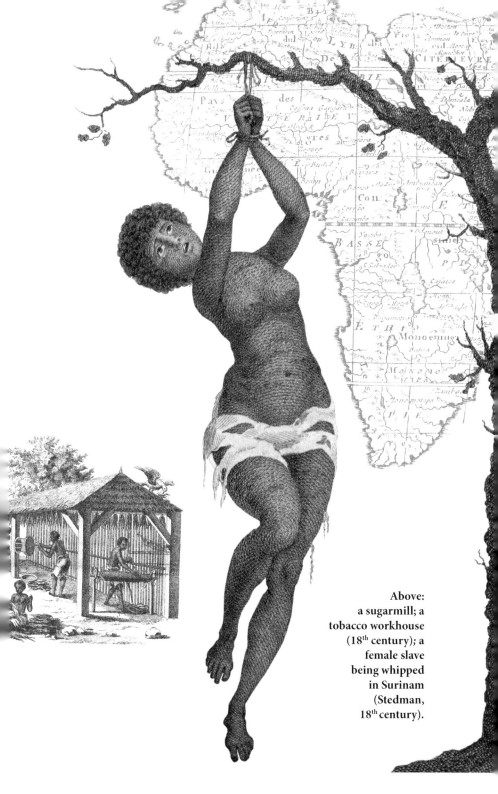

Above:
a sugarmill; a
tobacco workhouse
(18th century); a
female slave
being whipped
in Surinam
(Stedman,
18th century).

their slaves in the Christian religion (...) and do their utmost to fit them for baptism." In 1735, 2 articles were added to the code; the first one granted the slaves the right to carry a reasonable quantity of goods; the second one circumcised the barbarous deeds of some masters: "*No slave to be dismembered at the will and pleasure of his owner, master, or employer, under penalty of 100l. payable to the informer.*" This is the law evoked above by Long. But it was obviously not enough, as a new article of 1751 reads: "*To prevent the bloody, inhuman, and wanton killing of slaves, any person, so offending, to be adjudged, for the first offence, on conviction, guilty of felony, and have benefit of clergy, and suffer the further punishment of imprisonment (...) not exceeding the term of 12 months; and for the second offence, (...) to suffer death (...).*" What these articles silently tell us is that slaves were daily put to death for little or no reason, and that these laws were not actually applied. Long specifies that the last article was inspired by one Lockwood, a lunatic owner, who inhumanly butchered his slaves. The historian adds that it was used at least a second time against another violent master, who was burnt in the hand. There were indeed some sadistic masters in Jamaica, including Annee Palmer, in St James, who enjoyed torturing her slaves. In his diary, Lewis also notes a slave's song: *Take him to the Gulley! Take him to the Gulley! / But bringee back the frock and board. / "Oh! massa, massa! me no deadee yet!" / Take him to the Gulley! Take him to the Gulley! / Carry him along!* It's a direct reference to one Bedward, owner of the Spring Garden plantation around 1785. "*It was his constant practice, whenever a sick Negro was pronounced incurable, to order the poor wretch to be carried to a solitary vale upon his estate, called the Gulley, where he was thrown down, and abandoned to his fate; which fate was generally to be half devoured by the john-crows* (vultures—editor's note), *before death had put an end to his sufferings.*" If the Age of the Enlightment brought *more humanity*, according to Edwards, it was still the scene of many enormities that even the planters could not seal: "*That the narratives (...) of excessive whippings, and barbarous mutilations, which have lately awakened the sympathy of the public, are all 'absolutely false'—though it has been asserted by others, shall not be asserted by me. (...) I, on the other hand, aver that, although such enormities have certainly sometimes happened, and may happen again, yet that the general treatment of the Negroes in the British West Indies is mild, temperate and indulgent.*" According to Long, benevolence was a necessity. "*We are obliged to it,*" he says, "*both from reason and self-interest; bodily strength, and their adaptation to the climate, would enable them to pass from the lowest to the highest stations, and give the law to their masters, if they were willing unanimously to attempt it; but when those who fill the lowest rank, are used with equity and benevolence, so far from becoming dreadful, by flocking together in order to trample upon us, they comply with whatever we require of them; they offer themselves willingly to be our defenders, and are themselves the instruments made use of to restrain one another within the bounds of their allotted condition.*" Benevolence dictated the aforementioned articles of the slave code, then. But at a closer range, they appear to mainly protect the masters from other masters—slaves were costly, and needed to be preserved. Especially since the birth-rate was low in Jamaica.

To buy the best 'products', the masters studied the characters of the African slaves. The terrible Long coldly describes their respective qualities. The Coromantyns, he says, were roguish, fierce and stubborn; he likes the Minnahs better, being timid but with suicidal tendencies. The Mundigos would be perfect, would not it be for all their worms. He rejects the Ebos, as being lazy, sullen and trying to avoid any effort. For the fields, he praises the Congos, the Conchas, the Whidahs or the Angolas; though the latter happened to be stupid, contrary to the Negroes from Senegal, he recommends them as House Negroes, or foremen—especially since they were so ill adapted to hard work. Raynal, for his part, turns the mirror back: "*The masters from each European nation,*" he claimed, "*treat their slaves in their own way. The Spaniards make them the companions of their indolence; the Portuguese, the instruments of their debauchery; the Dutch, the victims of their avarice. The English consider them as strictly physical beings not to be uselessly used or destroyed; but they never socialize with them, never smile nor speak with them. As if they feared that it might appear that Nature had somewhat made them alike. That's why their slaves hate them.*"

Black customs

Slaves had to partly provide for themselves, and Leslie says that a lot of them could be found going through the masters' dustbins. In the countryside, they went naked, men and women, fed on herring and salt fish, the cheapest provisions. The masters encouraged them to chase the rats that infested the plantations by exchanging 100 dead rodents with 2 bottles of rum. They usually watered it down with brandy, added cinnamon and clove, nutmeg and egg yolk, in order to obtain the famous punch, also called the *kill-devil*. This dark picture got a little bit better as time went by, and as the masters gave 1 or 2 acres of land to their slaves. They cultivated it, and even sold the surplus at the market, on Sunday. In

Kingston, more than 10,000 slaves gathered every week on Parade. According to Lewis, who let them take care of their grounds on Saturday, some made good money out of it. When they died, they left their plot of land to whosoever they wished.

There were many holidays for slaves, who spent it celebrating. Every Sunday afternoon, they would dance or wrestle, says Leslie, *men and women promiscuously together*. They played hand-made instruments such as the Bangil, *not much unlike our Lute*; the Rookaw, *which is two sticks jagged*; and a Jenkgoviing, *a way of clapping their hands*. And, adds the historian, *the whole made a very terrible kind of harmony*. Long admits that they had a good musical ear, but despises their chants as being *without the least particle of poetry*. Yet, describing their dances as sometimes gay and sometimes graves, the historian seems to be fascinated: "*The female dancer is all languishing, and easy in her motions; the man, all action, fire, and gesture.*" Their songs about everyday life often bordered on satire. They described each other, especially the Overseer, if he happened to be around, *to add a poignancy to their satires and heighten the fun*. (Long) Lewis could not bear these ceremonies, which left him with a headache; he yet underlines that many revolutionaries chants were thus going around the island; and that slaves used them to spread various news. Edwards states that the chants varied according to the characters of the slaves, *those of the Eboes being soft and languishing; of the Koromantyns, heroic and martial. At the same time, there is observable, in most of them, a predominant melancholy, which, to a man of feeling, is sometimes very affecting*. The dances were not always as innocent as they appeared, as some were disguised fight trainings. Others were also used in pagan rites, such as *obeah*—it was the case for the Mayal (or Myal), a starter to the voodoo ceremonies. "*This is intended to remove any doubt of the chief Obeah-man's supernatural powers*," says Lewis. "*And in the course of it, he undertakes to show his art by killing one of the persons present, whom he pitches upon for that purpose.*" In fact, the victim drank a cold infusion of *calaloo*, which, after the agitation of the dance, threw her into a sort of profound sleep. Thus frozen into a trance, motionless, and her pulse being imperceptible, she only came back to life when rubbed with another decoction, *as yet unknown to the Whites,* notes Long. She had no memory of what had happened. This was a way for the Obeahman to demonstrate his ability to bring back to life his disciples, should they die at the hands of their master. This feeling of invulnerability played a key role in the revolt led by Tacky in 1760 (see chapter 10); this slave was said to be protected by *obeah*. Such a leader ought to scare the Whites—by necessity, they then started to investigate the customs of their slaves.

Duppy

The slaves had to bury their dead. Leslie describes their funerals as a grandiloquent procession. The slaves, he says, carrying the coffin on their shoulders, walked around the place, made a stop in front of every house, and pretended, *that if the deceased person had received any injury, the corps moves towards that house.* They usually sacrificed a hog and put the corpse in the ground while crying—not the effect of grief but of joy. Then, beating the drums and playing the rattles, they went back to their place, leaving a bottle of rum at the feet of the tomb, and some soup at its head. Forced to Christianity, the slaves appeared to welcome it—it's still deeply rooted into the Jamaican society today. Nonetheless, Lewis thought that the slaves did not care much about the Whites' religion. They patiently listened to the sermons, he says, but never acted accordingly. They believed in life after death, though; and in spirits even more—they called them *duppies*. "*I have not been able to ascertain exactly the negro notions concerning the Duppy,*" confesses Lewis. "*Indeed, I believe that his qualities vary in different parts of the country. At first, I thought that the term Duppy meant neither more nor less than a ghost; but sometimes he is spoken of as 'the Duppy' as if there were none but one, and then he seems to answer to the devil. Sometimes, he is a kind of malicious spirit, who haunts burying-grounds (...), and delights in playing tricks to those who may pass that way. On other occasions, he seems to be a supernatural attendant on the practitioners of Obeah, in the shape of some animal.*"

On the Plantation

Most of the slaves spent their entire life on the plantations, being unable to leave without permission. In this closed-door society, the roles were precisely shared out. A plantation required huge investments. The planter needed to build a sugarhouse, a boiler, stables, and houses for the blacksmith, the carpenters and the slaves. Aside, and usually upon some small hill, stood his own house. Most of the times, it showed off its owner's opulence; but the planters hardly lived on their plantation. Indeed, they spent their lives in Spanish Town or Kingston. "*The planters not only live in opulence,*" reads the *Voyageur François*, "*but in an opulence which equals the greatest Lords' in Europe. They have carriages drawn by six horses, preceded and followed by many people, as well as Negroes who run in front. In a word, Jamaica beats every colony as far as luxury and opulence are concerned. If I may believe one Mr Shirley, some inhabitants can be placed among the richest men in the world. One Mr Beckford, for instance, owns 22 plantations with more than 1,200 slaves; and he has more than 150,000 guineas in the banks."* The same book, dated from 1772, gives a flattering description of Spanish Town:

> Santiago de la Vega, called Spanish Town, though inferior in size to Kingston, is the actual capital of the island, as it used to be under the Spaniards. Many wealthy persons live there, who spend a lot. That's where the Governor and most of the officers live, too. There's a theatre, a troupe of actors, and even some play writers who are, it is said, quite talented (...) The Assembly of the Court house here stand. Their luxurious outfits and the quality of the food they eat distinguish the inhabitants. There are many carriages, and everything it takes to make a beautiful city. The balls are as frequent as in London, and people live as graciously as if at the Court of London.

The Governor's house, the famous King's House, stood in Spanish Town since 1762. It featured a paved portico made of white marble, some columns made of stone from Portland, and mahogany furniture— *the noblest and best edifice of the kind, either in North America or any of the British colonies in the West Indies*, claims Long. Only the 200 feet facade remains today.

But the wealthiest planters did not even live in Jamaica—some never set a foot on the island. They left their property in the hands of an *Overseer*, while living a high-profile life in London. They were so rich that the expression *rich like a West Indians planter* became a popular saying. Yet, all planters were not wealthy. Many ruined themselves in so demanding a business. The investments were so important that some lost everything in the course of a single year, when too many slaves died from disease for example. The investors did not hesitate to sue their debtors—sometimes, they demanded their money overnight, not even waiting for the first harvest. The English investors were merciless—the planters were expropriated, and sometimes thrown into the insane jails of Spanish Town. There, they were treated as petty thieves, and stayed among the rabble, white or black, receiving small money from their usurers to sustain their lives until their trial. Fearing such an extremity, many of them holed up in their houses, waiting for the authorities with a rifle—the confrontation was better than the humiliation. Though quite in favour of the planters, the Jamaican legislation also protected the merchants; when a plantation was seized, slaves were used as means of payment. They were sold without consideration of family ties or affinities, to various plantations throughout the island. Long denounces this process as barbarous and counter-productive; but in the middle of the chaos generated by the financial racing linked to sugar, nobody paid attention to his recommendation. Sugar had now become a trade for big investors. At the end of the 18ᵗʰ century, nothing much remained of the small 'officers turned planters', who cleared a few acres, 200 years earlier. Independent planters suffered under the yoke of the investors, and the pressure of their heavyweight competitors. Bryan Edwards notices that, between 1771 and 1791, 177 plantations went bankrupt and were resold; 55 others were simply abandoned, while 92 fell into the hands of the usurers. Sugar cane exploited 200,000 slaves, who cost so much, that Long advocates to replace them with machines. The industrial revolution was coming, the sugar colonies were living their last hours of prosperity.

Gangs and intendants

The absentee proprietors called upon white Intendants, or *Overseers*. to take care of their plantation. This crucial position was first reserved to some specialists from Barbados, the historical high place of sugar canes growing. They were taken in at high price, before the planters realized that they were usually at a loss in front of the geological specificities of Jamaica. It was quite hard to find a good *Overseer*, as there was no certified training. Those who came from Europe were not efficient, and Long says it took them years before they could understand the way a plantation worked. Furthermore, it was quite hard to keep them, as they were seeking fast results to negotiate a better pay in another plantation. As soon as they started to know a plantation, they left it for a new one. And to obtain rapid results, they forced the pace, exhausting both the slaves and the soil. Under such circumstances, happy was the owner who was not totally ruined when he got his plantation back. When he arrived in Cornwall in 1815, Lewis found his plantations in ruins, and his slaves on the brink of revolt. The Intendant he had been paying for several months from England, had subcontracted another *Overseer* without telling Lewis. The absentee proprietors were a plague to Jamaica; the Assembly even thought about taxing them at one point—especially since most of the benefits left for England without benefiting the island.

There were 2 categories of slaves in the plantations, the house Negroes and the field Negroes. The former took care of the domestic work—there were maids, cooks or grooms. These slaves, affirms Long, *live as well, or perhaps much better (...) than the poorer class of people do in England.* The latter worked in the fields, and were themselves divided into 3 gangs. The first one comprised the strongest men, who cleared the grounds, planted, cut and picked up the canes. They also worked at the mill—though a female slave usually worked it. They woke up at dawn, came out of their hut—usually lost among the fruit trees—, to answer the morning call. The late ones received a few lashes, *but I am happy to say that of late years a very slight excuse is generally admitted,* rejoices Edwards. During the first break, they had *calaloos,* yams and plantains for lunch. Around noon, they stopped working for 2 hours, the time for them to eat, to relax or to cultivate their personal grounds. The working day came to en end with the sun set, which is quite early in the West Indies. But during harvest, slaves worked day and night, so that the canes would not dry on them. The teen-agers and disabled formed the second gang; they usually weeded the fields. Finally, the children formed the third and last gang, devoted to small tasks.

Law and order

To maintain order, families were scattered upon arrival, and the planters were careful not to regroup too many Africans who spoke the same language. In his *Voyage to Guinea* (London, 1745), the English traveller William Smith notes: "*As for the languages of Gambia, they are so many and so different, that the natives, on either side of the* (Gambia) *river, cannot understand each other.*" He then advocates to trade with *the different nations, on either side of the river, and having some* (slaves) *of every sort on board,* (so that) *there will be no more likelihood of their succeeding in a plot, than of finishing the tower of Babel.* But as stated by Long, the slaves were the best instruments to constraint themselves. That's why the planters exacerbated rivalries between different estates. They also confided the newcomers to some elder slaves, who then took advantage of them, embracing the condition of master in the twinkle of an eye. "*The Negroes themselves,*" notices Edwards, "*when invested with command, give full play to their revengeful passions; and exercise all the wantonness of cruelty without restraint or remorse.*" He then evokes the way they treated their dogs: "*They seem to maintain these poor animals solely for the purpose of having an object whereon to exercise their caprice and cruelty.*" But this analysis is somewhat challenged by the numerous revolts that punctuate the history of Jamaica.

10

Rebellions and Liberty

B eyond the most formidable insurrections such as the Maroons wars or the one led by Tacky in 1760, incalculable slaves rebellions took place in Jamaica. They were sometimes well-coordinated projects, sometimes isolated and spontaneous acts of refusal, provoked by despair, or a once too often whipping. And they kept on happening until slavery was abolished in 1838. As late as March 1816, Lewis reports the details of a plot, which was uncovered on the plantation of Lord Balcarres. Above 1,000 slaves had decided to slaughter all the Whites— *and 300 had sworn to assist in it with all the usual accompanying ceremonies of drinking human blood, eating earth from graves, &c.* (Lewis) Once caught, far from denying, the leader claimed his responsibility, and threatened the Judge of retaliation. Consequently, the Whites kept the militia under arms until he was executed. Slaves in Jamaica scared their masters from the first day till the last one.

Tacky 1760

The most important insurrection took place in 1760. It was orchestrated by the Coromantyns, these untamed and dreadful enemies of servitude. Every author underlines their physical and mental vigour, including Edward Long, who admits their being superior to all other Africans. The generic name of *Coromantyns* derived from one of the first English trading posts in Africa, *which is now become an insignificant village, or factory, in possession of the Dutch.* (Edwards) The Coromantyns actually came from various peoples of the West coast, such as the Ashantis, the Fantins or the Quamboos. "*The circumstances which distinguish the Koromantyn, or Gold Coast, Negroes, from all others,"* says Edwards, *"are firmness both of body and mind; a ferociousness of disposition; but withal, activity, courage, and a stubbornness, or what an ancient Roman would have deemed an elevation of soul, which prompts them to enterprizes* (sic) *of difficulty and danger; and enables them to meet death, in its most horrible shape, with fortitude and indifference."* They were also secretive to an extreme. In certain plantations, they even refused to mingle with slaves from other tribes; and thus successfully concealed their pagan rites orchestrated by their spiritual leaders, the *obeahmen*. But this occult science eventually came to light. On the brink of Eastern Monday, 1760, 50 slaves from Port Maria, in the parish of Saint Mary, rebelled, dragging the rest of the island behind them. The white Jamaica was caught off-guard. This conspiracy was kept so secret, that *almost all the Coromantin slaves throughout the island were privy to it, without any suspicion from the Whites.* (Long) White people feared they might unite with the terrible Maroons to take control of the colony. In Kingston, the slaves even crowned a Queen, who wore her royal attributes during secret meetings.

The insurrection broke out on the Frontier plantation, in St. Mary's parish, belonging to the late Ballard Beckford, and the adjoining estate of Trinity, the property of my deceased relations and benefactor Zachary Bailey, details Edwards. In the morning, 50 slaves followed Tacky to Port Maria, where they murdered a sentinel and stole 50 rifles. Bailey, reputed for treating his slaves humanly, galloped towards them, convinced he could bring them to their senses. A shower of bullets hailed him, so he turned back, and rod round to all the different plantations in the neighbourhood, giving them notice of their danger. Joined by 50 more rebels, Tacky and his men marched to Heywood Hall to plunder it, setting the cane fields on fire and slaughtering all the Whites—*they literary drank their blood mixed with rum*, laments Edwards. Then the rebellious troop went to Esher, William Beckford's estate. En route, they came across *a poor white man, who was travelling on foot,* (Long) and murdered him. At Esher, they besieged a dozen of Whites, garrisoned inside the house. But the latter ran out of ammunitions, and were soon swarmed but the furious attackers. One of the Whites was a Doctor, and he was *mutilated* (Long), dragged by a foot and thrown on a pile of corpses. Betrayed by his breathing, he was shot 5 times in the back—but he miraculously survived to tell his story. *"In one morning, they murdered between thirty and forty Whites and Mulattoes, not sparing even infants at the breast,"* deplores Edwards. Back to Ballard's Valley, the rebels—

now around 400—*having a good magazine of hogs, poultry, rum, and other plunder of the like kind, they chose out a convenient spot, surrounded with trees, and a little retired from the road (...), and began to carouze* (sic), explains Long. Baily and 80 men from the militia soon rushed them. They retreated into the woods, and the skirmishes went on for several days—none was decisive, but they enabled 2 faithful slaves to give the alert in Spanish Town. Lieutenant-Governor Sir Henry Moore dealt with the situation with discipline and firmness. He dispatched a regiment to St Mary, and called upon the Maroons in Scott's Hall, since the 1739 Treaty obliged them to intervene against the rebellious slaves—they answered the call willingly. They usually showed no compassion for the slaves. "*In their treatment of fugitive slaves,*" says Edwards, who did not like them, "*they manifest a blood-thirstyness* (sic) *of disposition, which is otherwise unaccountable (...); it is notoriously true, that they wish for nothing more than a pretence to put the poor wretched to death, frequently maiming them without provocation (...) and oftentimes bringing home the head of the fugitive, instead of the living man.*" Yet, upon their arriving to St Mary, they behaved *extremely ill* (Long), requiring the payment of some arrears before entering the fight. The English complied. Yet, their charge was not as successful as expected, as they were repelled; and while Tacky and his men bravely resisted, the rebellion spread.

Muskets and Obeah

During the insurrection, the English discovered an unsuspected and dark side of their slaves' culture, *obeah*—or voodoo. A few historians dug out their beliefs before 1760, though; Leslie reports that they believed in 2 divinities—a good one, Naskew; and an evil one, Tunnew. But none went far enough to unveil the secret of their sorcerers. "*A veil of mystery is studiously thrown over their incantations, to which the midnight hours are allotted, and every precaution is taken to conceal them from the knowledge and discovery of the White people,*" explains Edwards. *Obeah* played a key role in the insurrection of 1760. Indeed, Tacky covered himself with a mysterious powder, which supposedly made him invulnerable—it even enabled him to catch the English bullets with his bare hands, before hurling them back to his enemies. Fearing such a belief might excite more slaves to rebel, the colonists rejoiced when they allegedly captured Tacky's *personal obeahman* in St Mary. "*This old impostor was caught whilst he was tricked up with all his feathers, teeth, and other implements of magic,*" triumphs Long, "*and his this attire*

suffered military execution by hanging: many of his disciples, when they found that he was so easily put to death, notwithstanding all the boasted feats of his powder and incantations, soon altered their opinion of him, and determined not to join their countrymen in a cause which hitherto had been unattended with success."
But as far as his men were concerned, Tacky remained invulnerable, since he came out of every fight without the slightest injury. This psychological influence disturbed the Whites, who hurriedly passed a law—article 21 of the slave code: *Obeiah-men, pretended conjurors, or priests, upon conviction before two justices and three freeholders of their practicing as such, to suffer death, or transportation, at the discretion of the court.*

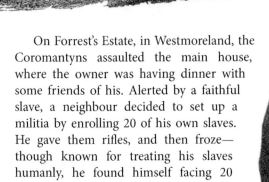

On Forrest's Estate, in Westmoreland, the Coromantyns assaulted the main house, where the owner was having dinner with some friends of his. Alerted by a faithful slave, a neighbour decided to set up a militia by enrolling 20 of his own slaves. He gave them rifles, and then froze—though known for treating his slaves humanly, he found himself facing 20

Above: the slaves leave Africa; the slaves are branded in the West Indies; portrait of Wilberforce, the abolitionist.

armed Negroes in the middle of an insurrection! Out of respect, they simply saluted him with their hats before walking away. Among them were some slaves recently captured in Guadeloupe, where they had been trained to fight by their former French masters. They looted and burnt several estates before retreating into the woods. A detachment of the militia soon caught up with them, but fell into an ambuscade. Long says: "*The whole party was thrown into the utmost confusion (...); each strove to shift for himself, and whilst they ran*

different ways, scarcely knowing what they were about, several were butchered, others broke their limbs over precipices, and the rest with difficulty found their way back again." This first victory excited the slaves and 1,000 of them joined the ranks of the Guadeloupians. But their entrenchment was eventually taken by the joined efforts of the 49th regiment of Captain Forsyth and the Leeward Maroons. During the fierce battle, the slaves first retired into the woods, and then rushed back their former camp to fire at the English. But the counter-offensive of the Maroons was decisive, this time. They defeated the rebels, slaughtering some and forcing the rest to flee disorderly into the woods. According to Long, this was the turning point of the insurrection in Westmoreland, as the following attempts of the rebels happened to be of no consequence.

The rest of Jamaica was still at war. At Val de Luides, in St John's parish, an insurrection was prevented, and the leaders were hanged. In St Thomas, a huge operation was dismantled thanks to an infiltrated slave. From the Carpenter's Mountains to St Dorothy to the short epic of Damon in Clarendon, Jamaica seemed about to burst out. In Kingston, the Whites shuddered upon hearing about the crowning of a Coromantyn queen named Cubah; her subjects honoured her as a sovereign. "*Her Majesty was seized, and ordered for transportation,*" ironically says Long. She succeeded in convincing the captain of her ship to put her ashore near Leeward, where she added some wood to the fire of revolt—but she was eventually captured, and then executed.

The colonists grew confident as they were gaining ground. In St Mary, Tacky's troops were now in a tough position. The English got organized, using the frigate of Admiral Holmes as a floating jail in Port Maria. Thus, the militia was discharged of all prisoners, and concentrated on the rebels' entrenchment. The violent assaults of the Maroons finally overthrew the rebels, who fled into the woods. "*Tacky (...) having separated from the rest,*" tells Long, "*was closely pursued by lieut. Davy of the Marons* (sic), *who fired at him whilst they were both running a full speed, and shot him dead.*" What a shot!—if this relation is true. Indeed, Edwards, who never spares an occasion to express his disdain for the Maroons, gives another version of Tacky's death. "*This unfortunate man, having seen most of his companions slaughtered, was discovered wandering in the woods without arms or clothing, and was immediately pursued by the Maroons, in full cry. The chase was of no long duration; he was shot through the head.*" As usual, the Maroons severed the head of their victim and handed it to the English, who proudly exposed it on a pike in Spanish Town. But the slaves soon deprived the arrogant winners of their trophy, which they stole and concealed. What Long does not speak about, and what Edwards asserts as certain—he says he learnt it from the Maroons themselves—, is what the Maroons did with the rest of Tacky's body. They, he says, *roasted and actually devoured the heart and entrails of the wretched victim!* Long draws a necessarily suspicious portrait of Tacky: "*He was a young man of good stature, and well made; his countenance handsome, but rather of an effeminate than manly cast. (...) He did not appear to be a man of any extraordinary genius, and probably was chosen general, from his similitude in person to some favourite leader of their nation in Africa.*" Desperate and cornered, the rebellious Negroes sought refuge into a nearby cave, where they were soon discovered by the Maroons, and slaughtered. It is said that they had not waited for their executioners, killing themselves instead. Anyway, the Maroons brought back their ears to get their reward—but then again, Edwards accuses them of having collected these particular ears upon other bodies, those of the rebels killed in Heywood Hall by the English, and whom they never had time to bury.

Finally, the remaining rebels surrendered on the condition of being spared. Some were still fighting in Westmoreland or in St James but the insurrection was now almost over. The Jamaican Assembly decided to make an example with 3 slaves, who had partaken in the *Frontier* massacre. The first one was chained to a stake erected on Parade, to be burnt alive. Edwards was there. "*He uttered not a groan, and saw his legs reduced to ashes with the utmost firmness and composure; after which, one of his arms by some means getting loose, he snatched a brand from the fire that was consuming him, and flung it in the face of the executioner.*" The next 2 ones were hung up alive in iron cages, and left to die. "*The Negroes who rebel and kill their master,*" explains Father Labat, "*are thrown into the rollers of a mill, burnt alive, or exposed in iron cages, so tightly pressed that they can make no motion; they are then hung to a tree, and left to die out of hunger and rage. We call it, putting a man on a dry diet.*" But the countenance of both victims awoke fear and respect in their executioners' mind. "*Until they expired, they never uttered the least complaint, except only of cold in the night, but diverted themselves all day long in discourse with their countrymen, who were permitted, very improperly, to surround the gibbet,*" reports Edwards. They even made fun at the historian, calling upon him on the 7th day of their torment, pretending to have some important revelations to make. Appointed by the officer in charge as an intermediary, Edwards went to talk to one of them. "*I endeavoured, by means of an interpret, to let him know that I was present; but I couldn't understand what he said in return. I remember that both he and his fellow-sufferer laughed immoderately at something that occurred—I know not what. The next morning, one of them* (named Fortune, NDLR) *silently expired, as did the other on the morning of the ninth day.*" Regarding the death of the second slave, named Kingston,

Long comments: "*The morning before* (he) *expired, he appeared to be convulsed from head to foot; and upon being opened, after his decease, his lungs were found adhering to the back so tightly, that it required some force to disengage him. The murders and outrages they had committed, were thought to justify this cruel punishment inflicted upon them in terrorem to others; but they appeared to be very little affected by it themselves, behaving all the time with a degree of hardened insolence, and brutal insensibility.*" Your slaves were insolent, Mr Long?

Embers

The inferno of 1760 was not fully quelled, and the breeze of revolt brought it back to life a few years later. In July 1765, several Coromantyns in St James secretly planned an insurrection for the day following Christmas. But the desire to rebel was apparently too strong. Urged on by his accomplices, Blackwall—a slave, who was a time suspected of being one of the rebels of 1760, but eventually relaxed for lack of evidence—started it all on November 29, on the plantation of Whitehall. He set a building afire in the middle of the night to bring out the inhabitants of the main house—where firearms were kept. Blackwall then pretended to fight the flames, urging the *Overseer* to climb up to the roof to reach the inferno. Meanwhile, 9 rebels rushed the house, *with the most hideous yells, and sharpened bills in their hands,* (Long). They came across a white man, whom Long calls Mr B—; he was out on the piazza with his sister, Mrs B-d, when the rebels *surrounded him and hacked him into a thousand pieces,* deplores Long. "*The pleasure they enjoyed in mingling the body of this unhappy gentleman (who had only lodged here, by accident, in his way to Spanish Town), afforded Mrs B—d an opportunity to jump out of the piazza, and run towards the bottom of the hill on which the house stood.*" Joined by 2 faithful slaves, she hid among the thick weeds on the riverside.

Now possessing firearms, Blackwall and his men ran after the Whites who had fled from Whitehall to the neighbouring estate of Ballard's Valley. They passed by Mrs B-d, taking no notice of her—she reached a safe haven shortly afterwards, thanks to a faithful Negro—, and surrounded the habitation of the *Overseer* of Ballard's Valley. Inside, a dozen of Whites expected the worst. But as he was closing in to set the house afire, one of the rebels' leaders was hit by a bullet *that struck against the lock of a gun, which the rebel had in his hand, and recoiling into his body, killed him upon the spot.* (Long) This unexpected turn of events somewhat embarrassed the assailants; taking advantage of it, the Whites came out of the house, and disbanded the rebels, who fled to the woods. The operation being a failure, Blackwall went to the Whites, telling them how he had hidden at the break of the insurrection in order to escape the wrath of the rebels. But the inquiry soon revealed his true responsibility in the plot, which concerned no less than 17 estates. Thirteen slaves were executed, including Blackwall, and 23 were transported. The Coromantyns were, once more, responsible for the upheaval. The Assembly introduced a bill to tax the Coromantyn slaves—it was never ratified, probably because the planters would rather be rich than safe. In 1766, 33 Coromantyns freshly disembarked from Africa rebelled, and killed 19 Whites within one hour's time. A bloody repression quickly put an end to the riot.

The Jamaican folklore remembers a few legendary figures, including the dreadful Jack Mansion—or Mansong—, aka Three-Fingered Jack, who led an insurrection in St Thomas, and then took leave in the woods, between Cane River Falls and Mount Lebanus. He was almost 7 feet tall, and walked around with a sword at his belt, a musket in his hand and a bag of *obeah* powder around his neck; he feared no one, attacked every one, and spread fear in the whole parish. But Quashie, the Maroon already responsible for his injured hand, found him, and put him to death after *a terrific fight*. (Black)

These revolts made considerable damages, and were a continuous threat to the colony—then at the peak of its prosperity. They were, as a matter of fact, very decisive in the abolition of slavery, proclaimed in 1838.

The end of slavery

The abolition was a two-step process. The Emancipation Act, approved by the English Parliament on August 29, 1838, provided that *as from 1 August 1834, all slave children under six years of age, and any which might be born after that date, were to be free. All other slaves became apprenticed to their former masters, the field-labourers, or predials, for six years (up to 1 August 1840), and the non-pedrials for four years (up to 1 August 1838), after which time all were to be completely free.* (Black) This historical reversal came after many fights and complicated debates, both moral and economical.

Slavery has always been a moral issue, and the religious were the first to denounce the servitude of the Indians in the New World. And if many first believed that the Africans were born to be slaves—so it was no sin to use them as such—, this sometimes-sincere belief slowly eroded. At the end of the 17th century, George Fox, founder of the Society of Friends—the Quakers—, urged to set all black people free after a few years in slavery. Slavery was even abolished in the colony of Pennsylvania, founded by the son of one of the conquerors of Jamaica, William Penn. But these were just a few voices in the middle of a pro-slavery chaos. The New and remote World enjoyed a blurry legal status, both embarrassing and convenient. Laws were passed according to circumstances, and Jamaica was jealous of her independence, and regularly fought royal directives. Slavery was legal in the West Indies. But what about Europe— where humanists had been denouncing it for so long? The question was raised as more and more black slaves arrived in England—by 1772, the planters had brought along more than 10,000 of them. The confrontation of the new and the old worlds had become inevitable.

Hostilities started when a slave named Jonathan Strong was beaten and left for dead by his master in the streets of London. Grandville Sharp, a key figure of the abolition, took Strong in, took care of him and even provided him with a job. But one day, Strong came across his former master in London, Mr Lisle, who claimed him as his property. He sold *him later for £30 to James Kerr, a Jamaican planter*, underlines Black. Upon learning about it, Sharp had Strong kidnapped in extremis, and kept him away from his new master. This story changed the fate of Grandville Sharp, who henceforth dedicated his life to the abolition of slavery. He wanted England to rule on slavery upon the soil of England. He had the opportunity to do it in 1772, when he took in another abandoned slave, James Somerset, who was again claimed back by his master. But this time, Sharp went to trial to force the English government to take an official decision: was slavery legal in England? Judge Lord Mansfield declared, on the contrary, that slavery was neither approved nor tolerated by the English law—the beginning of the end for the slave trade.

An abolitionist wind was blowing all over Europe— the Quakers and their abolitionist committees attracted influential people such as James Ramsay or Thomas Clarkson. The decision of Judge Mansfield was a first step—they now aimed at putting a definitive end to the trade. And they succeeded thanks to the support of people like William Wilberforce, a rich English heir made aware of abolitionism during the religious renewal underwent by England at the time. And when, in 1781, Luke Collingwood, the captain of the slave ship *Zong*, threw 132 slaves overboard alive in sight of the Jamaican coast to collect the insurance premium, Sharp made sure it would not go unnoticed. He published a relation of this horrid event, and had it distributed all over London—the public opinion was shocked. Nonetheless, it took a few more years, and a few setbacks before the law of 1803 was passed. From

January 1 onward, it says, the slave trade was abolished and forbidden by law; but not slavery, which was to die a quiet death along the years. In Jamaica, the planters were outraged; but it was just the beginning.

In England, slave drivers were now considered as pirates—hanged when taken. In Jamaica, things got stiff. The planters were threatened by the abolitionists, who covered the colony with anti-slavery tracts printed by the Anti-Slavery Society—founded by the Quakers; and they reacted with brutality and resentment. "*Indeed, they tended to treat their slaves more cruelly now in the belief that so doing would discourage any ideas they might get into their heads about freedom,*" says Clinton V. Black. Jamaica was the spearhead of the resistance of the sugar colonies. People there had fought hard against the English Parliament to enjoy semi-autonomy, and did not intend to give it up just like that. In more recent colonies, called the *Crown Colonies*, such as Trinidad or St Lucia, abolition was decreed through simple Orders in Council received from Europe, and naturally integrated to the main corpse of laws ruling the islands. In rebellious Jamaica, two successive Governors failed to pass the law. The island started to boil. The Whites talked about nothing else, and their slaves had big ears; the smell of freedom reached their nostrils. Some even figured out that slavery was *already* abolished, and that the Whites simply refused to set them free. In 1823, a series of secret meetings in St George ended up in a blood bath when the authorities found out. But nothing could have stopped the slaves, as they were now supported in Europe. In 1831, Samuel 'Daddy' Sharp, a Baptist priest, called people to arms in the Western part of the island—the fire broke out on the Kensington Estate, in St James. The infernos suddenly multiplied all through the island, causing considerable damages. Yet, the insurrection, the very last one in the history of Jamaica, was suppressed as all others—*retaliation was prolonged and terrible,* says Black. Sam Sharp was hanged in Montego Bay, in a square, which bears his name today—he was enthroned National Hero in 1975.

The planters' resistance lasted for 10 years; they had already lost the moral battle, but they fought the economical one for as long as possible. As usual, commerce triumphed. On the sugar market, Jamaican suffered competition from Brazil and Cuba. To support her planters, England placed a heavy duty on sugar from other sources, and by 1829 sugar had become a luxury commodity. Not to mention a new and young competitor from Europe, the much more profitable beetroot. Black concludes: "*If slavery could not produce cheap sugar, it was no longer necessary and it was therefore in the interests of the British public to have it abolished.*"

Apprenticeship

On August 1, 1834, many slaves were waiting for the blessed morning in churches, or in Spanish Town square, where the official ceremony was held. Some had climbed to the top of the Blue Mountains to witness the rising of a brand new day—yes, they were free at last. But back to Kingston, they had to integrate a program of apprenticeship which was supposed to facilitate the transition between 2 so contrary conditions in life. The most pessimistic foretold a blood bath, just like in Haiti. The more optimistic feared the creation of separatist black communities inland. The planters, for their parts, were afraid to see their estates deserted by their workers. Thanks to the influence of some missionaries and of some stipendiary magistrates—sent to Jamaica to make sure apprenticeship was effectively carried out—, the first times were concluding. But it did not last. The former slaves wondered: how could they be free since they still had to work for their masters? Not to mention that they now had to pay for everything, from their food to the rent of their huts. This was a confused and tensed period. The planters, fearing what would come next, behaved even more brutally. They thought about the time when the labour supply would drop out. They called upon immigrants. The first German settlers arrived in 1834. Some Irish and Scottish followed. But those who survived the tropical climate eventually deserted the plantations to become state servants, or to open their own business. This was another failure for the planters. Yet, between 1838 and 1844, 33,000 Indians came to the island, soon followed by Chinese and even 7,500 Africans, who freely came to the New World.

From 1835 to 1836, apprenticeship was going on well. But many problems arose, including the terrifying workhouses—some sorts of prisons where the reluctant apprentices were confined. Thrown into dark cells, they had to endure inhumane treadmill sessions, consisting of walking a huge wheel made of wood planks. The engineer Cubitt invented this punishment in 1818, to advantageously replace whipping. But when the apprentices stumbled, or fainted, they were still tied to the hip; driven by the wheel, the unconscious unfortunate were then hit by each plank as it went by. As a result of these ill treatments and tensions, the situation became critical, and England had to cut apprenticeship short. Thus, on August 1, 1838, all black people in Jamaica were declared unconditionally free.

Conclusion

The history of Jamaica in more recent times deserves a book by itself. From 1838 onwards, sources multiply and this might have prejudiced the uniformity of this work, which, hopefully, can be read like a journey through time. Moreover, the more recent history of Jamaica forms the background of another book in the same series, *Jamaican Greats* (DREAD Editions). The island became independent in 1962, and is surviving nowadays thanks to tourism or bauxite—a little; and maybe one day thanks to marijuana, or *ganja*, as it might be legalized soon. Unfortunately, the economical situation and the interests of many rogue politicians have created a strong criminal network in Jamaica. Ideally located on the drugs route between North and South Americas— always a matter of a geopolitical position—, Jamaica has become a drugs trafficking hub, and 120 tons of cocaine are said to transit each year in the island. Of course, this trade generates criminal activities. Jamaica is a Third World country with a young population and few opportunities. Thus, with 200 active gangs, and some 1, 500 murders a year for a global population of 3 million, Jamaica stands among the most dangerous countries in the world. This tells us of the challenges she faces today. But as this book demonstrates, the *island in the sun* has overcome many strives in the course of time; let us be confident that she will overcome those. This book now ends, but history *still a-gwaan*.

Finis

Printed in Great Britain
by Amazon